PROFILES
OF
EMINENT AMERICAN
CHEMISTS

RAYMOND B. SEYMOUR

and

CHARLES H. FISHER

FIRST IN A SERIES
"DISCOVERING THE DISCOVERERS"

Litarvan Enterprises Pty. Ltd. - Sydney

Raymond B. Seymour
Distinguished Professor of Polymer Science
University of Southern Mississippi
Hattiesburg, MS 39406-0076

and

Charles H. Fisher
Adjunct Professor of Chemistry
Roanoke College
Salem, VA 24153

Edited by
Sylvia Tascher

Litarvan Enterprises Pty. Ltd. - Sydney - 1988

This book represents either original work or information obtained from highly regarded sources. Reprinted material is quoted with permission and sources as indicated. The authors and publisher do not assume and hereby disclaim any liability to any party for any loss or damage caused by errors or omissions in *Profiles of Eminent American Chemists,* whether such errors or omissions result from negligence, accident or any other cause.

The authors regret that, owing to difficulties in acquiring information about some of those individuals profiled, a few profiles are brief.

©1986 Litarvan Literature
International Standard Book Number 0-937557-05-6
Library of Congress Card Number 86-082985

Printed in Singapore by Koon Wah Printing Pte. Ltd.

Profiles of Eminent American Chemists is dedicated to our wives: Frances B. Seymour and Lois C. Fisher.

The Authors

CONTENTS

PREFACE

Chemical pioneers - with pioneers in other sciences - have given us our exciting, wonderful, and fantastic 20th century! American pioneers have taken us into space, conquered diseases, defended us, improved our quality of life, transformed our agriculture into the food basket of the world, and made the 20th century uniquely productive and important. Our average life span increased from forty-nine years in 1900 to nearly seventy-five years in 1986; our standard of living improved approximately four-fold during the same period.

The American Institute of Chemists has responded appropriately to the successes of the pioneering chemists and engineers. In keeping with its objectives of promoting the interests of chemists and chemical engineers for the benefit of humankind, the American Institute of Chemists initiated programs decades ago to recognize those who have significantly advanced the status and beneficial use of chemistry. The prestigious Gold Medal Award was created for this purpose in 1926. Florence E. Wall, early member and honorary fellow of AIC, wrote about the Gold Medal in the May, 1979, issue of *THE CHEMIST*:

"Sometime in 1925, Albert P. Sachs, one of the most active of the founding members of the Institute, was appointed a committee of one to produce a design for a Gold Medal. It had been decided that the Institute should bestow a major award annually to someone in government, industry or education who had the good of chemists at heart and who had done something notable for the benefit of this professional group.

"How well the medal has fulfilled its purpose is obvious to anyone who studies the roster of distinguished recipients. The Gold Medal is one of the highest awards of long standing in the chemical profession. It is the Institute's most prestigious award and is given annually to a person who has stimulated activities of service to the science of chemistry or the profession of chemist or chemical engineer in the U.S."

Dr. William Blum of the National Bureau of Standards was the first to receive the Gold Medal. Other early recipients were Lafayette B. Mendel, Francis P. Garvan and his wife, George Eastman, Andrew W. and Richard B. Mellon, Charles H. Herty, Henry C. Sherman, James B. Conant, Marston T. Bogert, and James F. Norris.

At its forty-third annual meeting held in New Orleans in 1966, the American Institute of Chemists started its annual Chemical Pioneer Program. The inaugural remarks entitled "Chemical Pioneers Who Shape Industry" were presented by distinguished scientist Dr. William J. Sparks, co-inventor of butyl rubber, President of the American Chemical Society, and recipient of many well-deserved honors. Dr. Sparks was also Chairman of the 1966 Chemical Pioneers Award Committee; the other members were Drs. William E. Hanford and John L. Hickson. Those who received the 1966 Chemical Pioneer Awards were Carl E. Barnes, Herman A. Bruson, Charles H. Fisher, Robert M. Joyce, Charles C. Price, and Eugene G. Rochow. Since the first meeting, the AIC has named at least four Pioneers annually.

Twenty years later, New Orleans was again the site for the AIC gathering. At that time, in his speech "Look What the Chemical Pioneers Started," C. H. Fisher stated that these and other pioneers began the greatest science revolution in all history. Naming but a few of the remarkable individuals to receive the Pioneer award, he briefly outlined the scientific achievements of Battista, Hass, Haensel, Hall, Idol, Levine, Marvel, Phillips, Plunkett, Rochow, Simons, Sparks, Tishler and Toland.

Most of the Gold Medalists and Chemical Pioneers have received several or more imporatnt honors. Fifteen received the National Medal of Science, the highest science award given by the United States government. And fourteen of the living honorees have the great honor of being elected members of the National Academy of Sciences or National Academy of Engineering. Some of the deceased Medalists were also members of the Academy of Sciences or Engineering. H. C. Brown, Calvin, Flory, Libby, Pauling, Seaborg, and Urey are recipients of the Nobel Prize. Many of the Medalists have received various other honors, including the Priestley Medal or the distinction of holding high office, such as President of the American Institute of Chemists or the American Chemical Society.

In 1968, Marquis Who's Who, Inc., published a biographical dictionary entitled *World's Who's Who in Science*. This book lists the more eminent scientists in all the world in all history (to 1968). Interestingly, about half of the Medalists and about a third of the Pioneers are listed in it.

Partly because they are or have been personally acquainted with many of the individuals profiled in this book, the authors have enjoyed reviewing the careers and achievements of the AIC Gold Medalists and Chemical

Pioneers. The authors hope that their book will give further recognition to those profiled and increase appreciation of the importance of research and innovation. Perhaps it is not too much to hope that the general process of benefitting humankind through creative research also will be encouraged.

Gratitude is expressed to the many individuals and organizations that contributed in one way or another to the preparation of this book of profiles. This includes the Medalists, Pioneers, and others* who provided information, reviews, and photographs. We are particularly grateful to David A. H. Roethel, Executive Director of the American Institute of Chemists, who helped us acquire many photos and provided useful advice. Professor James D. Navratil of the University of New South Wales and Litarvan's staff are thanked for their valuable assistance.

We owe special thanks to Professor Harold F. Walton, University of Colorado, who made time in his busy schedule to critically review the book prior to publication.

Raymond B. Seymour
Charles H. Fisher

*D. Y. Curtin and Tim O'Neill, University of Illinois; D. Stanley Tarbell, Vanderbilt University; K. A. Beal, National Bureau of Standards; Thomas Flynn, Wadsworth Laboratories Photo Unit; Walter Frommer, Olin Corp.; Harvard University; Max Tishler, Wesleyan University; Research Corporation; Thelma McCarthy, The Center for History of Chemistry; Debra Koret and Wallace Pringle, Wesleyan University; Mrs. Margaret C. Clark, Cosmos Club; Linda S. Thompson, Mobil Mining and Minerals Co.; E. N. Brandt and J. S. Nichols, The Dow Chemical Co.; M. Lois Gauch, Eastman Kodak Co.; Mary L. Good and A. O. Braun, Allied Signal Engineered Materials Research Center; Helen C. Adams, Bradford Stanerson and Michael Heylin, American Chemical Society; D. W. Meek, Ohio State University; R. J. Riley, Fordham Law School; Vladimir Haensel, University of Massachusetts at Amherst; M. M. Bursey, University of North Carolina; M. N. Ackermann, Oberlin College; Mary W. Buck, MacMurray College; D. J. Cook, DePauw Archives, DePauw University; L. J. Noe, University of Wyoming; Ella Putman, Monsanto Chemical Co.; M. W. Yeats, MIT Museum; Mrs. George McFarland, daughter of W. K. Lewis; Robert E. Berry, USDA Citrus and Subtropical Laboratory; Helen MacDowell, widow; Mellon Bank, Pittsburgh; Richard W. Jackson, Peoria, IL; Aura G. Wilson, Yale University; George Foster, Institute of Food Technology; John H. Nair (son), Clifton Park, NJ; D. Poland, Johns Hopkins University; S. W. Campbell, Clark University Archives; R. D. Dresdner, University of Florida; Dr. Meredith Sparks (widow), Coral Gables, FL.

FLORENCE WALL

Florence Wall has been a member of the American Institute of Chemists since 1923. Remarkably fit and able for a woman of her years, she serves The Institute as historian.

THE AMERICAN INSTITUTE OF CHEMISTS

The American Institute of Chemists was founded in 1923 to improve public recognition of the chemical profession. One of the key ways it met this objective was to establish a nationally prominent award to recognize chemists and chemical engineers who make outstanding contributions to the advancement of chemical science. Thus was created the Gold Medal Award in 1926. AIC's highest honor, the Gold Medal, was and is still regarded as one of the top three awards in American chemistry. Its list of recipients reads like a *Who's Who in American Chemistry*, including as it does Nobel Prize winners, leading industrialists, major researchers, esteemed academicians, and others.

Sensing the need for a more specialized honor, in 1966 the Institute created the Chemical Pioneer Award. This award recognizes chemists, chemical engineers, and their associates who have made outstanding contributions which have had a major impact on advances in chemical science and industry and/or the chemical profession. The emphasis is on creative innovation, often by invention, in the world of chemical technology. From a large number of nominations, no more than four recipients are chosen annually. These individuals represent the panoply of the chemical profession. It is noteworthy that Charles H. Fisher and Raymond B. Seymour, the authors of this book, have been so honored. Dr. Fisher is widely regarded as the architect of the Chemical Pioneers program, having instigated this award following his term as AIC President in 1962-63. In recognition of his work, Dr. Fisher was awarded the AIC Presidential Citation of Merit Award in 1986.

The American Institute of Chemists salutes all those notable practitioners who have received the Gold Medal or Chemical Pioneer Award, and thanks Drs. Seymour and Fisher for their efforts in assembling these profiles.

David A. H. Roethel
Executive Director

(Photograph courtesy of the University of Illinois.)

ROGER ADAMS

*"To the large group who had done research with him or had taken his classes, and to the thousands who had known him in his varied activities, his death meant not only the passing of a great man but also the end of an era."**

In September of 1954, more than five hundred people gathered at the University of Illinois at Urbana-Champaign to pay homage to the leading organic chemist of his generation. For Roger Adams, who had served the university for thirty-eight years, was retiring at the age of sixty-five.

*Tarbell, D. Stanley and Ann Tracy, *Roger Adams: Scientist and Statesman*, American Chemical Society, 1981.

Considered by any measure of ability and achievement, Adams was easily one of the most versatile and talented chemists of all time. Those students, colleagues and friends who flocked to Urbana from distant places did so not merely to honor an outstanding scientist - they were drawn by a combination of respect and personal affection for a man who was unique in his time; and his friends planned this occasion to attempt to show him what he meant to them and to recognize his service to American chemistry and to science in general.

Adams had a remarkable ability for attracting and educating young people, and their achievements were as important to him as his own success. This interest in his students as individuals was obvious, and was one of the major reasons for the respect and affection they felt for him. Fondly known as "The Chief" to generations of students, he was responsible for educating numbers of them so that many would achieve high positions in the academic world and in industry, and the impact of their achievements on science and society would be felt for decades to come.

In 1916 Adams accepted an offer from William A. Noyes to become assistant professor of chemistry at the University of Illinois, little realizing that within ten years he would mold the department into one of the most outstanding in the country and would also become its head, to succeed Noyes.

His brilliant researches, described in over four hundred papers (which included the research of 184 doctorates, fifty postdoctorates, and countless master's and bachelor's candidates), had both theoretical and practical value. Before Adams entered the scene, scientists had been able to demonstrate that platinum and palladium were the most active catalysts for hydrogenations at low temperatures and pressures, but no easy method had been discovered for preparing active palladium and platinum catalysts and no method was known for preparing with certainty, in successive experiments, platinum or palladium catalysts of uniform activity. Adams prepared platinum and palladium dioxides by fusing chloroplatinic acid or palladium chloride with sodium nitrate. The resulting metallic dioxides were isolated by cooling the melt and digesting with water. He discovered when he added a small charge of the brown metal oxide to the solution of the unsaturated compound and treated it with hydrogen, the oxide was promptly reduced; and a suspension of the black finely divided metal resulted. The metal then catalyzed the hydrogenations of the organic compound. The convenience in preparation and the great effectiveness of the Adams catalyst under mild conditions have been widely recognized.

Adams also made extensive studies on the elucidation of the structure of many naturally occurring compounds. In collaboration with Ralph L. Shriner at the University of Illinois, he investigated (1925) the composition of chaulmoogra oil, a mixture of fatty-acid glycerides once used to treat leprosy. He established the structure of hydrocarpic and chaulmoogric acids obtained by saponification of the oil and demonstrated the presence in each of a cyclopentene ring. Following this work, he synthesized many analogous acids that, in the form of esters, exhibited physiological action similar to that of chaulmoogra oil.

Adams determined the structure of gossypol, the toxic yellow pigment of cottonseed, the presence of which limited for many years the full utilization of cottonseed oil and meal.

His studies clarifying the structure of the narcotic principle of marijuana demonstrated that the test commonly used at that time by the Federal Bureau of Narcotics for detection of marijuana actually indicated the mere presence of an innocuous companion product. Adams' clarification led to the development of methods for synthesizing analogous substances with similar narcotic properties and a variety of interesting products.

Adams' research was also directed to the toxic alkaloids that cause cattle poisoning. Commonly found in plants on Texas ranches, these compounds occur especially in various species of *Senecio, Crotalaria, Trichodesma* and *Heliotropium.*

Among Adams' many other investigations were the synthesis of local anesthetics, studies on anthraquinones, organic arsenic compounds, and the synthesis and reactions of a new class of compounds with exceptionally high reactivity - quinone mono- and di-imides. Moreover, while serving as a major in the Chemical Warfare Service during World War I, he synthesized phenarsazine chloride, a sternutatory substance better known as Adamsite.

He also investigated extensively steric hindrance due to restricted rotation about a single bond as found in substituted biphenyls, diphenylbenzenes, phenylpyrrols, bipyrryls, arylolefins, and arylamines. He demonstrated that substitution in the *ortho* positions of the bond between the rings was effective in hindering rotation and that the *ortho* substituents could be arranged in sequence of effectiveness. For example, in the biphenyl series he studied the relative stability of several compounds by measuring the rate of conversion of an optically active form of the substance into its racemic modification. He demonstrated that the effectiveness of the groups to slow up the rate of racemization falls into the following order

with the bromine atoms showing the greatest effect:
$Br>CH_3>Cl>NO_2>CO_2H>OCH_3>F$.

Synthetic polymers also received some of his attention. In 1929 he (with William Lycan) found that the polymerization of omega-hydroxydecanoic acid causes the formation of linear polymers and a large dimeric cyclic ester containing a ring with twenty-two carbons.

Adams' countless contributions to science garnered him numerous honors, including: ten honorary degrees, a total of twenty-four medals and awards from American and foreign scientific societies and honorary membership in nine chemical societies and the National Academy of Sciences (1929). Some of his most notable tokens of esteem were: the Davy Medal of the Royal Society of London (1945); A. W. Hoffman Medal of the German Chemical Society (1953); American Chemical Society medals - W. H. Nichols (1927), Willard Gibbs (1936), T. W. Richards (1944), and Priestley (1946); Franklin Medal of the Franklin Institute of the State of Pennsylvania (1960); National Medal of Science (1964); and Gold Medal of the American Institute of Chemists (1964). In addition, he was awarded the U. S. Medal for Merit and was appointed Honorary Commander of the British Empire (C.B.E.) for his achievements as a member of the National Defense Research Committee during 1941-46.

He was very active in the American Chemical Society, serving as president in 1935 and chairman of the board of directors from 1944 to 1950. He was also president of the American Association for the Advancement of Science in 1950.

Adams was co-author of *Elementary Laboratory Experiments in Organic Chemistry* (5th Ed. 1963), for twenty years editor-in-chief of *Organic Reactions*, and editor of two volumes of *Organic Syntheses.*

Roger Adams, the youngest of four children, was born January 2, 1889, in Boston, Massachusetts. He was educated at Harvard University, where he received his B.A. in 1909, A.M. in 1910, and Ph.D. in 1912 under C. L. Jackson. The following year he spent in Germany, studying with Otto Diels and Richard Willstatter - the leading exponents, respectively, of synthetic organic chemistry and the chemistry of natural products. In 1913 he returned to Harvard as a post-doctoral fellow with Jackson (then emeritus). He became an instructor in organic chemistry at Harvard in 1914.

Adams died in Urbana on July 6, 1971. In their book, *Roger Adams: Scientist and Statesman*, the Tarbells stated: "Adams is a prime example of Samuel Johnson's definiton of genius: 'A mind of large general powers, accidentally determined to some particular direction'."

(Photograph courtesy of the American Institute of Chemists.)

FREDERICK EUGENE BAILEY, JR.

"For his pioneering studies of alkylene oxide polymers and his discovery of polymerization mechanisms for making very high molecular weight poly(ethylene oxide)."[*]

Ethylene oxide was synthesized by Wurtz in 1859 by the reaction of sodium acetate with ethylene dibromide. The production of ethylene oxide by the reaction of potassium hydroxide on ethylene chlorohydrin, reported in 1863, has been replaced by the

[*]The citation of the Chemical Pioneer Award.

direct silver-catalyzed oxidation of ethylene. Union Carbide, which was one of the first producers of ethylene oxide, continues to use this oxide for the production of its Prestone antifreeze and automotive coolants. This reactant is used also to produce polyester fibers and polyurethane. Polyethylene glycols, which Wurtz produced by the reaction of ethylene oxide and ethylene glycol, have been produced for many years by Union Carbide under the trade name Carbowax. Since ethylene oxide continues to be an important product for Union Carbide, it is not surprising that one of its leading research scientists, Dr. Frederick Eugene Bailey, Jr., has focused his studies on ethylene oxide and its high molecular weight polymers.

The son of Frederick Eugene and Florence Berkeley Bailey, Fred was born in Brooklyn, New York, on October 8, 1927. He entered Amherst College as an Addison Brown Scholar to receive his B.A. degree in 1948. Thereafter, he was a Forrest Jewett Moore graduate fellow at Yale (M.S., 1950; Ph.D., 1952).

Dr. Bailey then began his long career with Union Carbide at South Charleston, West Virginia. He is now a senior research scientist. He has further demonstrated his dedication to polymer science by serving Marshall University, West Virginia University, and Morris Harvey College as adjunct professor and by chairing Gordon Research Conferences.

The recipient of AIC's 1987 Chemical Pioneer Award, Fred has been a fellow of the American Institute of Chemists since 1970. He is also a fellow of the American Association for the Advancement of Science and the New York Academy of Sciences. He has served the American Chemical Society as national councilor, chairman of the Polymer Division, and general secretary of the Macromolecular Secretariat.

Dr. Bailey is the author of some sixty scientific reports and is the author, co-author, or co-editor of *Polyethylene Oxide, Initiation of Polymerization, Urethane Chemistry and Applications,* and *Interactions in Macromolecules.* He has been awarded sixty-one patents by the U. S. Patent Office.

Fred married Mary Catherine Lowder in 1979.

WILLIAM OLIVER BAKER

William Baker joined Bell Laboratories in 1939 and his advancement was rapid. By 1955 he had been appointed Vice-President of corporate research. The goal of his research program at Bell was an understanding of the science of polymers used for telephonic communication. He developed x-ray techniques to demonstrate lateral ordering of parallel chains in fibers. He also developed light scattering molecular weight determination techniques and contributed to a better understanding of the properties of polyolefin sheathing used as a replacement for lead for the protection of metallic cables. His other meritorious contributions include high frequency pizoelectric transducers; temperature induced conductivity of nylons and proteins; polymeric carbon, which led to ablative structures; satellite communications; masers; lasers; superconducting (jointly with J. Paul Hogan) for the invention of crystalline polypropylene.*

In 1978 the American Chemical Society Award in Petroleum Chemistry was presented to Banks in recognition of his discovery of olefin disproportionation. The original catalysts for this reaction are molybdenum carbonyl and molybdenum oxide supported on alumina. This discovery, described in a joint paper with Dr. Grant C. Bailey,** has been cited in over 200 publications since it first appeared.

The disproportionation reaction, which is used for the interconversion of light olefinic hydrocarbons, was widely recognized as "the outstanding development in fundamental industrial chemistry in recent years." But in spite of its importance, this discovery was much less significant than that of catalytic polymerization of olefins to produce crystalline polyethylene, polypropylene and poly(4-methyl-1-pentene), for which three key patents were issued to Robert Banks and J. Paul Hogan. Sulfuric acid, hydrochloric acid and sodium hydroxide were called "heavy chemicals" in the 1930's because their annual production in the United States exceeded one million tons. Today, the "new heavy chemicals" - polyethylene, polypropylene, polystyrene and polyvinyl chloride - are produced at an annual rate of over one million tons. Although an olefin polymer was known in the nineteenth century, the credit for polyolefins is given to Fawcett and Gibson, who accidentally produced low density polyethylene in the early 1930's. C. S. Marvel, F. Mayo, J. P. Hogan and R. L. Banks produced high density polyethylene

*The 1956 Nobel Prize was awarded to Dr. Giulio Natta for his discovery of polypropylene.
**Ind. Eng. Chem. Prod. Res. & Div., 3, 170 (1964).

solenoids; solid state diodes; and transistors. His research efforts resulted in thirteen U. S. patents and over one hundred research publications in scientific journals.

Dr. Baker retired as Chairman of the Board of Bell Telephone Laboratories in 1980.

The son of Harold May and Helen Stokes Baker, Bill was born July 15, 1915, in Chesterton, Maryland. There he attended secondary and high school, receiving a B.S. degree from Chesterton's Washington College in 1935. In 1957 he received an honorary Sc.D. degree from his alma mater. He also received honorary degrees from over twenty other institutions of higher learning: Stevens Institute of Technology (1962); Georgetown University (1962); University of Pittsburgh (1963); Seton Hall University (1965); University of Glasgow (1965); University of Akron (1968); University of Michigan (1970); Saint Peter's College (1972); Monmouth College (1973); Polytechnic Institute of New York (1973); University of Pennsylvania (1974); Clarkson College of Technology (1974); Trinity College, Dublin (1975); Kean College of New Jersey (1976); Northwestern University (1976); University of Notre Dame (1978); New Jersey Institute of Technology (1978); Lehigh University (1980); Drew University (1981); Tufts University (1981); New Jersey College of Medicine and Dentistry (1981); and Farleigh Dickinson University (1982).

Bill accepted a Harvard fellowship at Princeton University. There, while working as a graduate student under Dr. C. P. Smyth, he developed new information on solid state science. He was able to relate molecular rotations to entropy of fusion and explain the high melting points of symmetrical organic molecules. He extended these investigations to eutectics, multiphase crystallizations and aliphatic and biological compounds which exhibited mobility in the solid state. Bill was awarded his Ph.D. in physical chemistry at Princeton in 1938. He spent another year at Princeton as a Procter postdoctoral fellow before joining Bell Laboratories.

Bill is a member of the National Academy of Sciences, National Academy of Engineering, Institute of Medicine, American Academy of Arts and Sciences, American Chemical Society, American Philosophical Society, Industrial Research Institute, Sigma Xi, Omicron Delta Kappa, Phi Lambda Upsilon, Cosmos Club, Chemists Club, and Princeton Club. He is a fellow of the American Institute of Chemists, American Physical Society, and Franklin Institute.

He has served on: the advisory boards of *General and Applied Polymer Science, Carbons, Information and Society,* and *Science, Technology and Human Values*; the Visiting Committee on Science and Mathematics of Drew University, and the Commission on the Humanities. He has been an extensive lecturer, including: the National Institute of Health (1958); Notre Dame - Arthur J. Schmitt Lecturer (1968); North Carolina State University - Harrelson Lecturer (1971); University of Pennsylvania - Herbert Spencer Lecturer (1974); American Iron and Steel Institute - Charles M. Schwab Memorial Lecturer (1976); the Metallurgical Society of AIME - American Society for Metals Distinguished Lecturer (1976); National Federation of Abstracting and Indexing Services - Miles Conrad Memorial Lecturer (1977); University of Texas Medical Branch - Cecil and Ida Green Visiting Scholar (1980); Oklahoma Section of American Chemical Society - Logue Lecturer (1981); University of Wisconsin, Laboratory of Chemistry - Centennial Lecturer (1981); Johns Hopkins University - Lecturer for Semi-Centennial of Library (1981); and Delaware Section of American Chemical Society - Carothers Lecturer (1981).

Bill was named as one of the nation's leading industrial scientists by *Fortune Magazine* in 1954. He received the AIC Honor Scroll (1962) and Gold Medal (1975).

He has also been awarded the: Perkin Medal (1963), Priestley Medal (1966), Edgar Marburg Award (1967), ASTM Award to Executives (1967), Industrial Research Institute Medal (1970), Frederik Philips Award (1972), Industrial Research Man of the Year Award (1973), Procter Prize of Sigma Xi (1973), Princeton University's James Madison Medal (1975), Mellon Institute Award (1976), Franklin Institute of Fahrney Medal (1977), ACS Willard Gibbs Medal (1978), Materials Research Society von Hippel Award (1978), ACS Madison Marshall Award (1980), New Jersey Science and Technology Medal (1980), Vannevar Bush Award (1981), New Jersey Patent Law Association's Jefferson Medal (1981), Sarnoff Prize (1981), and National Security Medal (1982).

Dr. Baker has served as a trustee for Carnegie-Mellon University, Princeton University, Rockefeller University, the Andrew W. Mellon Foundation, the Harry Frank Guggenheim Foundation, the Fund for New Jersey, General Motors Cancer Research Foundation, the Newark Museum, and the Charles Babbage Institute. He is director of Annual Reviews, Inc., Council on Library Resources, Summit and Elizabeth Trust Company, Johnson & Johnson and Health Effects Institute Clinical Scholars Program of the Robert Wood Johnson Foundation, Third Century Corporation, Babcock & Wilcox Company, American Dow International Inc., Dow Chemical Laboratories, Inc., Sandia Corp., Western Electric Co., and Western Electric International. He has also served as the vice president of the President's Committee on Science and Technology, Advisory Board on Military Personnel Supplies, Evaluation Panels of the Advisor to the National Bureau of Standards, and Commission on Sociotechnical Systems. This last produced the widely read report *A Nation at Risk.*

Dr. Baker has authored the following books: *High Polymers* (1974); *Second Rate Brains* (1985); *Symposium on Basic Research, AAAS* (1959); *Rheology,* Vol. III (1960); *Technology and Social Change* (1964); *Listen to Leaders in Engineering* (1965); *Science and Society: A Symposium* (1965); *Chemistry, A New Look* (1966); *Perspectives in Polymer Science* (1966); *Research in the Service of National Purpose* (1967); *Research in the Service of Man: Biomedical Knowledge, Development and Use* (1967); *Washington Colloquium on Science and Society* (1967); *Science: The Achievement and the Promise* (1968); *1942-1967, 25 Years at RCA Laboratories; Materials Science and Engineering in the U.S.* (1970); (Edited) *Proceedings of the 23rd National Conference on the Administration of Research* (1970); *A Look at Business in 1990 . . . A Summary of the White House Conference on the Industrial World Ahead* (1972); *The Technological Catch and Society* (1975); *Annual Review of Materials Science* (1976); *The Random House Encyclopedia* (1977); and *Science and Technology in America - An Assessment* (1977).

In addition to his vocation as a scientist, Bill has demonstrated a broad interest in social progress, medicine, economics and the future. He enjoys the environment outside the laboratory and is an ardent hiker, traveller and photographer.

Bill married Frances Burrill in 1941. They have one son, Joseph Burrill Baker.

CLARENCE KENNETH BANKS

Leprosy or Hansen's disease, which is the result of an infection by *Mycobacterium leprea*, has been known and feared for several thousand years. It is now possible to arrest this disease by treatment with dapsone or promacetin. The latter was synthesized by Chemical Pioneer (1971) Clarence Kenneth Banks.

Kenneth was born in Kansas City, Missouri, on June 1, 1914. After graduating from high school, he enrolled in the University of Missouri (Kansas City) and received an A.B. degree in 1936. He attended graduate school at the University of Nebraska where he received his M.S. and Ph.D. degrees in 1938 and 1940, respectively.

In 1940, he accepted a position as research chemist with Parke, Davis and Company where he advanced to Research Division Head. Nine years later, Dr. Banks was named Director of Research for M & T Chemicals Inc. He was promoted to Vice President in 1950 and Assistant to the President in 1967. The next year he accepted employment with American Can Company, the parent of M & T Chemicals Inc.

Kenneth is a member of the American Chemical Society, American Association for the Advancement of Science, Pharmaceutical Association, Electroplating Society, British Chemical Society, Sigma Xi, and Phi Lambda Epsilon. He has published several reports in scientific journals and has been granted a number of patents by the U. S. Patent Office.

Dr. Banks married Lucille Evelyn Baker in 1940. Two children were born of this union. He is now retired and living in Sedona, Arizona.

ROBERT LOUIS BANKS

When Henry B. Hass introduced Robert L. Banks at the 1981 meeting of the American Institute of Chemists, he recited the following limerick:

> "There is a fine Phillips chemist named Banks
> And he's in the very front ranks
> With a brand new reaction
> He gave satisfaction
> And has earned our most sincere thanks."

This honor* had a long gestation period. But the Patent Office was even slower in recognizing Bob's talents: he had to wait thirty years before being granted a patent

*The 1981 Chemical Pioneer Award.

but it was not produced commercially until it was rediscovered by Nobel Laureate K. Ziegler in the 1950's. A. Zletz of Standard Oil of Indiana and Hogan and Banks of Phillips Petroleum were granted patents for high density polyethylene in 1951 and 1953.

The youngest of seven children, Bob was born November 24, 1921, to Dr. James A. and Maude (McAlister) Banks in Piedmont, Missouri, a small midwestern town. Bob's father was a dentist; his mother a former music teacher. Bob entered Southwest Missouri State College in 1940, two years later transferring to the University of Missouri at Rolla where he received a B.S. degree in chemical engineering. He earned his M.S. degree at Oklahoma State University (1953) and received an honorary professional degree (1976) and an alumni merit award (1980) from his alma mater.

Bob was first employed as a process engineer for Co-op Refinery of Coffeyville, Kansas. In 1946 he left this wartime aviation gasoline plant to accept a position as a research chemist/engineer with Phillips Petroleum, where he is still employed as a senior research associate. He and Hogan were part of a Phillips group which was successful in the late 1940's in converting natural gas to gasoline.

Banks served briefly as a visiting professor at the University of Missouri (Rolla) in 1981 and has presented lectures throughout the United States and in Austria, Canada, France, Ireland, and the Soviet Union. Awardee of 48 U. S. patents and close to 150 patents in foreign countries, he is author or co-author of more than thirty-five technical publications. He is a member of the American Chemical Society and the Catalyst Society and a fellow of the American Institute of Chemists.

For his outstanding contributions to applied chemistry, Banks shared the 1987 Perkin Medal with J. Paul Hogan.

Banks married Mildred Kathleen Lambeth in 1947. They have three daughters, Susan Lee, Mary Kathleen, and Melissa Anna, and four grandchildren. Bob is an enthusiastic golfer and outdoorsman.

CARL EDMOND BARNES

Carl Barnes discovered in 1951 that nylon-4 could be produced by the alkaline catalyzed polymerization of 2-pyrrolidone and has spent considerable effort since that time in his attempts to commercialize this polypyrrolidone. In 1963, he formed his own company, Barnes Research Associates. Four years later, he started a new company, Alrac Corp., and supplied limited samples of nylon-4 yarn to garment manufacturers. Since 1977, he and others have invested in Barson Corp. in the hopes of producing, by means of a polymerization process, a commercial hydrophilic fiber which will have the dyeing characteristics and the feel or "hand" of silk or cotton.

While artificial fibers, such as rayon (artificial silk) were produced in the nineteenth century, no truly synthetic fiber was available until the late 1930's. It was Wallace H. Carothers who produced polyamide which he called nylon-66. In addition to this dyadic polyamide, obtained by the condensation of adipic acid and hexamethylenediamine, a monadic nylon-6 was also made in the laboratory of Carothers in the early 1930's. This polymer, which was obtained by the polymerization of carprolactam, was marketed under the trade name Perlon-L by Paul Schlack in Germany in 1937. Other dyadic nylons, viz 44 and 610, have been produced, but nylon-66 remains the most widely used synthetic polyamide fiber. Silk and wool are also polyamides which, because of the high percentage of polar amide groups, have higher moisture absorption and better feel than nylon-6 or nylon-66 in which the amide groups are separated by at least four carbon atoms. Substituted nylon-1, which has a high percentage of polar amide groups, has been produced in the laboratory but not on a commercial scale. Nylon-2 (polyglycine), which has a high percentage of polar groups and resembles silk, was produced by Leuchs in 1902. Nylon-3 fibers have been produced by a molecular rearrangement of acrylamide. Dimethyl nylon-3 has also been produced from the lactam, 4,4-dimethylazetidin-2-one, but none of the monadic nylons (1, 2 and 3) have been produced commercially.

Prior to Dr. Barnes' discovery that carbon dioxide-initiated, acyl activated, polymerization of 2-pyrrolidone produced a heat stable polymer, he had made several important discoveries in polymer chemistry. Some of these were polyvinylcarbazole used as a mica substitute, "uvinol" uv light absorber, polyvinylpyrrolidone, a microfilm reader-printer, a protective coating for silverware ("Tan-I-Shield") and "Scotchgard."

Carl Edmund Barnes was born to N. Eugene and Grace E. (Fogg) Barnes in Lewiston, Maine, February 16,

1908. After graduating from the local high school, he entered Bates College. There he received his B.S. degree magna cum laude in 1930; his Ph.D. degree in chemistry was obtained from Harvard in 1935.

He spent four years as a research chemist with Polaroid Corporation (1936-1940) and then accepted a position as group leader of polymer research with General Aniline and Film Corp. He advanced to Associate Director of Research at GAF's Central Research Laboratories in Easton, Pennsylvania, leaving in 1950 to accept a position as Director of Research for Arnold, Hoffman and Co., Inc., in Providence, Rhode Island. He joined 3M Corp. as Assistant to the Research Vice President in 1953 and in 1961 was promoted to Research Corporate Vice President.

Dr. Barnes is a fellow of the American Institute of Chemists; a member of the American Chemical Society, and American Association for the Advancement of Science; and a director of Industrial Research, Armed Forces Chemical Association, Society of Motion Picture and Television Engineers, America's Future Inc. and American Economic Foundation. He has published several reports in scientific journals and has been granted over seventy-five patents by the U. S. Patent Office.

Carl married Sadie Boatnar Edwards in 1938. They have four children - Richard, Robert, Arthur and Louise. For some years Arthur has been working with his father at the Barson Corporation.

(Photograph courtesy of University of Texas at Arlington.)

ORLANDO ALOYSIUS BATTISTA

*"Money is like knowledge - the more
you have of it, the less you need to brag about it."**

Few chemists have had the distinction of receiving
four national awards from the American Chemical Society
and three awards from the American Institute of Chemists.
Dr. Orlando "Landy" Aloysius Battista is one of these rare
species. He received ACS's James T. Grady Award for
scientific writing (1973), Anselme Payen Award (1983),
Creative Invention Award (1983) and Phillips Award in

*From *Quotoons*, a collection of 60,000 original epigrams,
written by Battista.

Polymer Science (1986). AIC bestowed Honor Scrolls upon him (1965 and 1967) and the Chemical Pioneer Award (1969). Moreover, he was recipient of the Captain of Achievement Award from the American Academy of Achievement (1971), the Boss of the Year Award from the National Secretaries Association (1972), was named a Pioneer in Polymer Science by *Polymer News* (1981), and has received three IR-100 Awards from *Industrial Research*.

One of eight children, this twentieth century scientist, inventor, author and corporate executive, was born to James L. and Carmel Infante Battista in the small town of Cornwall, Ontario, Canada, June 20, 1917. He received the B.Sc. degree with class honors from McGill University in 1940. That same year he joined American Viscose Corporation,* where he was to spend the next thirty-three years of his professional life. In 1947 he became a United States citizen. He was transferred in 1970 from his position of assistant director of Central Research to Fort Worth to take on the responsibilities of vice-president for science and technology for Avicon Inc.**

Upon retiring from Avicon at the age of fifty-seven, Landy has accomplished more than most have in an entire lifetime. He served as adjunct professor of chemistry and director of the Center for Microcrystalline Polymer Science at the University of Texas at Arlington. In 1977 he resigned this appointment to found the O. A. Battista Research Institute and Research Services Corporation. He serves as chairman and president of these enterprises as well as of Knowledge, Inc., and Fastcrete Corporation.

*Later the FMC Corporation.
**A company formed to market his discovery of Avitene Hemostat.

Landy is a member of the American Chemical Society and served as chairman of its Cellulose, Wood and Fiber Division (1959-60). He was president of the AIC (1977-79) and is a lifetime fellow; he was certified as a Professional Chemist in 1977. He is also a fellow of the New York Academy of Sciences and a lifetime fellow of the National Association of Science Writers.

Since receiving his first patent for a process for forming porous artificial masses (1948), Dr. Battista has been granted over eighty patents by the U. S. Patent Office and over five hundred patents in foreign countries. He is probably best known for his accidental discovery of high solids aqueous suspensoids of cellulose microcrystals (1955). Millions of pounds of this product (Avicel) are produced annually by FMC in three large commercial plants in the United States, Japan and Ireland. It is estimated that about 500,000,000 pounds of Avicel have been sold since the original patent was issued in 1961.

Other important products of Landy's research are: a partial acid salt of microfibrillar collagen, used as a life saving hemostat in hospitals around the world; disposable contact lenses, patented in 1983; simulated marble or ivory based on protein hydrogels; new forms of graphite produced by the calcination of microcrystalline cellulose; recycled fibers from waste fibers; transparent burn and wound dressing based on crosslinked polymeric hydrogels; bioassimilable protheses - bone, sutures, selective fluid scavengers; and unique non-drug weight control products based on an expandable form of gelatin with a matrix of natural fiber.

Dr. Battista's first book, *Fundamentals of High Polymers* (published by van Nostrand-Reinhold, 1958) was the first of some twenty-one books he was to write. Others include: *Microcrystal Polymer Science* (McGraw-

Hill, 1975), *The Challenge of Chemistry* (Holt, Rinehart and Winston, 1959), *Olympiad of Knowledge* (1984) and *Research for Profit* (1986). He has also authored such popular books as *How to Enjoy Work and Get More Fun Out of Life* (Prentice-Hall), *The Power to Influence People* (Prentice-Hall), and *Quotoons* (G. P. Putnam & Sons), which were major factors in his having been presented the Grady Award.

In addition, Landy has published more than one thousand scientific articles. Also a composer of songs, his *Fort Worth* has been made the official song for his adopted city; an album of eight of his lyrics is soon to be published.

This outstanding chemist, who has long admitted to being a workaholic, maintains that "every great thing Americans have achieved occurred only because they were very respected overworkers." He subscribes to Sir Francis Bacon's formula: "Knowledge is not to be sought either for pleasure of the mind or for contention, or for superiority over others, or for profit, or for fame, or power of any of these inferior things, but for the benefit and use of life."

Landy married Helen Keffer in 1945. Neither son, William Battista, nor daughter, Elizabeth Ann, have followed in their father's footsteps, although his daughter serves as Chief Financial Officer of Research Services Corporation and Knowledge, Inc.

ARNOLD ORVILLE BECKMAN

Crude electrochemical cells were made in 1800 by Volta, who used an electric pile of zinc and silver disks separated by paper impregnated with an aqueous sodium chloride solution. In the 1920's, chemists used litmus paper to determine whether an aqueous solution was acidic (red) or alkaline (blue). During this period, a galvanometer was used to measure the potential of a balanced electro chemical cell, such as a hydrogen, silver chloride cell. The negative log of the hydrogen activity of the balanced cell was expressed as pH. In 1934, Arnold Beckman, who was a consultant for a Southern California citrus processing plant, decided to simplify the measurement of the pH of lemon juice by developing an "acidimeter" which would provide pH values directly. This resulted from a chance encounter with a classmate,

Dr. Glenn Joseph, with whom Beckman had attended the University of Illinois. Dr. Joseph had been trying unsuccessfully to measure the acidity of lemon juice that was heavily dosed with sulfur dioxide.

In October, 1936, the U. S. Patent Office granted Dr. Beckman a patent for his pH meter. The Beckman pH meter, or acidimeter, immediately became an indispensable tool for the citrus industry in Southern California. Soon, the pH meter, the first product in Beckman's long and illustrious career in the field of scientific instrumentation, became an invaluable tool for analytical chemists working in medicine, science, agriculture and industry.

In 1940, Dr. Beckman introduced a quartz photoelectric DU spectrophotometer for automated chemical analyses and a precision helical potentiometer, or Helipot. Prior to the introduction of the DU Spectrophotometer, a month's time instead of minutes was required to make Vitamin A assays with an accuracy of +/-25 percent. The Helipot, which was to be used as a component of the pH meter, became an essential component of RADAR in World War II. Subsequently, it was used within a wide variety of other electronic equipment.

For his invaluable contributions to science, in 1987 Dr. Beckman was inducted into the National Inventors Hall of Fame and named American Institute of Chemist's Gold Medalist. He is recipient of the California Institute of Technology's Distinguished Alumni Award (1984) and Milliken Award (1985). He has also received honorary doctoral degrees from six universities, and has been elected chairman emeritus of the Board of Trustees of the California Institute of Technology.

The son of George W. and Elizabeth E. Jewkes Beckman, Arnold was born in Cullom, Illinois, on April 10, 1900. He received his B.S. and M.S. degrees from the University of Illinois in 1922 and 1923, respectively. After spending two years as a research associate at the Bell Laboratories, he entered the California Institute of Technology, where he received his doctorate in 1928. While serving on the chemical faculty at the California Institute of Technology (1926-39), he also served an executive officer of the National Technical Laboratory (1935-40). He was president of Helipot Corporation (1944-58), of Arnold O. Beckman, Inc. (1946-58), and of Beckman Instruments (1940-65). After his company was merged with Smith-Kline, he served as Chairman of the Board of the Smith-Kline-Beckman Corporation. At the time Beckman's fledgling company first began to produce the pH meter, the firm consisted of two employees, one of whom was Dr. Beckman. Today the company employs over seven thousand people worldwide.

Dr. Beckman is an honorary fellow of the American Institute of Chemists, a fellow of the Royal Society of Arts, and a member of the American Academy of Arts and Sciences, National Academy of Engineering, American Chemical Society, American Association for the Advancement of Science, Instrument Society of America, Newcomen Society, Sigma Xi, Delta Upsilon, Alpha Chi Sigma, and Phi Lambda Upsilon. He also holds membership in the Jonathan Club, Newport Harbor Yacht Club, and is a member of the board of directors of several organizations.

Dr. and Mrs. Mable S. (Meinzer) Beckman, whom he married in 1925, are parents of Gloria, Patricia, and Arnold Stone. The Beckmans are widely known for their generous contributions to the advancement of education and research; his largest public gift was $50 million to California Institute of Technology.

JOHAN A. BJØRKSTEN

Johan Bjørksten's most dramatic research contributions have been in the field of gerontology. He advanced the concept of irreversible cross-linking of body proteins and nucleic acids as a principal cause of the aging process. Since, in the half century to follow his research on gerontology, he has not discovered any facts incompatible with this theory, he maintains that the problem of extension of human life span can only be solved by the application of the enzyme, chelation and hydroxyl free radical approach. He further believes that a basic understanding of the biochemistry of the aging process must be achieved before there can be a real breakthrough in therapy.

Born to Walter and Gerda E. A. Ramsay Bjørksten in Tammerfors, Finland, on May 27, 1907, Johan attended the University of Helsingfors where he received M.S. and Ph.D. degrees in chemistry in 1927 and 1931, respectively. He spent the next academic year as a guest researcher at the University of Stockholm. During the academic years 1931 and 1932, he conducted postdoctoral research, as Rockefeller Foundation Fellow, at the University of Minnesota under the direction of R. A. Gortner.

From 1933 to 1935, he served as a research chemist for Felton Chemical Company in Brooklyn and then moved to the midwest where he was in charge of development at Pepsodent (Clearing, Illinois, 1935-36) and chief chemist for Ditto, Inc. (1937-41). He was co-founder of A-B-C Packaging Machine Corp. (Tarpon Springs, Florida, 1940) and chemical director of Quaker Chemical Products (Conshohocken, Pennsylvania, 1941-44).

Since 1944 he has been associated with Bjørksten Research Laboratories in Madison, Wisconsin, and from 1953 with Bjørksten Research Foundation. He also served as chief executive officer (1945-48) and chairman of the Board (1948-56) of Bee Chemical* (Lansing, Illinois). He was co-founder (1956) and director of Griffolyn Company** in Houston.

Dr. Bjørksten received AIC's Honor Scroll (1959), the Chicago Technical Society Merit Award (1964), the Cosmetic Industry Buyers and Suppliers Association Award (1964), the Alfthan Prize of the Finnish Chemical Society (1972) and AIC's Pioneer Award (1977).

*Sold to Morton-Thiokol in January 1986.
**Now called the Reef Company.

He is author of *Longevity: Past - Present - Future* (JAB Publishing, 1987) and co-author of *Polyesters and Their Applications* (Reinhold, 1956). He has also been granted several patents by the U. S. Patent Office and has published numerous reports in scientific journals.

Johan is a lifetime fellow and past president of the American Institute of Chemists. He is a member of the American Chemical Society, American Association for the Advancement of Science, American Association of Cereal Chemists, Society of Cosmetic Chemists, American Leather Association, American Oil Chemists Society, American Society of Metals, American Society for Testing Materials, American Geriatrics Society, Technical Association of Pulp and Paper Industries, Finnish Chemical Society, Society of Paint Technology, Electrochemical Society, New York Academy of Science, Society Pro Faun et Flora Fennica, and American Institute of Aeronautics and Astronautics. He is also a member of Alpha Chi Sigma, Gamma Alpha, and Sigma Xi, as well as the Cosmos, Chemists and Rotary Clubs.

Johan married Bettina Feitler in 1938. Their daughter, Sybil Joan Jurgen von Rennenfampff is now deceased; her daughter, Julia, is a graduate student in New York. Their son, Dr. Oliver J. W. Bjørksten, is a professor of Psychiatry of the Medical University of South Carolina at Charleston. Johan married Christel Svedlin in 1963. Their three sons, Dargaa William, Nils Johan and Lennard Allen, are college students.

By continuing his research on life expectancy, Johan aptly demonstrates that there is life after sixty-five.

(Photograph courtesy of National Bureau of Standards.)

WILLIAM BLUM

The distinguished William Blum, who received the American Institute of Chemist's first Gold Medal in 1926 for his notable work in government service, was an expert in the atomic weight of cadmium, complex inorganic acids, electrochemistry, electrodeposition, electrotyping, electro-plating, electroforming, and corrosion. The Gold Medal was presented to him by retiring AIC president Dr. M. L. Crossley, who gave an address entitled "Science for Humanities Sake."

William received his B.S. degree in 1903 and Ph.D. degree in chemistry in 1908 from the University of Pennsylvania. Prior to beginning his career with the

Bureau of Standards, he was an instructor in chemistry at the University of Utah from 1903 to 1909. In 1951, Dr. Blum was made chief of the Bureau's Electrodeposition Section and assistant chief of the Chemistry Division.

Dr. Blum was president of the Electrochemical Society in 1926; he received the Society's Acheson Medal in 1944. He was an honorary member of the Electroplaters Society and was made an honorary member of the AIC in 1949. He was also a member of the American Chemical Society, Electrochemical Society, American Society for Testing Materials, Washington Academy of Science, Faraday Society, Electrodepositors Technical Society, Cosmos Club, Washington, D.C., and Chemists Club in New York.

Blum was co-author of *Principles of Electroplating and Electroforming*, which was published in three editions (1924, 1930, and 1949).

Born in Philadelphia on December 28, 1881, to Jacob and Katherine (Hoffman) Blum, William married Willetta Carr Baylis on September 20, 1910, and became the father of William, Jr.

Dr. Blum's hobby was fishing.

(Reprinted from *A History of the ACS*, with permission.)

MARSTON TAYLOR BOGERT

Dr. Bogert received many honors during his prestigious career, including honorary doctorates from Clark University and Columbia University; medal and an honorary degree from the Charles University in Czechoslovakia; medal of the Comensky University in Bratislava; Nichols Medal, 1905; Gold Medal, 1936; Priestley Medal, 1938; AIC honorary membership, 1945; and Chandler Medal, 1945.

The citation of the Gold Medal read:

". . . courageous explorer of the unknown realms of chemistry, lucid

interpreter of the significance of the results
of research in the advancement of
civilization, inspiring teacher, brilliant
scholar and valued friend, The American
Institute of Chemists awards you this medal
for your noteworthy and outstanding
services to the science of chemistry and to
the profession of chemist in America."

Dr. Bogert's address was entitled "The Onward March of
Synthetic Organic Chemistry."

Marston Bogert was active in several organizations
and held important positions in many of them. He was the
first American to be elected president (1938) of the
International Union of Pure and Applied Chemistry. After
World War II, he helped rebuild the organization and
continued as its president until 1947. He helped found the
Chemists Club and served as its president (1908). He was
president of the American Chemical Society (1907 and
1908). He was a colonel in the U. S. Chemical Warfare
Service (1918-19), president of the Society of Chemical
Industry in 1912, and member of Theodore Roosevelt's
White House Conference on Conservation of Natural
Resources. Moreover, he was on the Board of Managers of
the New York Botanical Gardens and was a consultant
(1926-1931) for the American Perfumer and Essential Oil
Review.

Dr. Bogert authored some 400 publications, of
which approximately 300 described original work,
involving: organic compounds, including perfumes; the
relation between odor and molecular structure;
heterocyclic compounds, such as quinazolines and
thiazoles; derivatives of pyrogallol, thiophene, terephthalic
acid, phenacetin, cinnamic aldehyde, and unsaturated
ketonic acids; dyestuffs; pharmaceuticals; and terpenes.

He was also an associate editor of the *Journal of the American Chemical Society* (1909-19 and 1924-29); he held a similar position with the *Journal of Organic Chemistry*.

His diversity of interests is indicated not only by his achievements in chemistry, the chemical profession and botany, but also by his connections with the Board of Criminal Science of the Police Department of New York City (1925-26), the Consulting Board of the Institute of Cancer Research, Rutgers Theological Seminary (1903-13), and vice president of the National Institute of Social Science.

Because of his gentlemanly manner and appearance and attractive personality, Marston was unusually effective in dealing with people, lecturing in classrooms, and chairing meetings. The latter he conducted with great tact and without using notes; he could introduce foreign speakers in their own languages. A man highly interested in the international aspects of chemistry, in 1927-28 he was visiting Carnegie Professor of International Relations at Charles University in Czechoslovakia.

Dr. Bogert's Dutch ancestors settled in the New York City area in 1668. He was born in Flushing on April 18, 1868, to Henry A. and Mary B. (Lawrence) Bogert. After attending Flushing Institute, he attended Columbia where he was granted an A.B. degree (1890). The next four years he spent studying chemistry at Columbia's School of Mines to complete requirements for his Ph.B. While a student, he became prominent as president of his class and chairman of the student body. He was active in shot putting, rowing, high jumping, and ice skating, and played the flute in the college orchestra. Of his several degrees, the only one about which he boasted was the C.Q.D. - "Doctor of Complicated Queerazolines" - awarded by a group of chemists.

Following receipt of his doctorate, he joined the faculty at Columbia to become the first professor of organic chemistry. He remained at Columbia until his retirement in 1938 as emeritus professor. Over these years, he also served as a lecturer on organic chemistry at New York University.

Dr. Bogert died of pneumonia in a Long Island convalescent home on March 21, 1954.

WILLIAM CALVIN BRENEMAN

William Breneman, at the age of forty-three, was the youngest individual to receive the American Institute of Chemist's prestigious Pioneer Award (1985). This award was presented to Bill for his design of a pilot plant to produce high purity silicon.

Although over twenty-five percent of the earth's crust consists of compounds of silicon - the world's second most abundant nonmetallic element - silicon has been known to man only since early in the nineteenth century. In 1811, Joseph Gay-Lussac and Baron Louis Thenard prepared amorphous silicon by the reaction of silicon tetrafluoride with potassium. But Joens Jakob Berzelius, who repeated this experiment in 1823, is usually credited with the discovery of this element.

Pure silicon, which does not occur naturally, has many uses. When doped with traces of boron or phosphorus, it is an excellent semiconductor. Single crystals of silicon are widely used in power rectifiers, transistors, diodes and solar cells. Since silicon for the latter use costs over fourteen dollars per watt capacity, the U. S. Energy Research and Development Adminstration funded a low cost silicon solar array project in an attempt to demonstrate the production of silicon-based flat plate photovoltaic systems with a capacity of 500 megawatts and a manufacturing cost of fifty cents per watt of capacity. William Breneman was appointed principal investigator of this project.

Breneman's pilot plant design was based on Union Carbide's process for catalytic redistribution of chlorosilane which converts trichlorosilane to silane and silicon tetrachloride. The latter is reduced by hydrogen in the presence of metallurgical grade silicon to trichlorosilane which, in turn, is converted to silane and thence to silicon in a close cycle process.

After successful operation of the pilot plant in Sisterville, West Virginia, Bill moved to Carbide's Linde Division laboratory at Tonawanda, New York, where he consulted on the design of a semi-works plant built in Washougal, Washington, to provide market development quantities of high purity polycrystalline silicon from the silane process. This unit became operational in 1983. In 1982, Bill had been appointed chief design engineer for a 1,200 ton-per-year commercial-scale polycrystalline silicon plant at Moses Lake, Washington, which became operational in 1985.

With the exception of two years service as a lieutenant in the U. S. Army Signal Corps (Vietnam, 1964-

66), Bill has been employed by Union Carbide continuously since 1963. In addition to his work with a wide variety of silanes and silicon, he has worked with silicone copolymers and phenyl ethyl methyl silicones.

Bill is a professional engineer in West Virginia and Washington and served as chairman of the Mid-Ohio Valley Section of American Institute of Chemical Engineers for two terms. He is the recipient of NASA's Certificate of Recognition (1981 and 1982).

The son of Calvin and Mary Murrow Breneman, Bill was born in Braddock, Pennsylvania, on July 9, 1941. He graduated from Greensburg High School and enrolled in the Carnegie Institute of Technology, where he received his B.S. degree in chemical engineering in 1963. That same year he began employment with Union Carbide's Silicone Technical Center in Sisterville and attended Ohio University, receiving his M.S. in chemical engineering in 1971 and M.B.A. in 1975.

As a student, Bill played bagpipes in the Carnegie Institute Kiltie Band. He has a pilot's license and commutes by plane from his home in Vancouver, Washington, to the plant at Moses Lake, Washington. His other hobbies include cabinet making, spelunking, and sports car road rally racing.

Bill married Gracie E. Craig in 1968. He and his wife have one son, William Jr.

(Photograph courtesy of Coating Consultants.)

GEORGE E. F. BREWER

As evidenced by the success of New Orleans' annual Mardi Gras Conferences on Waterborne and Higher Solid Coatings sponsored by the University of Southern Mississippi and the Southern Association of Paint Technologists, the science of organic solventless coatings is an important segment of the polymer industry. The acceptance of this technology is due, to a large degree, to the pioneering efforts of George Brewer, recipient of the American Institute of Chemists Chemical Pioneer Award in 1978.

George, like most creative scientists, has always asked questions in order to catalyze his creativity. Years ago, he questioned why his grandfather's 1912 Model T Ford had less tendency to rust than did his 1953 model auto. George discovered that one possible solution to the nonuniform coating problem was the use of a solventless paint. Like Archimedes, George was able to cry out "Eureka" when he incorporated the idea of baking the solventless coating.

When George approached the executives of Ford Motor Company to explain his concept of the uniform application of paint, he realized the meaning of Mark Twain's statement, "The man with a new idea is a crank until the idea succeeds." For the following remarks issued from the Director of Research and the Chief Engineer, respectively: "Not a dime for the lunatic!" and "What? The _ _ _ wants to put holes or slits in my car bodies!"

One may have better insight of the reluctance of these two men to have initially accepted Brewer's suggestion when one considers that the proposed process would have required 50,000 gallons of paint in a tank 300 meters long by three meters wide by three meters high. However, because of George's tenacity, this electrodeposition coating process is now used in over four hundred installations for protection against corrosion of automobiles, toys, furniture, and many other objects. Moreover, unlike previously used coating processes, the electrodeposition process does not contribute to air pollution.

The history of George Brewer's invention started in 1808, when a Russian scientist by the name of Reuss observed the movement of clay particles toward the anode in an electric cell containing an aqueous suspension of clay. This process, called "electrophoresis" by Reuss, was attempted in the 1920's and 1930's by several investigators for the deposition of beeswax, asphalts and rubber. Finally, in 1948, Arne Tiselius received the Nobel Prize for his successful application of electrophoresis in protein characterization.

Dr. Brewer was also able to apply his electrocoating process to an aqueous emulsion containing ten percent paint. Before this could be successfully accomplished, however, more than 150 man years went into experimentation, more than 75,000 paints were tested, 10,000,000 wheels were painted, and 150 experimental cars were coated and tested. The first automobile using the Brewer process was electrocoated at the Ford plant in Wixam, Michigan, in 1963. By 1972, over 500 electrocoating units had been installed around the world. It is interesting to note that today the automobile industry considers the invention by "the _ _ _ who wanted to put holes and slits in car bodies" the greatest breakthrough since the invention of the spray gun.

Born on January 23, 1904, in Austria, George attended local secondary school, receiving his Ph.D. degree from the University of Vienna in 1933. His doctoral thesis was on the physical-chemical aspects of dyestuffs for textiles. The three postdoctoral years were spent as a lecturer at his alma mater. He also spent some time as technical manager for a textile mill in Vienna. In 1939, he became a lecturer at the Institute of Textile Industries in Brussels, Belgium. A year later he emigrated to the United States to serve as a professor of chemistry at Rosary College in River Forest, Illinois, and research chemist for the state of Illinois on a NAC project. In 1944, he became head of the Department of Chemistry for Detroit's Marygrove College.

During the 1940's he also served as a consultant for Goge Products Company. In 1958, he consulted for Ford Motor Company. His first patent on electrodeposition of paints was issued in 1965. In 1968, he left Marygrove to become a staff scientist for Ford, leaving Ford in 1972 to open his own consulting firm.

George is a member of the American Chemical Society, American Institute of Chemists, and Society of Paint Technology. He served as president of the Michigan College Chemistry Teachers' Association (1954), was president of the Association of Analytical Chemists (1959), chairman of the Michigan Institute of AIC (1964), and Chairman of the Detroit Chapter of ACS (1960). He also served as the ACS Director of Organic Coatings and Plastic Chemistry (1974).

Dr. Brewer received the Midgeley Medal from the ACS Detroit Section (1964), Best Speaker Award from Western Coatings Society (1971), ACS A. K. Doolittle Award for best paper, and the AIC Chemical Pioneer Award (1978). He was the J. J. Mattiello Memorial Lecturer (1973) and was named a Pioneer in Polymer Science by *Polymer News* (1982). He has been awarded twenty-three patents by the U. S. Patent Office and is the author of one hundred scientific publications.

George married Frances Joan Werner in 1933. The Brewers live in Brighton, Michigan, where for recreation they swim and play bridge and tennis. George also teaches an electrocoating laboratory course at the University of Detroit.

(Photograph courtesy of Purdue University.)

HERBERT CHARLES BROWN

American writer Horatio Alger's over 100 tales of fiction, with such titles as *Ragged Dick* and *Pluck and Luck*, described the "rags-to-riches" success of young men. Had this Unitarian minister been born a century later, he could have written a true account of Herbert Charles Brovarnik (later anglicized to Brown) which would, without doubt, have outsold the rest of the Alger stories - this in spite of the fact that none of Alger's heroes became scientists and he himself probably did not know the formula for borane.

Had Alger written about Herbert, he would have told of a boy whose education in one of Chicago's predominately black ghetto schools was interrupted by the untimely death of his father; a boy who overcame this and many other obstacles to persevere and receive the Nobel Prize in Chemistry in 1979.

This "Cinderella" story started in the early party of the twentieth century with the migration of Herbert's grandfather and parents-to-be from the Ukraine because of the Czar's pogroms. Herbert's grandfather went to Chicago; his parents-to-be to London. In 1908, his father married Pearl Gorinstein; the couple lived in an apartment project provided by the Rothschilds for Russian Jews who had fled mass annihilation. Herbert was born in London on May 22, 1912. When he was two years old, his family moved to Chicago. Because there was little work for a skilled cabinet maker in the United States during this period of rapid transition to mass production, Herbert's father became a carpenter. There was, alas, little work for a carpenter in the years following World War I. As a result, he started a small hardware store; he and his family lived above the store.

His father's death brought a temporary halt to his son's education. Herbert re-enrolled in school, to graduate in 1930 - the same year his mother sold the store. This was the time of the Great Depression and the young man was unable to obtain but odd jobs. For this reason, he decided to enter Crane Junior College to major in electrical engineering. Unfortunately for engineering and fortunately for science, he became fascinated with his first course in chemistry, which fascination has lasted to this day.

For financial reasons, Crane was closed in 1933 and its students and faculty dismissed. Herbert then obtained a part-time job as a shoe clerk, one rung higher than that of Alger's shoeblacks. He also enrolled in night classes at

Lewis Institute.   Luckily, a former instructor at Crane, Dr. Nicholas Cheronis, had in his back yard a commercial laboratory.   He invited some of his more promising former students to make use of the laboratory to continue their studies.   Sarah Baylen was one of these students. Sarah, who had been Crane's outstanding chemistry student at the time of Herbert's arrival, did not immediately welcome Brown.   In fact, in a book published a half century later,* Sarah wrote that initially she had "hated his guts."   But Fate stepped in and the twosome joined forces.   They enrolled in Wright Junior College (established in 1934) to graduate a year later.   At that time Sarah wrote in Herbert's yearbook, "To a future Nobel Laureate."   Forty-four years later she accompanied him to Stockholm to realize her predilection.

Herb received a scholarship to the University of Chicago, which he attended with fiancee Sarah.   In 1936 he graduated with a B.S. in chemistry.   Little realizing she was only amplifying her earlier prognostication, Sarah presented Herbert a graduation gift - Alfred Stock's book on *The Hydrides of Boron and Silicon.*   Sarah's gift of the book fostered Herb's interest in boranes.   Although Herbert and Sarah planned to be married at that time, Professor Emeritus Julius Stieglitz urged him to accept a graduate teaching assistantship for the annual grand sum of $400 - scarcely enough for one to live on, let alone two.   In spite of their wish to be married, Herb had no choice but to undertake graduate research with Dr. H. I. Schlesinger at the University of Chicago.   A secret wedding followed. Alas, the "secret," published in the *Chicago Tribune,* added to the young couple's financial problems and Sarah was compelled to accept a position with Billings Hospital. So that she might obtain her B.S., Herb attended lecture

*Sarah Baylen Brown, *Remembering Herb*, Department of Chemistry, Purdue University, West Lafayette, Indiana (1978).

classes for her while at the same time conducting graduate work toward his doctoral degree, which he received in 1938.

Many individuals have found themselves in industrial work because they were unable to secure an academic appointment. The reverse was true for Brown, who at this time reluctantly accepted a postdoctoral position at the University of Chicago. One year later he was appointed Schlesinger's assistant, making the grand salary of *$2,400 annually.*

During World War II, Brown and his graduate students worked on volatile uranium compounds. The most desirable compound was uranium(IV) borohydride, more volatile than uranium hexafluoride. After four successful years of experimentation, Brown was informed that his chances of advancement with the department were slim. As a result, he accepted a position of assistant professor at Wayne State University. In 1947, he became a full professor at Purdue University, being promoted to Wetherill Distinguished Professor (1959) and Wetherill Research Professor (1960). He was granted emeritus status in 1978 and continues to work with a large group of postdoctoral students.

Brown's research involved the development of quantitative methods for the determination of steric effects in organic chemical reactions and the chemical effects of steric strain. He also investigated the non-classical ion problem, the basic properties of aromatic hydrocarbons and the development of a set of electrophilic constants which correlated aromatic substitution data and a wide variety of electrophilic reactions. He is probably best known, however, for his discovery (with B. C. Subba Rao) of the room temperature additon of diborane to olefins in ether solutions. This hydroboration reaction, which occurs without skeletal rearrangement to produce addition of H-B at the less hindered side of the double bond, forms H-C-C-B. (Herbert likes to point out that his parents were farsighted in naming him.) The hydroboration reaction earned him the Nobel Prize.

Dr. Brown was also recipient of the Nichols Medal (1959), Linus Pauling Medal (1968), National Medal of Science (1969), Roger Adams Medal (1971), Charles Frederick Chandler Medal (1973), CCNY Scientific Achievement Medal (1976), Albert Cresson Medal (1978), Priestley Medal (1981), Perkin Medal (1982), and Gold Medal of the American Institute of Chemists (1985). He received the ACS Award for Creative Research in Synthetic-Organic Chemistry (1960) and the Madison Marshal Award (1975). He was Harrison Howe Lecturer (1953), Centenary Lecturer of the Chemical Society of London (1955), Baker Lecturer (1969), and Ingold Memorial Lecturer (1978), which included the Ingold Medal. He was elected to the National Academy of Science (1957), the American Academy of Arts and Science (1966), and the Indian National Academy of Sciences (1978). He received an honorary D.Sc. degree from his alma mater and was elected an honorary fellow of the Royal Society of Chemistry (1978) and the Chemical Society of Japan (1982).

Dr. Brown's associations played a major role in his career. His destiny was interestingly foretold, as noted. This extraordinary individual, often said to be more of an inventor than scientist, is father to Charles Allen Brown, also a Ph.D. in organic chemistry. Son Charles married Israeli Dalia Stockelman in 1975 and they have two daughters, Tamar and Ronnie. In his work at IBM, he has established the remarkable reactivity of potassium hydride and has used that reactivity to make available potassium triisopropoxyborohydride, a very mild reducing agent, and potassium trisiamylborohydride, the most stereoselective reagent known. He established the reaction product of potassium hydride and trimethylenediamine, KAPA, to be a "Super-Base," the strongest base currently available to the organic chemist. He discovered the "Zipper" reaction, an almost instantaneous isomerization of triple bonds from the center of the chain to the end, even in molecules with a chain length of 32 carbon atoms. Could it be Charles is destined to follow in his famous father's footsteps?

(Photograph courtesy Wadsworth Laboratories/Photo Unit
New York State Department of Health.)

RACHEL FULLER BROWN

Rachel Brown's co-discovery (with Elizabeth L. Hazen) of the fungal antibiotic Nystatin made available the first safe antifungal antibiotic for human therapy. It was for this co-discovery that she received the Chemical Pioneer Award in 1975.

Nystatin, a boon for the treatment of certain candida infections, such as thrush and vaginitis, and for the correction of disordered intestinal flora caused by broad spectrum antibiotics, can also be incorporated in veterinary vaccines and used to prevent a fatal fungal infection in turkeys. Because of its fungistatic and fungicidal properties against a wide variety of fungi *in vitro*, there are many nonmedical applications for Nystatin. For example, it has been used to treat bananas before shipment and as a feed additive for livestock. When art treasures were damaged by floods in Florence, Italy, moldy growths were successfully controlled with the drug. A recent very significant use is the overcoming of Dutch elm disease in infected American trees.

Because Nystatin was discovered and described at the Division of Laboratories and Research of the New York State Department of Health where there was no policy for handling patents or royalties, the expertise of the Research Corporation was sought. The rights to the patent were assigned to them and an exclusive license to develop and manufacture the antibiotic was awarded to E. R. Squibb and Sons. The royalties, in excess of $13,000,000, are divided equally between the Brown-Hazen fund and other agencies of the Research Corporation for the support of scientific research. In this connection, Brown and Hazen, both of whom served on the Brown-Hazen Awarding Committee, are to be highly commended for their monentary unselfishness. These two women launched the career of many a young investigator, or gave another young person the necessary academic experience for subsequent research.

The Brown-Hazen support funds have taken many forms: an International Symposium on Medical Mycology, remodeling of the mycology laboratories of the College of Physicians and Surgeons of Columbia University, publication of Hazen and Reed's Laboratory Manual for Identification of Pathogenic Fungi, and a number of special short term courses for physicians and technicians and postdoctoral exposure to laboratory and clinical problems. The first Dalldorf Postgraduate Fellowship in Medical Mycology, funded by the Brown-Hazen Program

of Research Corporation, was awarded to Thomas M.
Kerkering by the Infectious Diseases Society of America.
The purpose of the fellowship, which is for a term of two
years with annual $14,000 stipend and $1,000 toward
laboratory and scientific travel expenses, is to encourage
young doctorate holders to undertake research and further
training in medical mycology leading to professional
careers in the combat of fungal diseases. The fellowship
was named in honor of Gilbert Dalldorf, who was director
of the Division of Laboratories and Research of the New
York State Department of Health in 1949 when Brown and
Hazen discovered Nystatin.

Rachel was born in Springfield, Massachusetts, on
November 23, 1898. She received her A.B. degree from
Mt. Holyoke College in 1920; M.S. and Ph.D. in chemistry
from the University of Chicago in 1921 and 1933,
respectively. From 1921 to 1924 she was a teacher at the
Frances Shimer School. Thereafter, she held the following
positions with the Division of Laboratories and Research,
New York State Department of Health: assistant chemist
(1926-29), assistant biochemist (1929-36), senior
biochemist (1936-51) and associate biochemist (from
1951). After forty-three years with the New York State
Department of Health, she retired in 1968.

Dr. Brown's researches were in the chemistry of
bacteria, particularly in the extraction and purification of
the numerous antigenic polysaccharides of the
pneumococcus, and production of specific antisera to
these; immunochemistry; serology of syphillis, for which
she developed quantitative precipitation tests with
cardiolipin antigen; isolation of antibiotics, in particular
Nystatin and Phalamycin. She was a member of the
American Chemical Society, Society for Experimental
Biology, American Association of Immunology, New York
Academy of Science, and American Association for the

Advancement of Science. Honors include membership in Sigma Xi and Phi Beta Kappa; Squibb Award (1955); Distinguished Service Award of the New York State Department of Health (1968); Honorary Doctor of Science Degree, Hobart and William Smith Colleges (1969); Honorary Doctor of Science Degree, Mount Holyoke College (1972); and Rhoda Benham Award of the Medical Mycology Society of the Americas (1972). She was further honored by being included in Edna Yost's 1959 book *Women of Modern Science*. Her work and the work of Dr. Hazen are the subject of the book *The Fungus Fighters: Two Women Scientists and Their Discovery* by Richard S. Baldwin (1981).

Rachel Brown, who believed opportunities for women in the profession had improved since the time of Marie Curie, offered these words of encouragement to women hopeful of pursuing a career in science:

"Currently, the best of educational opportunities are open to men and women alike. In teaching, in research, in the laboratory, in industrial and managerial areas many women with equal scientific abilities are doing much the same work as men and assuming similar responsibilities. More and more rapidly this situation will improve and sex discrimination will overcome with remuneration being the last barrier to yield.

"In a nation such as The People's Republic of China women scientists in all fields will progress from the present with much less of a handicap than those in western nations have known because of a desperate need for trained personnel to make up for their lost years. Equalization of the sexes may occur at an early stage of development. To reach the degree of sophistication of the western world, however, will take more time. In other communist countries that have not fallen behind scientfically, women scientists are well on the way to full recognition.

"It is imperative that the average woman scientist recognize her own potentials, believe in herself, and determine to give unstintingly of herself to her chosen career. Only then can she expect to achieve on a par with her male counterpart. No legislation can bring this to pass."

Following a brief illness, Dr. Brown died at the age of 81 on January 14, 1980, in Albany, New York.

(Photograph courtesy the Olin Corporation.)

HERMAN ALEXANDER BRUSON

The Chemical Pioneer Award of 1966 went to Herman Bruson with the citation: "...outstanding pioneer research in industrial organic chemistry which has done much to elucidate the complex chemistry of dicyclopentadiene and has resulted in many valuable industrial contributions in the fields of oil additives, surface active chemistry, antioxidants, and plasticizers, reported in more than 500 U. S. patents."

In the 1930's, Dr. Bruson observed that motor oil containing polymeric higher alkyl methacrylates would stay at about the same viscosity at either high or low temperatures. It has been claimed this development, which has benefitted all motorists, earned more than one billion dollars for major oil companies.

During World War II, Russian tanks became immobile in extremely cold weather. At the request of the U. S. Army, Dr. Bruson provided his special oil to the Russians for testing and use. As the result, their tanks could move when Nazi tanks were immobile.

Herman Bruson's subsequent chemical discoveries were also very valuable: dyes for polyester fibers, heat-resistant polyester coatings, unique nonionic surfactants, non-migratory plasticizers, cyanoethylated products, antioxidants, flame-retardant polyurethane foams, bactericides, and pesticides. These researches led to his receipt of the Award of the National Association of Manufacturers (1965), Wisdom Hall of Fame Award of Honor (1970), American Chemical Society's Award for Creative Invention (1977), Eli Whitney Award of the Patent Law Association (1981), and "for improving the quality of life through chemistry" the Maurice R. Chamberland Award (1981). He was a lecturer at Temple University from 1939 to 1948, Priestley Lecturer at Penn State College in 1944, lecturer at Cheng Kung University in Taiwan in 1970, and consultant to U. S. and foreign firms. He also served as section editor of *Chemical Abstracts* from 1947 to 1960 and was a contributor to *Organic Reactions* in 1949. He was a member of various organizations, including the American and British Chemical Societies, American Association for the Advancement of Science, American Institute of Chemists, and the Chemists Club in New York. In 1968 Dr. Bruson was listed in *World's Who Who in Science* as one of the most distinguished scientists in the history of all the world.

Herman was the author of many research publications and was named on several hundred patents.

From his vast experience, he was able to offer sage advice to budding scientists: "(1) Invent something to fill a specific need; (2) invent something for which there is no known present need, but for which the invention itself is valid enough to warrant a patent that may be of value for future products; and (3) take a known patent and work around it, thereby developing one that's better."

Dr. Bruson was born July 20, 1901, in Middletown, Ohio, to Samuel J. and Rebecca (Arnovitz) Bruson. He received the B.S. degree at the Massachusetts Institute of Technology in 1923 and the D.Sc. degree at Zürich's Federal Polytechnic Institute in 1925. From 1925 to 1928 he performed research for Goodyear Tire and Rubber Company. The next twenty years were spent with Rohm and Haas Company. Thereafter, he was manager of high polymer research at Industrial Rayon Corporation (1948-52) and vice president, chemicals research, of the Olin Corporation (1952-66).

Herman Bruson married Virginia Haber in 1929. Born to them were three daughters: Rita (later Mrs. Howard Vactor), Dorothy, and Barbara. Dr. Bruson died in 1981 in Woodbridge, Connecticut.

(Photograph courtesy of General Electric
Research & Development Center.)

ARTHUR MAYNARD BUECHE

*". . .the man who has surely set some kind
of record in terms of service to professional
organizations, valued consultation to government,
unwavering support of and assistance to
educational institutions, and unstinting devotion to
the communities in which he has lived as well as
the world technological community."**

*Spoken by Dr. Charles E. Reid, Senior Vice President-
Emeritus of General Electric, in commemoration of Bueche at the
Gold Medal ceremony.

The distinguished and deserving Arthur Bueche was the 1980 recipient of AIC's Gold Medal. Receiving honors was not new to Bueche; during his lifetime he received many, including seven honorary degrees.

Arthur embarked upon a career in chemistry partly because his mother thought being a chemist sounded like an honorable way of making a living. "Better than being a lawyer," is what she was reputed to have said. His entrepreneurial spirit was derived from his father - himself an entrepreneur. In school Arthur was a scholar, football player, and poet. Two lines from one of his verses reflect his own philosophy for achievement:

"Dream, then do;
To make dreams come true."

Bueche was born in Flint, Michigan, on November 14, 1920. A graduate of Flint's Junior College, he went on to obtain his B.S. degree in chemistry from the University of Michigan in 1943 and doctorate in physical chemistry from Cornell University in 1947. He remained on Cornell's staff the next three years. Then, in 1950, he accepted employment with General Electric. There, working with Nobel Laureate Peter Debye, he made key contributions to the nation's crash program to synthesize rubber following World War II.

Arthur's research was not limited to rubber and energy. Other principal areas of research were: increased efficiency of management, and development, materials science and engineering, physics and chemistry of polymers, and effects of high-energy radiation on plastics. His achievements in research management equalled his many successes in research. He aptly demonstrated unique understanding of the chemistry of human endeavor, the reactions of interpersonal cooperation, and the cross-linking of good ideas from diverse disciplines and wonderfully non-similar people. With these splendid attributes, he was able to weld General Electric's research laboratory and engineering laboratories - which for years had gone their separate ways - into a truly unified research and development center. Following this accomplishment, he was rightly promoted to the position of senior vice president and top technical officer.

Bueche's contributions to professional and related institutions included his leadership at Gordon conferences, president of the Industrial Research Institute, a leading role in helping reestablish the President's Science Advisory Committee, establishing the Commerce Department study of industrial innovation, active trusteeship at Rensselaer Polytechnic Institute, and devoted membership on hospital boards and service to similar community activities. He was active in the American Institute of Chemists, American Chemical Society, American Institute of Physics, and American Association for the Advancement of Science. In 1971 he was elected to the National Academy of Sciences for his distinguished and continuing achievements in original research. He was also a member of and active participant in the National Academy of Engineering, and served as Chairman of the Council for Cornell University's College of Engineering. In 1973 he delivered the Electrochemical Society Lecture, in 1974 the Faraday Lecture and in 1978 the IEE Kelvin Lecture. He received medals from the American Society of Metals (1978) for the advancement of research, the Industrial Research Institute (1979), and the American Society of Mechanical Engineer's Centennial Medal (1980).

Two children were born as a result of Bueche's 1945 marriage. Following his death in October 1981, the National Academy of Engineering established a memorial fund in his name.

(Reprinted from *THE CHEMIST*, with permission.)

OLIVER W. BURKE, JR.

Oliver Burke, recipient of the AIC Chemical Pioneer Award in 1971, received his B.S. degree from Harvard College in 1932, a Ph.D. in chemistry from the University of Munich in Germany, and a Ph.D. in economics and business administration from the University of Innsbruck, Austria, in 1940. Dr. Burke was with the Office of Rubber Reserve of the Reconstructive Finance Corporation in Washington, D.C., from 1942 to 1950; he was named Deputy Director in 1948. In 1951 he organized the Burke Research Company to conduct fundamental chemical research on synthetic rubber, plastics and petrochemicals.

Dr. Burke received the Pioneer Award "for recognizing the importance of type of carbon black to the manufacture of synthetic rubber of high quality and for setting up the cooperative research which enabled scientists to achieve this goal; for discovering how to make a form of silica capable of producing high-tensile GRS; for being one of the great chemical inventors of our time."

Oliver Burke passed away on August 9, 1975.

(Photograph courtesy of Lawrence Berkeley Laboratory,
University of California.)

MELVIN CALVIN

Receipt of the Gold Medal from the American Institute of Chemists in 1979 represented to amiable Melvin Calvin, also known as "Mr. Photosynthesis," a "clean sweep" of every high honor that can be bestowed upon an individual by the chemistry profession. His other honors include the Nobel Prize (1961), Priestley Medal (1978), Gibbs Medal (1977), and Nichols Medal (1958), Sugar Foundation Award (1950), Flintoff Medal (1953), Stephen Hales Award (1956), Richards Medal (1956), Davy Medal (1964), Vitanen Medal (1976), Oesper Award (1981), Feodor Lynen Medal (1983), and Sterling B. Hendricks Medal (1985).

Melvin was born in St. Paul, Minnesota, April 8, 1911. His parents were Elias and Rose (Hervitz) Calvin. After graduating from St. Paul High School, he enrolled in the Michigan College of Mining and Technology, receiving his B.S. in 1931. M.S. and Ph.D. degrees from the University of Minnesota followed in 1934 and 1935, respectively.

He was a research fellow at the University of Manchester (1935-37) and joined the faculty of the University of California at Berkeley in 1937. Positions held have been instructor, assistant professor, associate professor, professor, university professor, director of the Biodynamics Laboratory and associate director of the Lawrence Berkeley Laboratory. From the following list of lectureships, it has to be taken for granted that Melvin Calvin enjoys prelection. He was Peter Reilly Lecturer at Notre Dame, Harvey Lecturer at the New York Academy of Medicine, Harrison Howe Lecturer, Donegani Foundation Lecturer, Max Tishler Lecturer, Karl Folkers Lecturer, Baker Lecturer, London Lecturer, Willard Lecturer, Vanuxem Lecturer, Prather Lecturer, Dreyfus Lecturer, Barnes Lecturer, O'Leary Lecturer, and Eastman professor at Oxford.

Melvin first became interested in photosynthesis (for which he was awarded the Nobel Prize, i.e., for tracing the chemical reactions that occur when a plant changes carbon dioxide and water into sugar) when carbon-14 became available in 1945. He showed that phosphoglyceric acid was formed in photosynthesis and that this 2-carbon acceptor was regenerable. To link Calvin entirely with photosynthesis is erroneous, however; his research has encompassed such diverse subjects as blood chemistry, fuel from plants, chemical evoluton and carcinogen screening. The Calvin Cycle bears his name.

Dr. Calvin is a member of the National Academy of Sciences, the American Academy of Arts and Science, Royal Dutch Academy of Science, Japanese Academy of Science, American Philosophical Society, American Institute of Chemists, American Chemical Society, Sigma Xi, Tau Beta Pi, and Phi Lambda Upsilon. He served as president of ACS in 1971. He is the author of seven books and over 500 scientific publications. He has served on twenty-eight scientific boards for the U. S. government.

Melvin married Marie G. Jemtegaard in 1942. Born to them were Elin, Karole and Noel.

The following quotation, taken from the address delivered at the time he received the AIC Gold Medal, allows one insight into this extraordinary man:

"Science contributes a primary input to our understanding of the meaning of our lives, and I would like to illustrate that with a series of historical illustrations, right up to and including today.

"Copernicus, Kepler: Three or four hundred years ago our concept of the universe was rather circumscribed. The earth was its center and man was the important creator on the earth and therefore in the universe. Copernicus and Kepler recognized that this was not so, that the earth was not the center of our universe, that the earth was near the edge and the sun was the center of our local universe. That concept initiated an enormous change in our view of the world. The sun became the center and the earth one of several objects moving around the sun.   This was not only a tremendous change in our view of the world, it has had an enormous impact on human thinking.   Galileo's telescope, of course, confirmed this idea by actually viewing and seeing the various planets that were moving around the sun, allowing precise calculation of the planetary orbits.   This ultimately led to the equations which describe the planetary motion, which had to be understood in more fundamental terms, and this, in turn, gave rise to Newton and his law of gravity and motion.

"Darwin: A second step in the impact of science on our view of the world - and all of these things effect the quality of our lives today - was taken later, a little over a hundred years ago, when Charles Darwin removed man from the center of things, and moved him to the edge of the stream of life, to being a component in the stream of living things.   In other words, man was removed from the center and made part of the evolutionary stream of life, after Darwin. This was an even more profound change in our view of ourselves and the world in which we live.   There is even today some slight argument about this.

"Einstein: In the twentieth century, particularly in this year (1979), I cannot help but call your attention to the man who revised our view of the universe in a fundamental way.   He gave microscopic and macroscopic explanations for Newton's laws of gravity and motion, and changed our whole view of how the universe is organized. I am speaking, of course, of Einstein.

"In a very real sense, chemistry today seems to be passing through a critical phase of its history. This is true not only of the basic science of chemistry but of chemistry as an applied science and technology in the construction of modern society. So much of applied chemistry meets us in our everyday lives that we cannot avoid knowing it. In a positive way, chemistry has contributed to the growth of western society in the form of new materials for both food and fiber, as well as materials for construction of homes and transportation and the improvement of human health and longevity. At the same time, in doing this, chemistry has brought a larger number of synthetic materials into the environment that had been there in nature. We as chemists are adding to the natural risks and disadvantages other risks that were not present before.

"In terms of basic science, however, chemistry is also at a critical point in that it is losing a bit of its identity as a science to physics, on the one side, and to biology on the other. In a sense, chemistry is central to all the physical sciences, since it is a science of materials at the molecular level of which both the world of physics and the world of biology are made. Chemistry is also losing something of its identity as an empirical science, in terms of the progress that has been made in understanding the nature of the atom and the molecule of which materials are made. Here the chemists give way somewhat to the physicists who can to some extent improve our understanding of the behavior of atoms and molecules and aggregates of molecules. This leads us into not only the structure of materials but into the structure of living things themselves.

"As we learn the laws of these new behaviors, we will begin to approach somewhat the understanding and the reproduction of some of the very specific processes that occur in biology today which we can only examine and try to understand. I think this understanding is likely to come in the next few decades, and it will help us not only to understand but to construct those parts of living things that we may choose. We will, for example, be able to construct materials which will allow us to collect the sun's energy in almost any form and to store that energy either as chemical energy or in some other useful form.

"With the natural green plant as our model it seems feasible to try to construct a purely synthetic system capable of capturing solar quanta and storing them in some stable form. This synthetic system, which we call 'synthetic chloroplasts,' would not resemble the natural entity in detailed construction, but would be capable of a similar function, that is, it would mimic the way the green plant membranes capture solar quanta to generate oxygen on one side and reducing power on the other side of the membrane. The potential reactants could be separated and stored and brought together later in a suitably constructed physical system for future energy recovery. These artificial systems could be used to generate hydrogen which could be used in chemical processing or as an energy source, thus releasing some of the petroleum products now used in this way for other purposes."

EMMETT BRYAN CARMICHAEL

During the past ninety years, much progress has been made in science and medicine. Emmett Carmichael, a farm boy from Shelbyville, Missouri, made major contributions to these advances, particularly in the state of Alabama where he resided since 1927. Emmett was born September 4, 1885. His parents, George Frank and Amelia Grant (Tingle) Carmichael, were hardworking and this trait was passed on to Emmett.

After graduating from high school in 1914, Emmett spent two years at Central College and then transferred to the University of Colorado to earn A.B. and M.S. degrees in 1916 and 1922, respectively. There he also served as an instructor in organic chemistry (1919 to 1924). For the next three years he was an instructor at the University of

Cincinnati where he received his Ph.D. in 1927. He then accepted a position at the University of Alabama. In the years to follow, he conducted postdoctoral work at Northwestern (1935) and at Harvard (1936).

Emmett spent over half a century in his adopted state. His first position was as an instructor in physiological chemistry. Eighteen years later he became professor of biochemistry at the Medical College of Alabama and then professor emeritus. Following retirement, he actively collected documents and wrote about deceased members of the Alabama health team for the Alabama Museum of Health Sciences. (This collection is housed in a room dedicated to Carmichael in the Lister Hill Science Library in Birmingham).

Dr. Carmichael was unusually active in the Alabama Academy of Science, American Association for the Advancement of Science (of which he was a fellow), American Institute of Chemists and American Chemical Society. He organized the Alabama chapter of AIC in 1950 and served as its chairman that year and in 1962. He was elected national president (1967-69) and served as chairman of the board and director at large (1969-71 and 1971-73, respectively). He served as vice-chairman (1932-34) and chairman (1934-36) of the Alabama chapter of ACS and chaired the committee on arrangements for the southeastern regional meeting of the ACS in 1954. He also served as the abstractor for all biological abstracts in the biochemical journal (1929-32). Emmett was secretary (1932-33) and president (1930-31) of the Alabama Academy of Science and editor of the *Journal of the Alabama Academy of Science* (1942-48). He was a charter member and served as chairman (1957-73) of the Gorgas Scholarship Foundation which conducts the University of Alabama science talent scout search.

Dr. Carmichael founded the Sigma Xi club at the University of Alabama at Tuscaloosa in 1928 and served as its first president. He was also a charter member of the Sigma Xi chapter at the University of Alabama Medical Center at Birmingham. He served as national president of Alpha Epsilon Delta, the honorary premedical society (1932-38) and was counselor of this society (1938-51). He was also national president of Phi Beta Pi, the professional medical fraternity (1950-57), served as editor of *Phi Beta Pi Quarterly* (1945-80), and was elected Man of the Year by this fraternity in 1954. He was a member of Alpha Chi Sigma, American Medical Association, International College of Anesthetists, American Association of Medical Chemists, American Board of Clinical Chemistry, American Society of Biological Chemistry, Society of Experimental Biology, American Physiological Society, Sigma Phi Epsilon, Order of the Golden Heart, and Gamma Sigma Epsilon.

Dr. Carmichael authored more than two hundred articles for scientific and medical journals. Ten editions of his *Laboratory Manual of Biochemistry* have been published.

The following awards were bestowed upon this distinguished individual: AIC's Honor Scroll (Alabama chapter) (1964) and Gold Medal (1971); Southern Chemists Award (1965); Wisdom Award of Honor (1960) and William Crawford Gorgas Award. He was inducted into the Alabama Academy of Honor (1973) and received honorary degrees from Central Methodist College (1979) and the University of Alabama in Birmingham (1981).

Dr. Carmichael enjoyed spectator sports, gardening, philately, writing and collecting documents. He married Lelah Marie Van Hook in 1921. At the age of ninety he passed away on November 15, 1985.

His philosophy, summed up in his biography in *Who's Who in America,* was: "Much of my success, as a scientist, is due to the training which I had on a Missouri farm, until I graduated from high school. Although there was hard work to perform, there was time for relaxation and thought. I had to decide what I did not wish to do, as an adult, and made plans to attempt the task of becoming the uncommon person."

KARL PALEY COHEN

Karl Cohen was a Columbia University graduate (A.B., 1933, M.A., 1934, Ph.D., 1937). Following brief postdoctoral studies at the University of Paris, Karl returned to his alma mater to begin his career as assistant to Harold C. Urey. Three years later, he was named Director of the Theoretical Division of the Manhattan Project at Columbia. His major contributions to the development of the gaseous diffusion and centrifuge processes for enriching uranium are summed up in his book *Isotope Separation* (one of the Nuclear Engineering Series), which remains today one of the standard reference works in the atomic field.

Following World War II, Karl served for four years as physicist and advisor on atomic energy matters to

Standard Oil Development Company*. From 1948 and 1952 he was Technical Director of the H. K. Ferguson Company, constructor of the Brookhaven reactor, synchrocyclotron and radioactivity laboratories. In 1952 he founded the Walter Kidde Nuclear Laboratories and served as vice president and general manager for more than three years. A prime advocate of the slightly enriched uranium, water-moderated reactor concept for power generation, he was instrumental in securing its acceptance by government and industry. His advice was sought in congressional debates, which led to the amendment of the McMahon Act.

In 1955 Cohen joined the General Electric Company and a year later became Manager of Advance Engineering of the Atomic Power Equipment Department. In this function he formulated the technical policy for the economic development of boiling water reactors, known in the industry as 'Operation Sunrise.' Recognizing the importance of reactor safety years before it became a matter of public concern, he recommended the establishment of a company-wide Reactor Safeguards Council, which he served as chairman for eight years. In July 1964 he was appointed manager of Advanced Products Section and placed in charge of GE's development of fast breeder reactors for central station power. His responsibilities included the design, construction and operation of the SEFOR reactor, an international fast reactor safety project. He also undertook development of gas centrifuges to separate uranium isotopes.** In 1965 Cohen was promoted to General Manager and his section enlarged and renamed successively the Advanced Products Operation, the Breeder Reactor Development Operation,

---

*Now Exxon Research and Engineering Company.

**Later pre-empted by the Atomic Energy Commission.

and the Breeder Reactor Department. Out of the work of the breeder reactor group came the concept of mixed-oxide fueled breeders (now universally adopted). Furthermore, a proposal was made to a group of New York utilities for a breeder reactor demonstration program, which became in due time the AEC's Clinch River Breeder Reactor Demonstration Program.

In 1971 Cohen was appointed Manager, Nuclear Energy Operational Planning, with responsibility for strategic planning for the Nuclear Energy Division, including the identification of goals and development of necessary strategies to enhance GE's nuclear opportunities. Two years later he assumed the position of Chief Scientist, his primary responsibilities being in the areas of new technology and business development, including uranium enrichment and the nuclear power aspects of technical and business relationships with the Soviet Union. Added to this incumbency in August of 1975 was that of establishing division-level design reviews for boiling water reactors.

Karl, who retired from General Electric in 1978, is currently a consultant on nuclear energy for General Electric, Exxon, and the Electric Power Research Institute.

This remarkable atomic scientist holds several patents in nuclear reactor technology and isotope separation. Moreover, he served as Regents' Lecturer during the winter quarter of 1970 at the University of California at Berkeley, Director of the U. S. National Committee of the World Energy Conference from 1972 to 1978, was consulting professor of mechanical engineering at Stanford from 1979 to 1981, and an advisor to the Energy Project of the International Institute for Applied Systems Analysis in Vienna. He was also a member of the Scientific Council of the Center for Theoretical Studies of the

University of Miami, consultant to the Atomic Energy Commission and other government agencies, and is currently a member of the National Research Council Review Panel for the Waste Isolation Pilot Plant at Los Medanos, New Mexico.

Karl was elected to the National Academy of Engineering in 1967. He is a founder, past president (1968-69) and fellow (1960) of the American Nuclear Society. He is also a fellow of the American Association for the Advancement of Science and the American Institute of Chemists, a senior member of the IEEE, and a member of the American Physical Society, Phi Beta Kappa, Sigma Xi, and Phi Lambda Upsilon. Karl was recipient of the Energy Research Prize in 1977 and the Chemical Pioneer Award in 1979.

The son of Joseph M. and Rose (Paley) Cohen, Karl was born in New York City on February 5, 1913. His 1938 marriage to Marthe H. Malartre produced Martine-Claude Lebouc, Elisabeth M. Brown and Beatrix Josephine Cashmore.

(Photograph courtesy of Harvard University.)

JAMES BRYANT CONANT

At the Diamond Jubilee of the American Chemical Society in 1951, the address of the day - widely quoted in the press - was delivered by James B. Conant.* The challenging nature of his address was suggested by the subject, "A Skeptical Chemist Looks into The Crystal Ball."

Harvard University played a major role in James Conant's life. It began with his enrollment in

*At which time Conant was President of Harvard.

undergraduate school in 1909. Fresh from graduate school seven years later, he accepted a position of instructor. Seventeen years later he became the school's President, which position he held for the next twenty years (until 1953). He left Harvard to undertake the appointment of U. S. High Commissioner for Germany; from 1955 to 1957 he served as Ambassador to West Germany.

Conant was one of the individuals responsible for blending organic and physical chemistry into the field of physical organic chemistry. Prior to his work, which included reduction and oxidation, hemoglobin, free radicals, superacid solutions, and chlorophyll, the two fields were regarded as distinctly different disciplines. He was widely published, including *Practical Chemistry*, with N. M. H. Black (1920), revised in 1927; *Organic Chemistry* (1928), revised with the assistance of Max Tishler in 1936; *The Chemistry of Organic Compounds* (1933), revised in 1939 and 1947; *Our Fighting Faith* (1942), revised 1944; *On Understanding Science* (1947); *Education in a Divided World* (1948); *Fundamentals of Chemistry*, with A. H. Blatt (1950); *Science and Common Sense* (1951); *Modern Science and Modern Man* (1952); *Education and Liberty* (1953); *Slums and Suburbs* (1961); *The Comprehensive High School* (1967); *Scientific Principles and Moral Conduct*, 1967; and his autobiography *My Several Lives* (1970). He was also the Editor-in-Chief of several volumes of *Organic Syntheses*.

Conant was visiting lecturer at the University of California in 1924, research associate at the California Institute of Technology in 1927, Sachs Lecturer at Teachers College in 1945, and Terry Lecturer at Yale in 1946. He also served as a major in the Chemical Warfare Service from 1917 to 1919.

He may have come close to setting a record in garnering honorary degrees, for he received the following: University of Chicago (1933), New York University (1934), Princeton University (1934), Yale University (1934), Boston University (1934), Columbia University (1934), Stevens Institute (1934), Tufts College (1934), University of Wisconsin (1935), Amherst (1935), College of Charles (1935), College of William and Mary (1936), Williams (1938), Dartmouth (1938), Tulane (1939), University of California (1940), University of Pennsylvania (1940), Bristol University, Queens University - England (1941), Cambridge University - England (1941), University of Algiers (1944), McGill University (1945), University of North Carolina (1945), University of Toronto (1945), Oxford University - England (1946), University of London (1946), University of Lyons - France (1947), Baylor University (1947), University of Illinois (1947), University of the State of New York (1947), Hamilton College (1947), Northeastern University (1948), University of Massachusetts (1948), University of Michigan (1949), Yeshiva University (1949), Wesleyan University (1949), Swarthmore College (1950), Jewish Theological Seminary (1951), Canterbury University - New Zealand (1951), University of Melbourne - Australia (1951), and Colgate (1952).

His list of honors includes but is not limited to Columbia University's Chandler Medal (1932); American Institute of Chemists' Gold Medal (1934) and Honorary Fellow (1949); American Chemical Society's Priestley Medal (1944) and Nichols Medal; Freedom House Award (1952); Commander, Legion of Honor, Most Excellent Order of the British Empire; and Medal for Merit, Oak Leaf Cluster (1948).

Conant was a member of the American Chemical Society; American Academy of Arts and Sciences; American Philosophical Society, National Academy of

Sciences; Massachusetts Historical Society; Royal Society (England); Royal Society of Edinburgh; Chemical Society (England); Honorary Fellow, Emmanual College, Cambridge (England); American Association for the Advancement of Science; American Society of Biological Chemistry; and American Institute of Chemists. His clubs were Tavern, Harvard and Algonquin in Boston; Century, Chemists, Harvard and University in New York; Cosmos in Washington; and Athenaeum in London.

He chaired the National Defense Research Committee from 1940 to 1945, and was a member of the Educational Policies Committee, the National Science Foundation Board, and the Committee on the Present Danger. From 1957 to 1962 he directed a study of the American high school and from 1962 to 1963 a study of the education of American teachers. He served as advisor to the Ford Foundation in Berlin in 1963 and 1964, was a member of the National Research Council's committee on scientific aids to learning from 1937 to 1942, and on Rockefeller Institute's board of science directors from 1930 to 1949. He was also with the Atomic Energy Commission from 1947 to 1952.

James was born in Dorchester, Massachusetts, on March 26, 1893, to James Scott and Jennett Orr (Bryant) Conant. He married Grace Thayer Richards on April 17, 1921; their children were James Richards and Theodore Richards. A New Englander by birth and Bostonian by advocation, Contant lived the last several years of his life in New York City.

RALPH ALEXANDER CONNOR

There is a section in southern Illinois known locally as "Little Egypt". It is here that several famous people were born, including Burl Ives, Reynold Fuson, Harold Snyder - and AIC's 1963 Gold Medalist Ralph Connor.

Ralph was born to Stephen A. and Minnie (Ross) Connor in Newton on July 12, 1907. His first chemical publication was based on work he did as a senior at the University of Illinois under the direction of Fuson. After receiving his B.S. in 1929, Ralph spent three years at the University of Wisconsin under the guidance of Homer Adkins. His work there was on high pressure hydrogenation and hydrogenolysis, including the early work on copper-chromium oxide catalysts. During his last year of graduate work (1931), he married a high school classmate, Margaret Raef.

Ralph then spent three years as an instructor in organic chemistry at Cornell, interspersed with two summers as an instructor in the University of Illinois summer school and one summer working with Wallace Carothers at Du Pont. He became an assistant professor of organic chemistry at the University of Pennsylvania in 1935 and associate professor in 1938. During these academic years, he collaborated with Fuson to write *A Brief Course in Organic Chemistry.** He also wrote a chapter on organic sulfur compounds for one of the first American advanced organic chemistry textbooks, authored by Henry Gilman. Ralph's research interests were on active methylene compounds and organic sulphur compounds.

When the Second World War occurred in 1941, Ralph took a leave of absence from Penn to join the staff of the National Defense Research Committee of the Office of Scientific Research and Development - a temporary civilian agency created to work on materials and instruments of warfare. James B. Conant was the Chairman of NDRC and Roger Adams was the supervisor of the chemical divisions. Ralph was initially Technical Aide but in 1942 replaced Frank C. Whitmore as Chief of the Organic Division of Division 8, the Division of Explosives. When George B. Kistiakowski joined the staff at Los Alamos, Ralph succeeded him as Chief of Division 8. The history of Division 8, written jointly by Kistiakowski and Connor, is contained in the book *Chemistry in World War II,* authored by W. Albert Noyes, Jr. For this work, Ralph was awarded the President's Medal of Merit, the King's Medal for Service in the Cause of Freedom, and the Naval Ordnance Development Award.

*Later Harold Snyder and Charles C. Price became co-authors; still later revisions were made by L. C. Behr.

After the war, Dr. Connor did not return to academic work but joined Rohm and Haas as Associate Director of Research on a part time basis, which association lasted until the above history had been written and most of the demobilization problems of Division 8 had been settled. This did not end his association with defense matters; Rohm and Haas was asked to organize and operate a research laboratory at Redstone Arsenal at Huntsville, Alabama (later known as the Guided Missile Center). For this work Ralph received the Outstanding Civilian Service Medal of the Department of the Army.

In 1948 Dr. Connor was appointed Vice President in Charge of Research of Rohm and Haas. He was elected to the board of directors in 1949 and in 1960, upon the death of Otto Haas, founder of the company, Ralph became chairman of the board. In 1970 he resigned as chairman and vice president and became chairman of the executive committee until his full retirement in 1973.

Ralph served on numerous committees of colleges and universities, the government, IUPAC and chemical societies. From 1954 to 1966, he served on the Board of the American Chemical Society and was Chairman for three years (1956-59). During this latter period, the sale of UOP by the Petroleum Research Fund was being initiated and the decision was made to make a big increase in the charges for *Chemical Abstracts*. Ralph continued on the board long enough to represent the Society in the UOP negotiations and then served several more years on the Finance Committee.

In addition to being AIC's Gold Medalist, Dr. Connor is an honorary member and recipient of the Chemical Pioneer Award. He also has received the Illini Achievement Award of the University of Illinois, the

Chemical Industry Medal of the Society of Chemical Industry, and the Priestley Medal of the American Chemical Society. Moreover, he holds honorary D.Sc. degrees from the University of Pennsylvania, the Philadelphia College of Pharmacy and Science, and Brooklyn Polytechnic Institute, an L.L.D. from Lehigh, and is an honorary member of Phi Lambda Upsilon. A life member of the Board of Ursinus College, he is a member of the University of Illinois Foundation, has served as Associate Trustee of the University of Pennsylvania, and is a member of Theta Chi, Alpha Chi Sigma, Sigma Xi, Phi Eta Sigma, and Phi Kappa Phi.

The Connors have one son, Stephen, a plant pathologist, and four grandchildren. In retirement, Ralph's interest has become genealogy and he has published four articles about his findings.

Not only is Ralph an accomplished trombone player, but it's rumored that he can hold his own vocally with singer/actor Burl Ives.

MELVIN ALONZO COOK

Harnessing the power of explosives has been the goal of many inventors. Alfred Nobel received 355 patents and millions of dollars by inventing dynamite, a mixture of Fuller's earth and glyceryl trinitrate. It was Melvin Cook who revolutionized the civilian explosives industry by producing a family of materials that are cheaper, safer, and more powerful than Nobel's dynamite.

Prior to this invention of slurry explosives, Melvin had served an an expert witness regarding an ammonium nitrate explosion at Texas City and an explosion of ammonium nitrate, aluminum and water at Knob Lake Mine in Quebec, Canada. He was well qualified to serve in such capacity. In 1947 he had accepted a position as professor of metallurgy and director of the Explosives

Research Institute at the University of Utah.

In 1958, Melvin founded IRECO Chemicals. He served as president and chairman of the board until 1972 when he became chairman of the Cook Slurry Company. Melvin's first slurry explosives were sensitized with trinitrotoluene; his first sensitized blasting agents were aluminized slurries. These have since been augmented by slurries containing a thickened and gelled oxidizer, such as ammonium nitrate and fuel oil. The U. S. Patent Office has awarded Cook six patents for his slurries. Moreover, Melvin was awarded the 1973 Chemical Pioneer Award for his discovery. Information on Cook's slurries may be found in his books *The Science of High Explosives* (1958) and *The Science of Industrial Explosives* (1974).

In addition to being a fellow of AIC, Dr. Cook is a member of the American Association for the Advancement of Science, Sigma Xi and the American Institute of Metallurgical Engineers. His other awards include the E. V. Murphree Gold Medal and the Nobel Gold Medal.

Melvin was born in Garden City, Utah, October 10, 1911, to Alonzo L. and Maude (Osmond) Cook. He received B.A. and M.A. degrees from the University of Utah in 1933 and 1934, respectively. Thereafter he accepted a Loomis fellowship at Yale, where he received his doctorate in 1937. Before joining the University of Utah, he was with Du Pont.

Cook married Wanda Garfield in 1935. Born to them were Barbara Jeane, Melvin, Virginia, Merrill Alonzo, and Krehl Osmond. Son Melvin, himself the father of nine children, is now president of IRECO Chemicals. He and his father co-authored *Science of Mormonism*.

HARRY WESLEY COOVER

Much of the world's technical progress has been adhesives, starting with waxes, natural resins and pitches. This one and one-half billion dollar industry is essential for many applications in modern construction, land, sea and air transportation, and packaging. One of the newer adhesives, which has been called "crazy glue," is a cyanoacrylate developed by Harry Coover. Coover's adhesives cure rapidly, in the presence of atmospheric moisture, by an ionic polymerization mechanism in which the ethylenic double bonds propagate leaving cyano and ester pendant groups on alternate carbon atoms in the cured polymer chain. The monomers for Coover's unique adhesive systems are obtained by the depolymerization of polymeric condensates of formaldehyde and cyanomalonic acid derivatives.

Harry was born in Newark, Delaware, March 6, 1919. His father was also Harry Wesley; his mother, Anna Rohm Coover. After completing Newark High School, Harry entered Hobart College. In 1941 he graduated with a B.S. in chemistry and was recipient of the Southerland Prize. He then entered graduate school at Cornell University and received his M.S. and Ph.D. degrees in 1942 and 1944, respectively.

Coover's career began with Eastman Kodak Company. He has held positions of leadership in the research function of the Tennessee Eastman Company. He was director of Research from 1973 to 1981, responsible for the investigations of some 1,300 scientists and engineers. This period saw sales of the chemical division grow from $3.9 million to $2.2 billion! He served as executive vice president of Eastman Kodak Company from 1981 to 1984. In 1985 he became president of the New Business Development Group for the Loctite Corporation.

Dr. Coover is a fellow of the American Institute of Chemists and a member of the American Chemical Society, Industrial Research Institute, American Association of Textile Chemists and Colorists, Association of Research Directors, and Directors of Industrial Research. He serves on the board of Georgia Tech and Tennessee Technical Foundation. He was selected AIC Chemical Pioneer in 1986.

Harry has published more than fifty reports in scientific journals and has been awarded over 400 patents by the U. S. Patent Office.

Children of his 1941 marriage to Murial Zumbach are Harry Wesley, Stephen R. and Melissa.

FREDERICK GARDNER COTTRELL

Frederick Cottrell was an unusually successful scientist and inventor. He received the AIC Gold Medal in 1938 and was named an honorary fellow in 1949. Cottrell was introduced at the Gold Medal Award ceremony by Walter A. Schmidt, a long-time colleague, whose remarks included the statement: "While Dr. Cottrell is internationally known as a chemist and metallurgist of outstanding originality and ability, he is probably best known in this country because of his unusual social outlook and general interest in social problems."

Born in Oakland, California, on January 10, 1877, Frederick was the son of Henry and Cynthia Cottrell and a descendant of Nicholas Cottrell who came to Rhode Island in 1638. Frederick's many interests and capabilities surfaced at an early age. As a boy, he showed proclivity toward science, invention and business enterprise. During his teen years, his several business cards identified him variously as a photographer, a printer, an electrician, and the publisher of a periodical called *The Boys' Workshop*. He possessed such vision that in his own time he was called visionary.

Young Fred was admitted to the University of California at Berkeley at the age of sixteen after four semesters of high schoool where, one acquaintance recalls, "he read textbooks like novels." Cottrell graduated in 1896 and was awarded a fellowship - only to have to resign it for economic reasons. Combining study with high school teaching, he worked toward the day when he could continue his formal education. In 1900 he went to Germany to work in Berlin with Jacob van't Hoff and in Leipzig with Wilhelm Ostwald, under whom he received his Ph.D. in 1902. Thereafter he returned to the University of California to begin his multifaceted career in physical chemistry. Laboring under economic necessity as well as interest, he began experimenting with electrostatic precipitation as a means of collecting sulphuric acid mists. The result was the precipitator, a device which could collect fly ash, dust and fumes, acid mists and fogs that belched from turn-of-the-century plants, and which became a primary means for controlling industrial air pollution.

In 1911 he accepted the position of chief physical chemist for the U. S. Bureau of Mines. He became chief metallurgist in 1914, assistant director in 1916, and director in 1919. He left the Bureau in 1921 to become chairman of the Division of Chemistry and Chemical Technology of the National Research Council. A year later he became director of the Fixed Nitrogen Research Laboratory of the

U. S. Department of Agriculture, which position he held until 1930.

In the early thirties Cottrell played important technical and legislative roles in the development of Muscle Shoals and the Tennessee Valley Authority. It is curious that he, with strong interest in the commercial value and use of inventions, held positions in academia and in government. Cottrell had many successes in research, but he was best known for his development of the electrostatic precipitator, which invention was adopted throughout the world to clean industrial gases and smokes, e.g., from power plants and cement kilns. Such operations diminished pollution and facilitated recovery of cement, potash, and minerals. Cottrell also played a major role in the development of industrial helium, petroleum processing, and nitrogen fixation.

Cottrell had no wish to profit personally from his valuable precipitator patents. At the ripe age of thirty-four, he resolved that science would be the principal beneficiary of his invention. However, his attempt to give the patent rights to the Smithsonian Institution and other non-profit organizations met with failure and he was forced to use his inventive genius to create an institution that could receive the gift, develop the patents commercially, and turn the rewards over to the further pursuit of scientific discovery. Thus the Research Corporation was created.*

Cottrell's motivation for establishing this entity was completely altruistic as evidenced by the words of associate Walter A. Schmidt - who also gave his patent rights on precipitation to help found the Research Corporation - "I do not think any man in the United States

*Chartered by the State of New York in February 1912.

had more fun in doing what he (Cottrell) has done without thought of monetary reward." As Cottrell hoped, the Research Corporation has played a potent role in advancing science and technology and helping scientists and inventors.

Robert H. Goddard's rocket research in the mid-twenties was supported in part by grants made to the Smithsonian Institution. The University of California received funds to assist Ernest O. Lawrence early in the development of the cyclotron. Grants to the Massachusetts Institute of Technology for the research of Robert Van de Graaff helped develop the high-voltage accelerator that bears his name. The Brown-Hazen Program of the Research Corporation produced valuable Nystatin. Other developments aided by the Research Corporation include Nicholas Milas' development of tasteless, odorless Vitamin A; blood fractionation work on a large scale by E. J. Cohn; and medical innovations by M. Kharasch on germicides. The royalties from all of these developments were redistributed to scores of institutions for continued research.

Among the many honors garnered by Cottrell were the Perkin Medal, Willard Gibbs Medal, Washington Award, and an honorary LL.D. degree from the University of California. When in 1937 he received the Western Society of Engineers Washington Award - an Award first given to Herbert Hoover - it was not primarily for engineering achievements but for the ". . . social contributions of his work." In receiving this award, Cottrell chose as his topic "Social Responsibility of the Engineer."

The first chapter of Harland Manchester's book *New Trail Blazers in Technology* is devoted to the life and works of Cottrell. He was selected by the author as one of ten inventors of the twentieth century whose work had a profound impact on modern-day life. Manchester describes Dr. Cottrell as "the man who lived a thousand lives." The characterization derives from the support of a multitude of researches he made possible through the foundation he established and through the counsel he gave to other scientists and engineers.

This most unusual man - one completely dedicated to the advancement of scientific knowledge, to helping other scientists, and to benefitting human kind - died November 16, 1948, of a heart attack at the age of 71. Fittingly, his death occurred at his alma mater and only a few miles from his birthplace while he was attending a meeting of the National Academy of Sciences at the University of California.

(Photograph courtesy of Mobil Mining & Minerals Company.)

EDWIN COX

Brigadier General Edwin Cox, senior partner of Cox and Gillespie, received the AIC Gold Medal Award and was named honorary fellow in 1965 with the citation:

"To Edwin Cox in recognition of rare talents as an outstanding leader in the chemical profession who has contributed importantly to technological advances in many areas, has given devoted efforts in the service of his country in peace and in war, and has striven constantly to increase the sympathy for scientific method and advances with a widening circle of citizens."

The speaker for General Cox at the award banquet was a long-time friend, Dr. Vannevar Bush, honorary chairman of the Massachusetts Institute of Technology and former director of the National Defense Research Committee and Office of Scientific Research and Development. Dr. Bush praised the excellent work General Cox had done while serving under him as secretary of the Joint New Weapons Committee of the Joint Chiefs of Staff in the latter part of World War II: "At the beginning of the war, there was a huge gap between the military men on the one hand and the scientists and engineers on the other. It took people with a good knowledge of both fields to bridge the gap. And Edwin Cox was the one that helped bridge the gap. World War II was the first war in which science and technology really became involved with the military and defense effort."

Born in Richmond, Virginia, on September 20, 1902, Edwin came from a long line of distinguished Virginians. He was descendent of Captain William Cox, who came to the colony in 1611. In his family tree are John Rolfe and Pocahontas. His mother, Sally Bland Clarke, was the daughter of Captain Maxwell T. Clarke and Ellen Scott, descendent of Richard Bennett, Governor of Virginia, and Richard Bland of the Continental Congress.

Cox distinguished himself while still a youth. He attended Scott and Talcott's Primary school and Richmond Academy, receiving two gold medals for academic excellence. In 1917, at the age of fourteen, Cox graduated from John Marshall High School as fifth in his class. He graduated with distinction from the Virginia Military Institute in 1920 with a B.S. in Chemical Engineering and an M.S. in chemistry upon completion of a thesis. He was only seventeen at the time and was said to have been the youngest graduate.

From 1920 to 1936, Edwin was active as a professional chemist. He was group leader in the analytical laboratory and foreman in a sulfuric acid plant of the Virginia-Carolina Chemical Company. In the subsidiary, Tobacco Byproducts and Chemical Corporation, he was chemist, foreman, night superintendent and chemist in charge of research and development. In 1924-26, Cox was an incorporator and officer of Phillps and Bird, Inc., which dealt in laboratory supplies and chemicals. Cox was transferred to another Virginia-Carolina subsidiary in 1928 where he supervised sales and technical development and became vice president. He aided in the establishment of the research department of the American Tobacco Company, and, at the governor's request, planned the laboratory and quality control of the Virginia Alcoholic Beverage Control Commission. Cox received patents on nicotine alkaloid, use of nicotine in sheep dips, and rancidity inhibitors. He published freely on these subjects, particularly on the synthesis of nicotine, protein precipitation, rancidity in wheat flour, and defluorination of phosphoric acid. In the period 1936-44, the Virginia-Carolina Chemical Company was reorganized and all chemical operations were combined into a division headed by Cox as division manager. Although these activities were largely managerial, he received six more patents on important developments.

Edwin's distinguished military career started early. Even before his graduation from the military institute, his father had enrolled the lad as a private in the First Virginia Infantry - the ninth generation to serve. He rose through the ranks and became Lieutenant Colonel in 1940. His varied and distinguished World War II service was highlighted by his assignment in May 1944 to the General Staff of the War Department, where he became Secretary of the Joint New Weapons Committee of the Joint Chiefs of Staff. Other appointments included Chairman of the Joint U.S. and the Combined U.S. and U.K. Intelligence committees, and member of the Committee on Disclosure of Technical Information to Allies.

Upon his return to civilian life, General Cox again became manager of the chemical division of the Virginia-Carolina Chemical Company. Later he was named vice president in charge of all research and development. He also had the responsibility of the Fiber Division, which had been organized to make protein fibers. During this period, there were many notable advances. The Chemical Division expanded twelve-fold, organic phosphate production was initiated, high-voltage phosphorus furnaces were put into operation, improvements were made in mining and processing phosphate rock, and new phosphate products accounted for seventy-five percent of sales. Cox resigned from Virginia-Carolina in 1957 and began a new career as a professional consultant.

In spite of pressing chemical, managerial, and military activities, the General was able to participate in civic and cultural affairs. He served on the State Library Board, of which he was chairman; on the Executive Committee of the Virginia Historical Society; and on the Executive Committee of the Diocese of Virginia. He was the author of both historical and scientific papers. Moreover, General Cox ran the farm where he lived in King and Queen County.

Cox was a member of the Virginia Chemists Club, American Chemical Society, American Institute of Chemists, American Institute of Chemical Engineers, and American Association for the Advancement of Science. In the American Chemical Society, he served as secretary, vice chairman, chairman of the Virginia Section, and co-chairman and councilor of the 1927 National Meeting in

Richmond. One of the organizers of the Virginia Academy of Science, he was chairman of the Chemistry Section. He was also chairman of the American Association of Cereal Chemists.

In addition to the two academic gold medals and the two honors bestowed upon him by the AIC, General Cox was presented the Distinguished Service Award of the Virginia Section of the American Chemical Society and the Order of Knighthood of St. John.

General Cox's only child, Edwin Cox III, born on October 31, 1931, graduated from the Virginia Military Institute in 1953; in 1960 he entered practice as a partner with his father.

The cordial and hospitable General died on February 22, 1977, of a heart attack.

GERALD JUDY COX

It has been known for over a century that high concentrations of fluoride in drinking water cause mottled, decay resistant teeth.   Today, nine states require fluoridation of water supplies.   In spite of this small percentage, the American Dental Association estimates that fluoridated water is supplied to about one-half the U.S. population.   Actually, while the concentration of natural fluorides is less than 0.1 ppm in water in the northeastern part of the country, in other regions this concentration may exceed 0.2 ppm.

It was Gerald Cox, working in collaboration with Mary L. Dodes, who discovered that fluorides were good for the teeth of rats.   These researchers, in work at the Mellon Institute, were attempting to produce mottled teeth in pregnant rats by using drinking water with fluoride concentrations as high as 40 ppm. The offspring of the rats were not given fluoridated water but were placed on a caries-producing diet. These offspring did not develop mottled teeth or dental caries. Dr. Cox reported these findings at a meeting of the American Water Works Association at Johnstown, Pennsylvania, in 1939. The paper was published in the AWWA journal along with an editorial taking the opposite viewpoint toward fluoridation of water. Dr. Cox's views were accepted by many and generated the gradual acceptance of fluoridation of water by many municipalities.

It was for this fluoride discovery that Gerald Cox was made the American Institute of Chemists' 1970 Pioneer.

Gerald was born in Sumner, Illinois, on April 27, 1885. He entered the University of Illinois to receive the B.S., M.S. and Ph.D. degrees in 1919, 1923, and 1925, respectively. Thereafter he accepted a faculty position with his alma mater. In 1929, he left the university and went with the Mellon Institute. During World War II he served on the War Production Board and National Research Council. In 1948 he resigned this position to join the faculty of the Dental School at the University of Pittsburgh, where he retired as professor emeritus in 1965.

In addition to being an AIC fellow, Gerald was a member of the American Chemical Society, American Association for the Advancement of Science, Society of Biological Chemists, Institute of Nutrition, Public Health Association, Dental Association and Association of Dental Researchers.

Gerald was married in 1919 and had one child.

MOSES LEVEROCK CROSSLEY

"His sterling character, soundness of purpose, and thought for others are shown in all that he undertakes, and are mirrored in his writings". *

Moses Crossley, a shy, gentle, and well-informed man, might well be called "Mr. AIC." He was a charter member, AIC president from 1924 to 1926 and 1934 to 1936, recipient of the Gold Medal in 1947, and made an honorary fellow in 1948.

*Attributed to Harry L. Fisher in describing Crossley's character.

Crossley was educated at Brown University where he received his Ph.B. in 1909, M.S. in 1910, and Ph.D. in 1911. His very active scientific life began at his alma mater as instructor in chemistry for two graduate years. Thereafter he served succeeding two-year periods at William Jewel College as instructor of chemistry, and lecturer, associate professor and acting head of the department of organic chemistry at Connecticut's Wesleyan University. He was also a consulting chemist to Barrett Company while at Wesleyan. He left university work to accept what was destined to be almost thirty years with Calco Chemical Company, where he started as chief chemist. He later became director of research and then director of research of the American Cyanamid Company at Calco and Stamford. Upon his retirement in 1949, Crossley was appointed a research specialist in the Bureau of Biological Research, Rutgers University, in which position he directed the chemotherapeutic phase of the Bureau's cancer research project.

Moses was presented the Gold Medal for his scientific work and leadership in research in the fields of dyes and pharmaceuticals and for his activities in behalf of the profession of chemistry. His early interest in dyes was shown the year after he received his doctoral degree in a paper "Improved Method for the Production of Mono-aminoanthraquinone."[*] This was only the beginning of a long active career in dyes: their study, preparation and manufacture, and constitution and the relation of that constitution to color. In his early studies, he became interested in the use of action of dyes on bacteria and their application in medicine. This interest soon became intense and the subject of his most important publications. He was very successful in research on

[*]Presented at the Eighth International Congress of Applied Chemistry, New York, 1912.

quinoline derivatives, the great field of sulfanilamides, magnesium salts, and the synergistic action of drugs. He conducted fundamental investigations of the chemistry of infectious diseases, especially the changes in certain constituents of the blood in pneumonia and in the chemotherapy of cancer. At the end of the European phase of World War II, Crossley was a member of a technical team sent to Germany to investigate the military uses of dyes and textile chemicals. He published more than one hundred papers on scientific and educational subjects and many patents resulted from his work.

As well as his deep commitment to scientific work and the management of a research laboratory, Crossley found the time to work on problems connected with the professional side of the chemist. He was particularly interested in the education of the chemist. In his words of 1920: "It is not the function of an educational institution to produce expert professional men, but rather to train men to think and to orient themselves advantageously in their environment. To qualify as an industrial chemist, a man's training must be augmented by experience gained in the chemical industry. . . An academic degree should be an endorsement of a man's character as well as an affidavit of the amount of training he has had." He was a member of the board of directors of Union Junior College and president of the Associated Alumni of Brown University. In 1940 he was awarded the Brown Bear for outstanding achievements, the award inscribed with the quotation from the university's charter of 1764: "Duly qualified for discharging the offices of life with usefulness and reputation." Brown also conferred upon him the honorary degree of Doctor of Science in 1944. Wesleyan University presented the same degree in 1947.

Crossley's work on methods of influencing the economic status of the profession helped to bring about greater compensation in some instances. His studies on the economic basis for the amortization of the service investment of chemists solved some   problems in the licensing of chemists. In this regard, he was instrumental in establishing a bureau of appointments where "the individual obtains the position which he is best qualified to fill, regardless of whether he is employed."

Moses was chairman of the Connecticut Valley Section of the American Chemical Society from 1915 to 1917 and president of the New York Academy of Sciences in 1950. He was an American delegate to many world scientific meetings, such as the International Union of Pure and Applied Chemistry (1926 and 1928).

Dr. Crossley was born July 3, 1884, of American parents at Saba Island, Dutch West Indies, where his father, an engineer, had gone to develop a sulfur mine. His hobbies were writing and sailing. His grandfather on his mother's side was a sea captain and Moses an expert sailor. Whenever possible he went to his summer home in Martha's Vineyard to sail. He died May 29, 1971, at the home of his son Evan in Hagerstown, Maryland.

CARL DJERASSI

In the medical profession, the name Djerassi is almost synonymous with the first oral contraceptive agent norethisterone, commonly known as "the pill," which is the most widely used contraceptive. It is taken for granted that Djerassi will long be remembered for his role in contraceptives since their use has been responsible, to a large extent, for the decline in population growth rate in the second half of this century. Carl's contributions to science are much more far-reaching, however; they include developments in the fields of antihistamines, anti-inflammatory agents, alkaloids, terpenoids, macrolide antibiotics and the application of optical rotary dispersion, mass spectrometry and magnetic circular dichroism to organic compounds.

Carl Djerassi was born in Vienna on October 29, 1923, the son of two physicians, Samuel and Alice (Friedmann) Djerassi. He emigrated to the United States in 1939 and attended Newark Junior College from 1940 to 1941, Tarkio College the next year, and then Kenyon College where he received his A.B. Summa Cum Laude in 1942. He then spent a year as a research chemist at Ciba Pharmaceutical Company in Summit, New Jersey. Thereafter, as a Du Pont Fellow, he commenced graduate school at the University of Wisconsin to receive his Ph. D. in 1945. The next four years he spent with Ciba but then accepted a position as Associate Director of Research for Syntex SA in Mexico City. In 1952, he returned to the United States to accept a position as Professor of Chemistry at Wayne State University. While on academic leave (1957-1960), he served as Vice President of Research for Syntex SA. Since 1959 he has served as Professor of Chemistry at Stanford.

Dr. Djerassi, who conducted investigations of antihistamines before and after graduate school, was the co-inventor of tripelenamine (Pyribenzamine), one of the first clinically effacacious antihistamines used in medicine. It was at Syntex that he became interested in natural products from the giant cacti. He has since determined the structure of over twenty of the pentacyclic triterpenoids and alkaloids from the cacti as well as that of cafestol obtained from coffee. He and his group have also isolated and determined the structure of over fifty alkaloids of South American plants, such as the apocynaceae species. Prior to formal studies made on the structure of macrolides, he and coworkers investigated erythromycin, mystatis, methymycin and neomethymicin, and established the first total structure of a macrolide.

Djerassi's systematic studies of optical rotatory dispersion, i.e., the variation of optical rotary power with wavelength, led to the use of this and circular dichroism in organic chemistry, which techniques are described in his book *Optical Rotatory Dispersion: Applications in Organic Chemistry*. He used the Cotton Effect curve based on the absorption of the carbonyl chromophore at 290 nm for assignments of absolute configuration and determination of the conformation. He described electron impact induced fragmentation of various organic molecules, including steroids, in many reports and four books, and extended these mass spectral results by use of computers. He also used magnetic circular dichroism (Faraday effect) to study organic compounds (notably porphyrins) and more recently examined the structure biosynthesis and biological function of novel sterols and phospholips in lower marine animals.

Dr. Djerassi's contributions to science have brought many honors. He received AIC's Freedman Foundation Patent Award in 1971 and Chemical Pioneer award in 1973; ACS's Award in Pure Chemistry in 1958, Baekeland Medal in 1959, Fritzsche Award in 1960, Award for Creative Invention in 1973, Alabama Section's Madison Marshall Award in 1973 and Award in Chemistry of Contemporary Technological Problems in 1983; National Medal of Science in 1975; Perkin Medal of the Society of the Chemical Industry in 1975; Wolf Price in Chemistry in 1978; Sixth Annual Exploratorium Award in 1982; the John and Samuel Bard Award in Medicine and Science in 1983; and was selected a member of the National Inventors Hall of Fame in 1978. He was also a Fellow at Bard College Center in 1982-83. On the occasion of the Freedman award, Dr. Louis Freedman summed up some of Djerassi's accomplishments with these words: ". . . for his years of service as an eminent organic and pharmaceutical chemist, professor and inventor and having made meritorious contributions to the art of chemical patenting."

Carl has been awarded honorary doctoral degrees by the Universities of Mexico, Wayne State, Columbia, Uppsala, Geneva and Ghent; by Kenyon and Coe Colleges; and by Worcester Polytechnic Institute. He has served on the editorial boards of *Journal of Organic Chemistry, Tetrahedron, Steroids, Proceedings of National Academy of Sciences, Journal of the American Chemical Society,* and *Organic Mass Spectrometry.* He was also a member and chairman of the Latin America Science Board and of the Board of Science in Technology Development of the National Academy of Sciences.

He is a fellow of the American Institute of Chemists and a member of the American Chemical Society, National Academy of Sciences, Swiss Chemical Society, American Academy of Arts and Sciences, Royal Society of Chemistry, German Academy of Sciences (Leopoldine), Royal Swedish Academy of Sciences, Royal Swedish Academy of Engineering Sciences, American Academy of Pharmaceutical Science, Brazilian Academy of Science, Mexican Academy of Scientific Investigation, Bulgarian Academy of Science, Phi Beta Kappa, Phi Lambda Upsilon and Sigma Xi. He has served on the Board of Directors of Syntex Corporation (1958-1972) and was Executive Vice President (1964-1968) and President of Syntex Research (1968-1970). He was also Chairman of the Board of Governors (1966-1978 and presently) and Chief Executive Officer (1968-1982) of Synvar Associates.

Moreover, he served as chairman of the Gordon Research Conference on Steroids and Natural Products; was a Camille and Henry Dreyfus Distinguished Scholar at Duke University; was Andrews Lecturer at the University of New South Wales, Phillips Lecturer at Haverford College, Centenary Lecturer for the Royal Chemical Society, Edgar Fahrs Smith Lecturer at the University of Pennsylvania, Francis Preston Veneable Lecturer at the

University of North Carolina, Edward Mack Lecturer at Ohio State University, Werner Bachman Lecturer at the University of Michigan, annual chemistry lecturer at the Royal Swedish Academy of Engineering, O. M. Smith Lecturer at Oklahoma State University, Debye Lecturer at Cornell University, L. C. Franklin Lecturer at the University of Kansas, Julius Stieglitz Lecturer at the University of Chicago, Redman Lecturer at McMasters University, Renaud Foundation Lecturer at Michigan State University, Arthur J. Schmidt Challenges in Science Lecturer at the University of Notre Dame, Scheele Lecturer for the Pharmaceutical Society of Sweden, annual Chemical Innovator in Industry Lecturer for the Norwegian Chemical Society, Dreyfus Lecturer at Dartmouth College, W. J. Probst Lecturer at Southern Illinois University, B. R. Baker Memorial Lecturer at the University of California at Santa Barbara, Lazenby Lecturer at Southern Methodist University, Gregory Pincus Lecturer at Worcester Foundation for Experimental Biology, Distinguished Visiting Speaker at the University of Calgary, Fairfield Osborn Memorial Lecturer at Rockefeller University, Purves Memorial Lecturer at Georgia Institute of Technology, Edward E. Smissman Memorial Lecturer at the University of Kansas School of Pharmacy, Annual Allan Guttmacher Lecturer for the Association of Planned Parenthood Professionals, Russel Marker Lecturer in the Chemical Sciences at Pennsylvania State University, Lewis Harris Distinguished Lecturer at the University of Nebraska, and the Haarmen and Reimer Distinguished Lecturer at Washington State University.

The author or co-author of seven books and over one thousand scientific publications, Carl has been awarded over 120 patents by the U. S. Patent Office.

(Photograph courtesty of Dow Chemical Company.)

WILLARD HENRY DOW

Willard Henry Dow, son of chemist and industrialist Herbert Henry Dow, was a man of vision. Such a gift was aptly demonstrated at the time of this country's entry into World War Two. It was then that the entire plastics industry had to be overnight revolutionalized, forcing chemists and engineers to find substitutes for metal and rubber and to develop new methods of producing and fabricating plastics products. Willard immediately rose to the occasion, learning how to make enough magnesium to produce thousands of airplanes and enough styrene to produce synthetic rubber on a large commercial scale. Without his leadership, it is almost certain that Dow Chemical would not have been able to generate instant solutions to the war years' critical needs. In fact, it was to a great extent because of Willard Dow's ability, viz. the Dow Chemical Company, to produce magnesium and styrene that this country won the war.

Willard was born in Midland, Michigan, on January 4, 1897, the year his father formed the company known as Dow Chemical. His education and early training were designed to prepare him for his future role as president of Dow. During vacations from high school and the University of Michigan, young Willard worked side by side with veteran chemists to learn all phases of his father's business. Once he graduated from university in 1919, he went to work for Dow. Three years later, he became a director and general manager of the company. With his father's death in 1930, Willard, at the age of thirty-three, became president and general manager. He also became head of several associated companies that had put into practical operation many of the company's inventions.

Willard inherited Dow Chemical at the onset of the Great Depression, when the company was producing (in spite of the hardships of the day) 150 chemicals at the rate of 800 carloads per month. Under Willard's leadership, the company rapidly grew and prospered. In the next seventeen years, Williard had lifted the company assets from $22,474,000 to more than $213,000,000 through research, the marketing of new products, and expansion of basic chemical production. Under his direction, Dow Chemical's seven-fold growth had brought it to a point far beyond his father's dreams and had established a potential for even greater growth. In the field of research, Dow's fiftieth anniversary saw fifteen hundred people working in more than thirty laboratories located in Midland, Ann Arbor and South Haven, Michigan; Freeport, Texas; and Pittsburg and Long Beach, California; with experts in chemistry, biology, botany, geology, medicine, mathematics, metallurgy, radiology, physics, and nuclear energy. Pharmaceutical chemicals accounted for ten percent of sales, agricultural chemicals for ten percent, magnesium and fabricated magnesium alloys for ten percent, and plastics for twenty percent - all of which could be attributed to Willard's extraordinary visionary role.

Willard Dow was a member of the Advisory Board of Chicago Procurement District, Chemical Warfare Service; director of the American Chemical Society; and member of the American Institute of Chemical Engineers. He was a thirty-third degree Mason and received a number of honorary degrees from various universities. For his countless contributions to mankind, Willard was selected American Institute of Chemist's Gold Medal recipient in 1944. At the banquet, M. E. Putnam, then vice president of Dow Chemical, lauded Willard with the following words:

"Practically all of the projects which have been developed by the Dow Chemical Company during the past fourteen years have been worked out under his personal guidance - enterprises such as the extraction of bromine from sea water, iodine from oil well brine, ethyl cellulose from cellulose and ethyl chloride, styrene and polystyrene, chemical servicing of oil wells and magnesium from sea water. Whereas Herbert Dow created the essential idea, Willard Dow has nourished and built that idea to greater and greater proportions. . . Without Dow's recovery of bromine from the sea, there could be no flood of 100-octane gasoline for the United Nations."

In early March 1949, Dow and his wife Martha

received an invitation from the Massachusetts Institute of Technology to attend the school's Mid-Century Convocation. They were to be among the honored guests who would hear an address by Sir Winston Churchill, former British Prime Minister. Tragically, before reaching Cambridge on March 31, the twin-engine plane carrying them crashed, killing both Willard and Martha.

In his memory, the company's world headquarters in Midland is called the Willard H. Dow Center.

HARRY GEORGE DRICKAMER

1983's recipient of the AIC Chemical Pioneer Award was Harry Drickamer, one of the pioneers in modern high pressure. In the period 1908-48, Nobel Laureate P. W. Bridgman developed the principles which are used in the design of all very high pressure experiments and made some measurement to pressures as high as 100,000 atmospheres. Bridgman was, however, interested primarily in macroscopic phenomena. It was Drickamer who not only extended the pressure range but first demonstrated that high pressure could be used to study phenomena at the molecular and electronic level. The basis of his work is as follows:

A fundamental effect of compression for condensed phases is to decrease interatomic and intermolecular distances and to increase overlap of the outer electronic orbitals. Since the spacial characteristics of various types of orbitals are different, their energies are perturbed in different degrees by compression. The study of these energy perturbations is well characterized as "pressure tuning spectroscopy" (PTS). Since the optical, electrical, magnetic and chemical properties of condensed phases depend on the characteristics and spacing of the energy levels, the applications and implications of PTS are very broad. They include such various topics as insulator-conductor transitions, the band structure and impurity levels of semiconductors, the electronic structure of alkali, alkaline earth and rare earth metals, the magnetic characteristics and spin state of metals and magnetic insulators, energies, efficiencies and rate processes in inorganic and organic phosphors, protein conformation in solution electronic excitations in metallorganic compounds and charge transfer complexes, electron transfer processes, photochromism and thermochromism and chemical reactivity in molecular crystals and solutions.

Drickamer's monograph (with C. W. Frank) on "Electronic Transition and High Pressure Chemistry in Physics of Solids" is a classic contribution to science.

Harry was born in Cleveland, Ohio, on November 19, 1908, to George H. and Louise (Stremple) Drickamer. He received his B.S., M.S., and Ph.D. degrees from the University of Michigan in 1941, 1942 and 1946, respectively. After graduation, he accepted a position as an engineer with the Pan American Refinery Corporation in Texas City. There he continued his graduate research, returning to Michigan to receive his doctorate in 1946. He then accepted a position at the University of Illinois as assistant professor of Chemical Engineering. He is presently professor of Chemical Engineering, Chemistry and Physics in the Center for Advanced Studies at the University of Illinois.

Dr. Drickamer is a member of the National Academy of Science, American Academy of Arts and Sciences, American Chemical Society, American Institute of Chemical Engineers, American Physical Society, Phi Kappa Phi, Psi Eta Sigma, Faraday Society, Iota Alpha, and a fellow of the American Institute of Chemists and the American Academy of Arts and Sciences. Among other awards, he has received the Bendix Award (1968), P. W. Bridgman Award (1977), Michelson-Morley Award (1978), Buckley Solid State Physics Award (1967), Colburn Award (1947), Alpha Chi Sigma Award (1967), Walker Award (1972), Ipatieff Award (1956), Langmuir Award (1983), Peter Debye Award in Physical Chemistry (1987), and Robert A. Welch Award (1987). He has been an invited lecturer for the Reilly Lectures at Notre Dame (1962), Frontiers in Chemistry Lectures at Western Reserve University (1963), W. N. Lacey Lectureship at California Institute of Technology (1971), and Kurt Wohl Memorial Lecture at the University of Delaware (1978).

Harry married Mae Elizabeth McFillen in 1942. Born to them were Lee Charles, Lynn Louise, Lowell Kurt, Margaret Ann and Priscilla.

(Photograph courtesy of Eastman Kodak Company.)

GEORGE EASTMAN

The life of George Eastman paralleled that of Thomas A. Edison in that George was also born poor and became a great inventor. He also became a successful industrialist and generous philanthropist.

Eastman was born in Waterville, New York, on July 12, 1854. His family moved to Rochester when he was six years old. Two years after the move, his father died and the family came upon hard times. George continued his formal education until he was fourteen when poverty forced him to leave school.

A chance suggestion started George in photography. For ten years he had worked first in insurance and then as a bank clerk. As he wanted to vacation in Santo Domingo, an engineer who worked in the basement of the bank told him he must make a photographic record of his trip. Accordingly, he bought a photographic outfit with all the paraphernalia of the wet plate days. He did not make the Santo Domingo trip, but when more competent with the difficult art of wet plate photography, he went to Macinac Island to photograph the natural bridges there.

George became completely absorbed in photography and wanted to simplify the complicated process, which at that time was still in its primitive stage. The camera itself was heavy; its plate was made of glass and the emulsion on its surface was unstable. As a result, it was necessary to make and apply the emulsion just before taking a picture. Eastman read in British magazines that photographers were making their own gelatin emulsions. Plates coated with this emulsion remained sensitive after they were dry in contrast to the wet plates that had to be exposed at once. While working in the bank during the day and experimenting at night in his mother's kitchen, he began to make his own gelatin emulsion.

In April 1880, George leased the third floor of a building in Rochester and started to manufacture dry plates for sale. The next year he left the bank to devote all his time to the new photographic dry plate business. The name "Kodak" was born in 1888 because he wanted a short word that could be spelled and pronounced easily. The letter "K" was a favorite and he liked the word beginning and ending with "K." The Kodak camera was placed on the market the same year and widespread publicity appeared in national magazines. Eastman coined a slogan for his new system: "You press the button - we do the rest."

In 1889 Eastman substituted celluloid (cellulose nitrate) film for the paper.　In contrast with the previously-used paper tape with the emulsion on the surface, the emulsion was now a part of the film.　The new film was well received, photography became more popular, and it became feasible to make movies.

Although Eastman's new film was vastly superior to the formerly-used coated film, it had the serious disadvantage of being flammable and hence hazardous. After much experimentation, Eastman was able to make a less flammable film using cellulose acetate.　In 1924 the cellulose acetate film replaced the cellulose nitrate film.

Mr. Eastman's company, which became Eastman Kodak Company in 1892, was one of the first American firms to establish a plant for the large-scale production of a standardized product.　It was also one of the first firms to organize a large and productive chemical laboratory. Eastman research led to many developments, including motion picture color photography in 1928.　As a result, photography became increasingly popular and the manufacture of cameras and films increasingly profitable. Consequently, Eastman found himself a very wealthy man.

George was far ahead of the thinking of contemporary management.　He became a pioneer in personal industrial relations by establishing the retirement, annuity, life insurance and disability benefit plans.　He also became known as a philanthropist.　One day in 1924 he signed away thirty million dollars to the University of Rochester, Massachusetts Institute of Technology, and Tuskegee Institute.

Dental clinics had been an interest close to his heart, and he founded a dental clinic in Rochester. Later he gave dental clinics to London, Paris, Rome, Brussels and Stockholm. He loved music. To share this love with others, he built Rochester's Eastman School of Music and the Eastman Theater, where he also funded a symphony orchestra.

Being a craftsman with tools, he liked working as a carpenter or repair man at his simple hunting lodge in North Carolina. For his many shooting and fishing trips and for safaris in Africa, he thoroughly organized his camping equipment, designing and making every pack and its contents. Moreover, he was an expert cook - his recipes were as accurate as chemical formulas - and he was always in charge of the camp cooking and personally produced special dishes, desserts and cakes.

The Synthetic Organic Manufacturers Association made Eastman an honorary member in 1925. Receipt five years later of AIC's Gold Medal brought with it congratulatory letters from President Herbert Hoover and S. W. Stratton, President of MIT.

George Eastman died in 1932, leaving his entire residual estate to the University of Rochester. In 1949, his Rochester home was opened as an independent public museum - International Museum of Photography at George Eastman House.

(Photograph courtesy of the American Institute of Chemists.)

JAMES ECONOMY

James, who was born in Detroit, Michigan, on March 28, 1929, to Peter George and Bessie Lalouise Economy, received his B.S. degree in chemistry from Wayne State University in 1950. Following receipt of his Ph.D. from the University of Maryland in 1954, he spent two years as a research associate with Chemical Pioneer "Speed" Marvel at the University of Illinois. The next four years were with Allied Chemical Company where he was a research chemist. In 1960, he joined Carborundum as a general research leader. Since 1975, he has been Manager of Polymer Science and Technology for IBM at San Jose, California.

While employed at Carborundum in 1972. Dr. Economy developed the moldable copolyesters of p-hydroxybenzoic acid, terephthalic acid, 4,4'-biphenol (EKONOL). A melt-spinnable aromatic copolyester fiber was reported by Carborundum in 1976 and this technology was used by Dartco to produce liquid crystalline polymers in 1984. Sumitomo also commercialized EKONOL fibers in 1985. Had it not been for Dr. Economy's pioneering spirit, most of these high performance polymer developments would not have been realized.

For his meritorious contributions to science, James is the recipient of fourteen IR-100 awards from Industrial Research and has been awarded some seventy patents by the U. S. Patent Office. In addition to being named AIC Chemical Pioneer in 1987, he has also received the Schoelhkopf Medal (1972), Southern Research Burn Institute Award (1976), and the American Chemical Society Phillips Medal (1985). He has published more than 135 scientific reports describing his work.

Dr. Economy is a fellow of the American Institute of Chemists and a member of the International Union of Pure and Applied Chemistry and of the American Chemical Society. He served as chairman of the Polymer Division of ACS.

James married Stacy Zapantis in 1961. They have four children: Elizabeth, Peter, Katherine and Melissa.

GUSTAV EGLOFF

For many years Gustav Egloff was the undisputed spokesman for the petroleum industry. At some meetings he would appear dressed entirely of petroleum derived synthetic clothing. He could easily explain the intricacies of petroleum refining to anyone, including taxi drivers, and usually did. To most people he was affectionately called "Gasoline Gus." His more than 650 publications and 280 patents described work on thermal reactions of aromatic hydrocarbons; pyrolysis, primarily to produce aromatics, alkenes, or gasoline; catalysis; sulfuric acid treatment of gasoline; physical properties; analytical procedures; processing natural gas, coal, and shale oil; and the development of petrochemicals. Two of his more economically important contributions were the multiple coil process for cracking petroleum to high-octane gasoline, and (with Carbon Petroleum Dubbs) the clean-circulation cracking process for continuous conversion of heavy oils to gasoline.

Gustav was born of Swiss parents on November 10, 1886, in New York City. He received the A.B. degree from Cornell in 1912, and the M.A. and Ph.D. degrees from Columbia in 1913 and 1916, respectively. At Columbia he was the Barnard Research Fellow and assistant curator of the Chandler Museum. He was employed by the U. S. Bureau of Mines and Aetna Chemical Company before accepting employment with Universal Oil Products in 1917. One of Egloff's proudest achievements was in persuading Vladimir Ipatieff, famous for his catalytic and high pressure research, to come to the United States in 1930 to organize a similar research program at UOP.

Egloff's contributions to chemical and petroleum science brought him many honors, including the AIC Gold Medal (1940), Octave Chamute Medal of the Western Society of Engineers (1939), Medal of Merit of Columbia University (1943), Washington Award (1953), and Carl Engler Medal of the German Institute of Petroleum and Coal (1954). Moreover, he received three honorary doctor of science degrees. In recognition of his outstanding work in petroleum technology, he was selected a delegate to eleven international meetings, several of which he presided over, to present papers dealing with refining processes. He was appointed a member of the Permanent Council for the World Petroleum Congress, chairman of the Petroleum Section of the Conference on Instrumentation in the Process Industry held in Pittsburgh in 1939, chairman of the Oil Processing Division of the Temperature Symposium held in New York in 1939, and chairman of the International Petroleum Exposition and Congress of Tulsa in 1940. The American Institute of Mining and Metallurgical Engineers appointed him to act in an advisory capacity to Chicago's Museum of Science and Industry.

Busy as Dr. Egloff was in his research activities, he was always willing to serve his fellow chemists through committees and association work and gave generously of his time and encouragement to young chemists, and anonymous financial support. He was well known as a lecturer, addressing national and local meetings of the American Petroleum Institute and American Chemical Society, as well as many universities and associations. He gave radio broadcasts for Science News Service, was elected American correspondent of the Institute of Petroleum, and wrote the yearly reviews of the cracking art for the proceedings of the Institute of Petroleum of London.

Egloff's books, some of which were co-authored, included *Earth Oil* (1933), *Reactions of Pure Hydrocarbons* (1937), *Physical Constants of Hydrocarbons* (five volumes, 1939-53), *Catalysis, Inorganic and Organic* (1940);,*Emulsions and Foams* (1942), and *Alkylation of Alkanes* (1948). An admirer once told Egloff he had "written more books than he had read."

Dr. Egloff was with UOP until his death in 1955.

(Photograph courtesy of American Institute of Chemists.)

HERBERT SOUSA ELEUTERIO

Prior to the mid 1930's, most polymer chemists maintained that unsaturated fluorocarbon compounds could not be polymerized. This was disproven by Roy Plunkett: Tetrafluoroethylene was polymerized by free radical chain polymerization, and the product (Teflon), which was essential for the development of the first atomic bomb, is widely used today as a heat and corrosion resistant plastic. Roy's "breakthrough" led to the development of many polymers and copolymers which are now widely used as elastomers, coatings, and piezoelectric materials. Over forty percent of the five thousand tons of fluorocarbon elastomers are used in this country; because of their unique properties, their use is increasing and new fluorocarbon polymers are being developed.

A novel class of perfluorinated monomers and polymers was developed by Dr. Herbert Sousa Eleuterio, who is credited also with the discovery of new catalytic reactions of olefins.

Herbert, who was born in New Bedford, Massachusetts, on November 23, 1927, received his B.S. degree from Tufts University in 1949 and doctorate from Michigan State University in 1953. After spending one year as a postdoctoral fellow at Ohio State University, he joined Du Pont, where he is now Technical Director of the Atomic Energy Division of Du Pont's Petrochemicals Department. Since joining Du Pont, he has been awarded twelve patents by the U. S. Patent Office. He has also published several articles in scientific journals.

Dr. Eleuterio has served on advisory panels to the National Science Foundation and National Research Council. A member of the American Institute of Chemists, American Chemical Society and Sigma Xi, he has served as national councilor of ACS and treasurer of the Sigma Xi Chapter of the Scientific Research Society of America. He received the Chemical Pioneer Award in 1987 with the citation:

> "For the discovery of a new catalytic reaction of olefins, and for the synthesis of a novel class of perfluorinated monomers and polymers."

Herbert was married in 1951. He and his wife are parents of four children.

(Photograph courtesty of American Chemical Society.)

ALDEN HAYES EMERY

Alden Emery's distinguished career consisted of two highly successful stages. First of all, Emery was active in chemistry and mineralogy and worked on sources of rock strata gases, sources and collection of dusts in mines, mineragraphic identification of minerals, microscopic mineralogy, treatment and utilization of non-metallic minerals, and mineral filters. The second segment of his career was with the American Chemical Society.

For thirteen years following his education at Oberlin College (A.B., 1922, Magna Cum Laude) and Ohio State University (A.M., 1923), Emery worked for the United

States Bureau of Mines. There he advanced to the position of assistant chief engineer. While employed at the Bureau's Pittsburgh laboratories, Emery studied dust suspensions in coal mines and obtained data that led to important improvements in mining operations and a great decrease in dust-explosion hazards. He received high praise for this work and for his past investigations to determine the origin of the asphyxiating gases emanating from certain rock formations in the gold mines of Colorado's Cripple Creek district.

In 1936 Emery left the Bureau of Mines to become assistant manager of the American Chemical Society. Within eleven years he had advanced to the prestigious position of executive secretary, which position he held until 1965 when he was named honorary secretary. He remained in this post for one year, retiring in July 1966.

Emery was assistant editor of *Chemical Abstracts* from 1930 to 1937, section editor of *Metal Abstracts* from 1931 to 1939, and lecturer on mineralogy at George Washington University. In addition to being a member of the American Chemical Society, he held membership in the Institute of Mineral and Metallurgical Engineering, Alpha Chi Sigma, Phi Beta Kappa, Sigma Xi, American Association for the Advancement of Science, Cosmos and Torch Clubs in Washington, D.C., and Chemists Club in New York.

The American Institute of Chemist's Gold Medal became his in 1961, the citation being: "To Alden H. Emery whose administration of the office of executive secretary of the American Chemical Society is outstanding for intelligence, tact, vision, and responsiveness to the desires of its members." In 1967 he received a special award - a bronze medallion - from the ACS Milwaukee Section in appreciation of his activities on behalf of the local sections of the American Chemical Society.

Alden Emery was born June 2, 1901, in Lancaster, New Hampshire, to Vernon and Carolina (Hayes) Emery. He married Dorothy Radde on June 16, 1924, which union produced Alden Hayes, Jr. and Robert Wilson.

FREDERICK J. EMMERICH

Frederick Emmerich, honorary fellow of the American Institute of Chemists, received AIC's Gold Medal in 1952 for distinction in the business field. That same year he was also awarded New York University's Madden Memorial Award.

It was Emmerich's distinguished leadership, interest in industrial affairs and human relations, and activities that have benefitted the chemical industry and profession and which propelled him one notch above others. Chairman of the Board of the Manufacturing Chemists' Association, he was a member of MCA's Defense Mobilization Committee and of the Chemical Industry Advisory Committee, U. S. Munitions Board. He was honorary vice chairman of the American Section, Society of Chemical

Industry; and president of the Chemists Club. He was also a trustee of New York University; a member of the National Industrial Conference Board, Committee for Economic Development; and of the U. S. Council of the International Chamber of Commerce.

In 1950, New York University awarded Emmerich the honorary degree of Doctor of Commercial Science. He received the Honor Scroll Award from the American Section of the Société de Chimie Industrielle in 1964, the citation reading: "An eminent leader of the chemical industry. His sound counsel and loyal participation have advanced international friendship and understanding. His devotion to his fellow man has won the love and respect of all who know him." Emmerich was honorary chairman of an "American Day Program" hosted by this section at the Faculté des Sciences de Bordeaux (France) in 1961.

A native of New York, Frederick received his education in the public schools and at New York University. After serving with the Army in World War I, he began his career (1920) as an accountant for National Aniline and Chemical Company.* Nine years later he became Comptroller and shortly thereafter was appointed Vice President. In 1946 he was elected President and in 1957 Chairman of the Board of Directors. Dr. Emmerich retired from active business the last day of December, 1957, but continued his close association with Allied as a Director. He died at his home on August 29, 1970, at the age of seventy-eight.

*National Aniline and Chemical Company became a unit of the Allied Chemical organization in 1920.

PAUL HUGH EMMETT

In 1835, Berzelius coined the words *catalyst* and *catalysis* from the Greek words *kata*, meaning entirely, and *lyo*, to loose. Though for many years it was generally accepted among scientists that a catalyst loosened the bonds in a reaction and thus altered the rate of reaction by way of a *catalytic force*, it is now believed that catalysts accelerate the attainment of equilibrium but do not alter the equilibrium constant.   In 1915, Irving Langmuir found that the amount of reactant adsorbed on an adsorbent was constant at a specific temperature and pressure.   Other information on catalysis was developed by Hugh Taylor, Eric Rideal and Paul Sabatier in the 1920's. It was studies by these latter individuals and graduate research under the direction of A. F. Bennett (a former student of Taylor) which sparked Paul Hugh Emmett's lifetime of research in the field of catalysis. In 1938, Emmett, in conjunction with Brunauer and Teller, developed and published the 'BET' equation for estimating surface areas for adsorption.

Paul was born in Portland, Oregon, on September 22, 1900, to John Hugh and Vina (Hutchens) Emmett. After graduating from Washington High School, he entered Oregon Agricultural College* where he received his B.S. in chemical engineering in 1922. He was granted his doctorate at California Institute of Technology in 1925. Paul spent the next year as instructor of chemistry at Oregon State College and then joined the U. S. Department of Agriculture, for the next decade working in the Fixed Nitrogen Research Laboratory. He left the Department of Agriculture in 1937 to accept a faculty position with Johns Hopkins University. In 1943, he worked with Harold Urey on the separation of uranium isotopes and consulted with W. T. Miller on the design of the Oak Ridge Fission Plant. Two years later, he joined the Mellon Institute. In 1956, he returned to Johns Hopkins as W. R. Grace Professor. After retiring from Johns Hopkins in 1970, he became Research Professor of Chemistry at Portland State University.

Paul was recipient of AIC's Chemical Pioneer Award and the Vollum Award from Reed University in 1980, the ACS Pittsburgh Section Award in 1953, and the Kendall Award in 1958. In 1964 he was awarded honorary doctoral degrees from the University of Lyons, the University of Hokkaido and was elected to the Consejo Superior in Spain; he was named honorary doctor of the University of Wisconsin in 1971. The Paul Emmett Award of the Catalyst Society of America was named for him. The University of Utah also established the Paul Emmett Lecture on Catalysis Series in his honor in 1984.

*Now Oregon State University.

Dr. Emmett was a lifetime fellow of AIC, a member of the American Chemical Society, National Research Council and National Academy of Sciences. He authored more than 150 reports in scientific journals, was co-author of *Catalysis, Then and Now* and editor of seven volumes of *Catalysis*.

Paul's 1930 marriage to Leila Lewis ended with her death in 1967. He was stricken with Parkinson's disease in the 1960's and confined to a special care home for the terminally ill until his death on April 22, 1985. He is survived by his second wife Pauline and a stepson Michael Ney.

WILLIAM LLOYD EVANS

*"William Lloyd Evans has been chairman of one of the greatest departments of chemistry in the United States, has received the Nichols medal, and is a past-president of the American Chemical Society, but only those who have been intimately associated with him can appreciate his stature as a man and as a chemist."**

*Introduction of Dr. Evans by Dr. Henry B. Hass, then Head of the Department of Chemistry, Purdue University, at the time Dr. Evans was awarded the Gold Medal.

In 1942 the AIC Gold Medal was awarded to Dr. Evans, chairman of the Chemistry Department of Ohio State University, in recognition of his outstanding accomplishments in the field of oxidizing organic compounds, particularly carbohydrates; and for his contributions to the profession as an educator.

Evans was widely known for his research on carbohydrates and the oxidation of organic compounds. His early work included studies on the mechanism of oxidation of compounds such as ethanol, acetaldehyde, isopropanol, and acetone. As attention was then given to the oxidation of carbohydrates, he synthesized previously-known sugars and studied dissociation phenomena in aromatic carbinols.

Evans was outstanding not only in research but also in teaching and lecturing, primarily in general chemistry. It is estimated he lectured to more than 45,000 students during his career.

Science was not his only talent. He was gifted as well in music, playing the violin as the youngest member of the Columbus Symphony Orchestra. He also directed the Ohio State Glee Club (while his wife directed the Women's Glee Club), organized choruses of men and women at Colorado Springs, and edited the Ohio State University song book.

William received his B.S. and M.S. degrees at Ohio State University in 1892 and 1896. He worked as a chemist for American Encaustic Tile Company in Lanesville, Ohio, in 1892-94. For two years after receiving his M.S. degree, he was an assistant in Ohio State's department of ceramics. The next four years were spent as an instructor in Colorado Springs. Evans received his doctorate in chemistry under John U. Nef at the University of Chicago in 1905 and returned to Ohio State as assistant professor of chemistry. In 1908 he was promoted to associate professor; in 1911 to full professor. Concurrently he served as lecturer in chemistry at Starling-Ohio Medical College. In 1928 he succeeded William McPherson as chairman of Ohio State's chemistry department and remained in this capacity until his retirement in 1941.

Evans received honorary degrees from Ohio State University and Capitol University. He was chairman of the Organic Division of the American Chemical Society (1928), president of the American Chemical Society (1929), honorary fellow of the American Institute of Chemists, and member of the National Research Council Committee on Carbohydrate Research (1926-27). During World War I he was head of the Laboratory and Inspection Division of Edgewood Arsenal, with the rank of major. A member of the Ohio Academy of Sciences, Evans served as its president from 1939 to 1940. He was also a member of the American Academy of Arts and Sciences, National Research Council Division of Chemistry and Chemical Technology (1934-1940), Torch Club (Columbus), Faculty Club of Ohio State University, Engineers Club (Dayton), Sigma Xi, Phi Beta Kappa, and Sigma Chi. Evans published many papers and was the co-author of several chemistry laboratory manuals and qualitative analysis texts with J. E. Day, A. B. Garrett, W. E. Henderson, W. McPherson, H. H. Sisler, and L. L. Quill.

The American Chemical Society bestowed the William H. Nichols medal upon Evans in 1929.

William Lloyd Evans was born on December 22, 1870. His parents, William Henry and Anne (Lloyd) Evans were Welsh immigrants. Dr. Evans married Cora Ruth Roberts on March 9, 1911; they became the parents of Lloyd Roberts, Jane Anne (later Mrs. A. H. Nielson), and

William Arthur (lost in action in the Pacific, U.S.N., 1944). Evans died on October 18, 1954, in Columbus, the city of his birth.

CHARLES HAROLD FISHER

When he returned to Salem, Virginia, for the fiftieth reunion of his high school class, "Hap" Fisher revealed to fellow students that a prophesy published in the school annual prior to graduation had come true. For it had been predicted that he would become a distinguished scientist and develop a synthetic leather; Hap said at least the second prediction had been realized.

Hap was born on November 20, 1906, in Hiawatha, West Virginia, to Lawrence D. and Mary M. (Akers) Fisher. When he was five months old, his family returned to their home in Salem, Virginia.

There were two things Hap particularly disliked as a boy - strenuous farm work and high school chemistry.

What he *did* like, in spite of his limited size, was football, basketball, track, and being editor of the high school annual, the *Oracle*.   Fortunately, his chemistry teacher, Dr. R. D. Cool, ignited a spark and Hap went on to Roanoke College to major in chemistry (B.S. 1928). He earned part of his expenses by playing a banjo in a dance band and working nights in a local post office.

One year later, thanks to a part-time teaching assistantship, he received his M.S. degree from the University of Illinois. His first taste of industrial research was in the summer of 1931, when he worked for the Pennsylvania Coal Products Company at Petrolia. After receiving his doctorate in 1932 under the direction of Professor R. C. Fuson, he worked again at the Petrolia firm where he developed a commercially successful antioxidant. Hap's formal education, following his graduate studies at Illinois, was not renewed until 1961 when he took a four-weeks course in management given by the American Management Association in New York.

In the fall of 1932, Fisher became a chemistry instructor at Harvard. Three years later he accepted a position in the group at Pittsburgh's U. S. Bureau of Mines that was investigating the production of liquid fuels by the hydrogenation of coal. The competent leader of the group, Dr. H. H. Storch, was later honored by the creation of the ACS Storch Award. Information was provided on the relation between the petrographic composition and rank of coal and its behavior on hydrogenation. It was suggested, with supporting evidence, that many valuable chemicals could be made by coal hydrogenation with the byproducts used as liquid fuels.

Although Fisher enjoyed his work on complex coal and coal tar, he preferred research on individual chemicals and organic synthesis. The opportunity to do such

research came in 1940 when he became head of the
Organic Acids Section of USDA's Eastern Regional
Research Laboratory, a new organization in Philadelphia
headed by Director P. A. Wells. In 1946, Hap was
promoted to head of the Carbohydrate Research Division.
The members of this Division developed improved
methods for making many derivatives of lactic acid, acrylic
acid, methacrylic acid, n-alkanoic acids, and starch. Vinyl-
type monomers and polyallyl compounds were
polymerized. Polyacrylate elastomers, with excellent oil
and heat resistance, were developed which are
commercially attractive. Such elastomers have been used
in many of the automobiles manufactured during the past
forty years; about 25,000,000 pounds of the polyacrylate
elastomers are made annually.

In 1950 Fisher was appointed Director of USDA's
Southern Utilization Research and Development Division,
which consisted of the Southern Regional Research
Laboratory with headquarters in New Orleans and six
satellite laboratories located in Texas, Louisiana, Florida,
and North Carolina. During his twenty-two years in New
Orleans, these Laboratories became internationally known
for their research on the chemistry and processing of
cotton, cottonseed, peanuts, sugar cane, pine gum, and
similar materials. The many commercialized products that
were based on or aided by this research include easy-care
and flame-resistant cotton textiles, improved methods and
machines for processing cotton, frozen citrus
concentrates, and plasticizers from vegetable oils.

Hap was named Chemical Pioneer in 1966 and
Pioneer in Polymer Science by *Polymer News* in 1981. He
was a member of the group in Philadelphia that received
USDA's Superior Service Award in the 1940's. He
received also the AIC Honor Scroll Award in 1960, Herty
Medal in 1959, and Southern Chemist Award in 1956.

Honorary doctoral degrees were bestowed upon him by by Tulane University (1953) and by Roanoke College (1963). He was presented with the Presidential Citation of Merit in 1986 by the American Institute of Chemists.

Dr. Fisher wrote the article on chemurgy for *Encyclopedia Britannica.* He is author of more than 180 scientific reports and has been awarded 72 patents by the U. S. Patent Office. His first paper, describing research done under the direction of Professor R. C. Fuson, was published in the *Journal of American Chemical Society* in 1930. He has lectured in many cities in the United States and in Canada, Mexico, and South Africa.

In addition to being a fellow and former president of AIC, Dr. Fisher is or has been a member of the American Chemical Society, American Association of Textile Chemists and Colorists, Southern Association of Science and Industry, Chemical Society (London), American Association for the Advancement of Science, American Oil Chemists Society, American Institute of Chemical Engineers, Institute of Food Technology, Louisiana Engineering Society, Virginia Academy of Science, Association of Consulting Chemists and Chemical Enginers, Commercial Development Association, Affiliate Member of International Union of Pure and Applied Chemistry, Sigma Xi, Gamma Alpha, Alpha Chi Sigma, Phi Lambda Upsilon, International House (New Orleans), Chemists Club (New York), Cosmos Club (Washington, D.C.), Town Club (Salem), and the Roanoke Valley Torch Club. He joined ACS in 1930 and has served as National Councilor (1946-1948 and 1951-1953), Chairman of the Philadelphia Section (1948-1950), Chairman of the Building Fund Campaign in the New Orleans area, and member of the Board of Directors, 1969-71.

Fisher was President of the Greater New Orleans Science Fair, Inc. (1968-69) and President of the Roanoke College Alumni Association (1978-79). He was a consultant in textile research for the Republic of South Africa (1967), in food technology for the Pan American Union (1968), and in paper technology for the Library of Congress (1973-76). He was a member of the Board, The Chemurgic Council (1966); member, National Academy of Sciences Committee on Scientific and Technologic Base of Puerto Rico's Economy (1966-67); member, National Academy of Sciences Panel on Development of Research Administrators and Technical Managers in Newly Industrializing Countries (1967-68); member, Cotton Task Group of President Eisenhower's Bipartisan Commission on Increased Industrial Use of Farm Crops (1950's); and member, Southern Regional Council on Graduate Education in Agricultural Sciences (1958-61).

Three of Hap's brothers received professional educations. Herman, graduate of the Virginia Military Institute, was a civil engineer for Du Pont when he died in 1957. Richard, M.D., is chief of the Orthopedic Group at the Lewis-Gale Clinic in Salem. Robert, recipient of the B.S. degree in chemistry (Roanoke College, 1936), was a postal inspector prior to his retirement. Brother Lawrence, Jr., is a businessman in Martinsville, Virginia. Sister Helen is the widow of Dr. Jack O. Rowell, member of the faculty at Virginia Polytechnic Institute prior to his retirement and death.

Hap married Elizabeth Dye in 1933. Following her death, he married Lois Carlin in 1968. Dr. Fisher returned to Roanoke College in 1972 as an adjunct professor. He and Lois established the Lawrence D. and Mary A. Fisher Endowed Scholarship at Roanoke College in 1978 in honor of his parents and the Lois Carlin Endowed Scholarship at Knox College, Galesburg, Illinois, in 1987.

(Reprinted from *THE CHEMIST*, with permission.)

LAWRENCE HUGO FLETT

"To Lawrence H. Flett - Outstanding leader in development in the chemical industry, who has devoted his lifetime to understanding and sympathetic human relations with his professional associates, and has unselfishly given a large part of his efforts to the furtherance of the profession of chemists, not only as an individual with individuals, but also through responsible positions in many professional organizations both national and international."

*Citation at the time Flett was made an honorary fellow of AIC.

Lawrence ("Mique") Flett developed the first commercial synthetic detergent prepared from petroleum. He did important research also on dyes, antiseptics, organic chemicals, insecticides, and intermediates. He had an outstanding record of service to and association with the American Institute of Chemists: he was president of the AIC from 1948 to 1952, served on many AIC committees, and represented the AIC as a delegate at the convocation celebrating the 125th anniversary of the College of the Holy Cross in Worcester, Massachusetts, in December 1968. He was named honorary fellow in 1957 and awarded the Gold Medal in 1958.

Mique served many professional organizations in many ways. He was a productive worker for the Western New York Section of the American Chemical Society; councilor several times representing either a local section or an ACS division; vice president of the ACS Western New York Section; one of the founders of the ACS Division of Chemical Marketing and Economics, of which he was the chairman in 1955-56; member of the Editorial Advisory Board for two ACS periodicals; president of the Chemical Market Research Association; vice president of the Commercial Chemical Development Association; member of the advisory committee of the Gordon Research Conference; member of the Board of Trustees of the Chemists Club, New York; two-term president of the American Section of the Société de Chimie Industrielle; and member of the advisory board for Documentation and Communication Research at Western Reserve University. Flett was a member of Kappa Sigma, American Association for the Advancement of Science, New York Academy of Science, Society of the Chemical Industry, Chemists Club, Bonnie Briar Club, Downtown Athletic Club, and Town Club (Scarsdale). He received about 75 patents and published a number of papers and books.

One of his books was entitled *Maleic   Anhydride Derivatives-Reactions of the Double Bond.*

The Gold Medal was awarded to Flett ". . . in affectionate recognition of his research achievements, his devotion to the profession of chemistry, and his long and unselfish promotion of the professional welfare of fellow chemists through the medium of the American Institute of Chemists and other societies." Fittingly, Dr. Flett's address that evening was "The Human Side of Chemistry." George L. Parkhurst, who spoke about Flett, investigated the spelling of his nickname. He discovered that Flett, who had grown up in an Irish community, learned to understand and love the Irish. Perhaps the change from "Mike" to "Mique" came at a later state in Flett's career when he came to know and love the French!

The Schoellkopf Medal is presented by the Western New York Section to a distinguished chemist working in the Buffalo-Niagara Falls area. Lawrence Flett received this honor. He was made an honorary member of the Société de Chimie Industrielle in 1956, at which time Dr. Flett was president of the American Section of the Société.

Lawrence was born on March 26, 1896, in Melrose, Massachusetts, to Charles Frederick and Alvina Flett. The tallest boy in his class, he played center on the basketball team. He received the B.S. degree in 1918 at the Massachusetts Institute of Technology and began his career as a chemist with the National Analine Division of the Allied Chemical and Dye Corporation. He married Dorothea Elizabeth Killough on November 24, 1920; their children are Sally and Ruth. In 1955, Flett retired in New London, New Hampsire, selected because "he had fallen in love with the place while attending Gordon Research Conferences." Flett's hobbies were golf, swimming, sailing and skiing. Death took him at the age of 83 in 1979.

PAUL JOHN FLORY

Since 1953, when septuagenarian Hermann Staudinger received the Nobel Prize, several other scientists have been so honored for work in the field of macromolecules. One of these was Paul J. Flory (1974) for "pioneering analytical methods for studying long chain molecules leading to the development of plastics and synthetic material."

Paul was born in Sterling, Illinois, on June 19, 1910, to sixth-generation American parents of Huguenot-German extraction. Ezra Flory was a clergyman-educator; Martha (Brumbaugh) Flory had been a school teacher; both of them were the first of their families to attend college.

After graduating from high school, Paul enrolled in Manchester College where his studies in chemistry were inspired by Professor Carl W. Hall. AIC Pioneer Roy Plunket also attended Manchester, and he and Paul conducted graduate studies together at Ohio State University. Paul received his doctorate in 1934 and accepted a position in the Central Research Laboratories of E. I. du Pont de Nemours and Company. Of this association, Flory later stated: "It was my good fortune to be assigned to a small group headed by Dr. Wallace H. Carothers . . . The time was propitious, for the hypothesis that polymers are in fact covalently linked macromolecules had been established by the works of Staudinger and of Carothers only a few years earlier."

Following Carothers' untimely death in 1937, Paul spent two years at the University of Cincinnati before returning to industrial research with Standard Oil and Development Company in New Jersey in 1940. In 1943 he joined Goodyear Tire and Rubber Company in Akron. In the spring of 1948 Paul left Goodyear at the suggestion of Nobel laureate Peter Debye to accept a George Fisher Baker non-resident lectureship at Cornell. He was appointed to full professor that fall and began to write a summary of his lectures entitled *Principles of Polymer Chemistry*, which was published by Cornell University Press in 1953. This was considered the first truly scientific polymer chemistry written in the English language and to this day ranks as the best of the many books now available to students of this discipline.

It was during the Baker Lectureship that Paul perceived a way to treat the effect of excluded volume on the configuration of polymer chains. He had long suspected that the effect would be non-asymptopic with the length of the chain; that is, that the perturbation of the configuration by the exclusion of one segment of the chain from the space occupied by another would increase without limit as the chain was lengthened. The treatment of the effect by resort to a relatively simple "smoothed density" model confirmed this expectation and provided an expression relating the perturbation of the configuration to the chain length and the effective volume of a chain segment. It became apparent to him that the physical properties of dilute solutions of macromolecules could not be properly treated and comprehended without taking account of the perturbation of the macromolecule by these intramolecular interactions. The hydrodynamic theories of dilute polymer solutions developed a year or two earlier by Kirkwood and by Debye were therefore reinterpreted in light of the excluded volume effect. Agreement with a broad range of experimental information on viscosities, diffusion coefficients and sedimentation velocities was demonstrated soon thereafter.

Out of these developments came the formulation of the hydrodynamic constant called *theta*, and the recognition of the theta point at which excluded volume interactions are neutralized.

Paul accepted a position at the Mellon Institute in 1957 but left four years later to accept a professorship in Stanford's Department of Chemistry. In 1966 he was appointed to the J. G. Jackson - C. J. Wood Professorship. Further investigations of the thermodynamics of solutions, in conjunction with Professor M. V. Volkenstein (U.S.S.R.) and Professor Kazuo Nagai (Japan) led to another book, *Statistical Mechanics of Chain Molecules*, published in 1969 (translated into Japanese and Russian in 1974). He also published over 300 scientific reports and was awarded twenty patents by the U. S. Patent Office.

Dr. Flory was a long-time member of the American

Chemical Society and served both as councilor and as a member of the Board of Directors. He was a fellow of the American Association for the Advancement of Science and the American Physical Society; a member of the National Academy of Science, National Research Council, American Academy of Arts and Sciences, and American Philosophical Society. He received honorary doctoral degrees from his alma maters (Manchester, 1950; Ohio State, 1970), University of Manchester (England, 1969), Politechnic di Milano, Indiana University, Clarkson College, the Weizman Institute of Science, University of Cincinnati, and University of Massachusetts.

Flory was recipient of the Joseph Sullivan Medal from Ohio State University (1945); Baekeland Award of the New Jersey Section of ACS (1947); Colwyn Medal from the Institute of Rubber Industry in Great Britain (1954); Nichols Medal from the New York Section of ACS (1962); High-Polymer Physics Prize from the American Physical Society (1962); International Award in Plastics Science and Engineering from the Society of Plastics Engineers (1967); Charles Goodyear Medal from the ACS (1968); Peter Debye Award in Physical Chemistry from the ACS (1969); Charles Frederick Chandler Medal from Columbia University (1970); First Award for Excellence - Chemistry, The Carborundum Company (1971); Cresson Medal from the Franklin Institute (1971); John G. Kirkwood Medal from Yale University (1971); J. Willard Gibbs Medal from the Chicago Section, ACS (1973); Priestley Medal, ACS (1974); Carl-Dietrich-Harries Medal from the German Chemical Society (1977); and the Erigen Medal from the Society of Engineering Science (1978). He was also named a Pioneer in Polymer Science by *Polymer News* in 1981.

Paul made at least one major contribution to polymer chemistry in each of his positions. His contribution to our knowledge of the mechanism of vinyl polymerization, i.e, via chain reactions, was published in the *Journal of the American Chemical Society* in 1937 when he was working with Carothers at Du Pont. Flory also proposed the chain transfer step that year. While at the University of Cincinnati, he provided a quantitative description of gelation through the formation of infinite networks by the condensation of multifunctional monomers. His solution theory, now summarized in the Flory-Huggins equation, was developed independently while he was at Standard Oil. He showed that swelling equilibrium could be used to estimate the crosslink density. He also introduced the term *theta temperature*, i.e., the temperature at which a polymer, in solution, obeys random chain statistics. He developed a relationship between intrinsic viscosity and molecular weight in which he introduced a new universal constant *phi (ø)*. He also provided a statistical mechanical theory of rubber elasticity.

Throughout his career, Flory maintained (1) that the chemical behavior of polymers is not intrinsically different from that of smaller molecules and (2) that polymer chains, in the solid state, are subject to the laws of random statistics. From an historical point of view, he credited H. Hlasiwtz and J. Habeman with the 1871 concept that proteins and some carbohydrates were polymers.

In spite of his busy schedule, Paul devoted a good deal of his time to human rights.

Three children resulted from Paul's 1936 marriage to Emily Catherine Tabor: Susan, Melinda and Paul John Flory, Jr. Susan is the wife of Professor George S. Springer, Department of Mechanical Engineering at the University of Michigan. Melinda is the wife of Professor Donald E. Groom, Department of Physics at the University of Utah. Paul Flory, Jr. is Doctor of Medicine, Department of

Human Genetics, Yale University.   There are five grandchildren: Elizabeth and Marie Springer; Suzannah and Jeremy Groom; and Paul John Flory III.

Paul Flory passed away on September 9, 1985.

DENIS FORSTER

Denis Forster, who published some forty articles while employed by Monsanto, was most deserving of the 1980 Chemical Pioneer award. His many publications and thirteen patents by the U. S. Patent Office are a credit to Monsanto, his employer since 1966. Denis was Group Leader (1970), Senior Group Leader (1974), Monsanto Fellow (1975), Senior Fellow (1980) and Distinguished Fellow (1984).

Denis was born at Newcastle-on-Tyne, England, on February 28, 1941, to Thomas Reginald and Margaret (Dobson) Forster. After completing Jarrow Grammar School, he enrolled in the Imperial College of Science and Technology at London University where, as an Imperial Exhibition and State Scholar, he received the B.Sc. and

Ph.D. degrees in 1962 and 1965, respectively. He then accepted a postdoctoral fellowship at Princeton where his research advisor was Professor W. Dew Horrocks.

Dr. Forster is a fellow of the American Institute of Chemists and a member of the American Chemical Society and the Racquet Club. In addition to the Chemical Pioneer Award, he has received the ACS Ipatieff Award (1980) and the Thomas and Hochwalt Award (1984), named for Charles A. Thomas and Carroll A. Hochwalt who started a research laboratory bearing their names in Dayton, Ohio.*   Forster has presented eleven plenary lectures in England, China, Belgium, and the United States and given fifteen seminars to American universities.

In contrast to several other Chemical Pioneers who have worked with heterogeneous catalysts, Denis has specialized in the use of homogeneous catalysts, particularly catalysts for carbonylation.   Geoffrey Wilkinson (Nobel Laureate 1973) demonstrated that rhodium complexes would function as hydroformylation catalysts under much milder conditions than the cobalt catalysts previously used, i.e., the cobalt catalyst system had been used for the commercial production of acetic acid by the carbonylation of methanol. W. R. Knowles and associates at Monsanto showed that carbonylation would take place with a selectivity of 99 percent under mild conditions (30-40 atm pressure at $180°$ C), in the presence of rhodium and iridium complexes, using an iodide promoter. Forster showed that rhodium III salts were reduced in these systems to rhodium I and $[Rh(CO)_2I_2]^-$ ions were found; that, in contrast to rhodium I, which is a poor nucleophile, $[Rh(CO)_2I_2]^-$ is an excellent nucleophile which attacks methyl iodide readily in an oxidative addition

*Acquired by Monsanto in 1938 to become its Central Research Laboratories.

reaction at room temperature. He demonstrated that the key to the selectivity of this process was related to the extremely short lifetime of the rhodium-methyl bond and an earlier rate-determining step prior to formation of the rhodium-organic compound. The first plant for the commercial production of acetic acid by this homogeneous catalytic process was built by Monsanto at Texas City. It is expected that this and other plants will produce more than one million tons of acetic acid annually.

Denis also proved that methanol can be carbonylated by iridium-catalysis, to wit: In the carbonylation reaction, the rate determining step is the methyl iodide addition to $[Ir(CO)_2I_2]^-$ which is in equilibrium with $[HIr(CO)_2I_3]^-$; and that iridium with an iodide promoter is also an efficient catalyst for the hydrocarboxylation of olefins for the production of carboyxlic acid.

Two daughters, Juliet and Rachel, were born to Denis and Hazel Frances (Onions), whom he married in 1964.

(Photograph courtesy of the American Institute of Chemists.)

DANIEL WAYNE FOX

Aromatic polycarbonates were described by Einhorn in 1898 and by Bischoff and von Hedenstrom in 1902. However, no attempt to commercialize these important high performance polymers was made until 1956, when Dr. Herman Schnell of Farbenfabriken Bayer AG and Dr. Daniel Wayne Fox of General Electric produced these plastics independently. Fortunately for progress in high performance polymers, the two producing firms agreed to cross license Schnell's interfacial and solution patents and Fox's transesterification patents. These clear, tough bisphenol-A-poly-carbonates are marketed under the trade names of Lexan, Merlon and Calibre by General Electric, Mobay, and Dow.

Daniel was born in Johnstown, Pennsylvania, on May 14, 1923, to Daniel Francis and Marie Alma Fox. From 1942-45, he served as a lieutenant in the U. S. Air Force. Thereafter, he enrolled in Lebanon Valley College to receive his B.S. degree in chemistry in 1948. He was awarded the M.S. (1951) and Ph.D. (1952) degrees by the University of Oklahoma. He then accepted a position with General Electric where he is now manager of Chemical Development Operations, Technology Division, Plastics Business Group.

Dr. Fox was named Chemical Pioneer in 1987 with the citation: "For his pioneering studies in the polymerization of polycarbonates, the invention of LEXAN resin, and outstanding entrepreneurship in the commercialization of engineering plastics." Recipient of more than forty-five patents on polymers and plastic subjects by the U. S. Patent Office, he is a member of the Plastics Hall of Fame. He is the author of several books in his field, including *Aromatic Polycarbonates.*

In addition to being a fellow of the American Institute of Chemists, Dr. Fox is a member of the National Academy of Engineers, American Chemical Society, Society of Plastics Engineers, Sigma Xi, and Phi Lambda Upsilon.

Daniel and Joyce Schmidt were married in 1948. The Foxes are parents of Barbara Ann and Daniel S. Fox.

Dr. Fox is an ardent tennis player and golfer.

(Photograph reprinted from "A Century of Chemistry,"
with permission.)

FRANCIS PATRICK GARVAN

*"This decision is a master stroke of
the Institute. No act in its past history could
merit greater approbation. It would be
difficult to find candidates more deserving of
this signal honor than Mr. and Mrs. Francis P.
Garvan."**

Chemists and the chemical profession lost a great
friend when Francis Garvan died from pneumonia in 1937.

*From the March 1929 issue of *THE CHEMIST* at the time
Mr. and Mrs. Garvan were awarded the Gold Medal from the
American Institute of Chemists.

Garvan's devotion to his country and his contributions to its economic life were outstanding. During his service in charge of investigations for the New York office of the Alien Property Custodian and as Alien Property Custodian in 1919, he conceived the idea of making the United States an economically self-sufficient nation through the establishment of a great chemical industry. Prior to that time, the United States had six chemical plants. With the authority of President Wilson, Garvan organized the Chemical Foundation, which purchased from the government the 4,813 patents that had been seized by the United States from Germany. These patents were leased to private individuals and corporations on a royalty basis. The Chemical Foundation had a capital of $500,000 in preferred and common stock with interest limited to six per cent each. Proceeds from the royalties were invested in research and in projects of importance to chemists or the chemical industry.

As president of the Chemical Foundation, Garvan directed the distribution of funds to worthy projects such as the establishment of 64 scholarships in chemistry; the donation of $850,000 to the Farm Chemurgie Council; the bestowal of $275,000 to *Chemical Abstracts*, published by the American Chemical Society; research on the production of paper and rayon from slash-pine to bring new industrial prosperity to the southern states; the support of research on the common cold; the publication of scientific books; contributions to the International Congress of Soil Science, to the National Research Council and to the U. S. Institute for Textile Research; and other projects for the benefit of chemistry. Garvan also contributed from his personal fortune to the financing of six four-year chemistry scholarships at Yale or Vassar in memory of his daughter Patricia.

Garvan conceived even greater benefits to this country through chemistry. He foresaw agriculture placed on a self-sufficient basis as a source of raw materials for the chemical industry. In his capacity as president of the National Farm Chemurgie Council, he planned the use of alcohol for fuel, and the extraction of chemical raw materials from agricultural products.

Garvan's great contributions to chemists and chemistry were recognized by various honors. Fordham, Yale, Trinity, and Notre Dame awarded honorary degrees to him. He has been the only layman to receive the Priestley Medal of the American Chemical Society. He received the Mendel Medal, awarded by Villanova College to the Catholic who has signally advanced the cause of science. The American Institute of Chemists awarded to him and his wife, jointly, its medal in 1929 for "noteworthy and outstanding service to the science of chemistry, or to the profession of chemist in America." In 1949, the Garvans were named honorary fellows of the AIC.

The announcement that the Gold Medal would be awarded to the Garvans was met with great enthusiasm. Dr. F. E. Breithut, then president of the American Institute of Chemists, received numerous letters and messages of approval. A letter from W. R. Whitney, then Vice President and Director of General Electric, began with the sentence, "I wish to add my little bit of commendation of the just presentation of the Institute's medal to Mr. and Mrs. Francis P. Garvan." A letter from F. W. H. Hobbs, then President of Arlington Mills, contained the sentence, "Certainly no one else so richly deserves this medal and I am sure your article will bring about universal satisfaction and especially to those of us who have the pleasure and privilege of association with Mr. Garvan. . . ." Dr. Charles H. Herty presided at the award ceremony and Dr. Finley made the presentation. The speakers were the Hon. John

W. Davis, representing the legal profession; Dr. John J. Abel, of Johns Hopkins, representing the medical profession; and Dr. John H. Finley, representing the general public. Robert L. Munger wrote a seven-stanza poem for the Garvans, which was published in *THE CHEMIST.*

Garvan, who was a lawyer rather than a chemist, had an outstanding legal career in addition to his work for chemistry. Nevertheless, he was one of the first Americans to realize the part chemists play in building a nation. In foreseeing a solution to his country's economic problems, he offered the services of chemists, who would utilize the agricultural products of America's rich earth to produce the raw materials for industry.

Born in 1875 in East Hartford, Connecticut, Garvan graduated from the New York Law School in 1899. He was dean of the Fordham Law School from 1919 to 1923.

MARY LOWE GOOD

Since relatively few women study advanced chemistry, there has been limited opportunity for the "fairer sex" to demonstrate brilliance in this field. Mary Lowe Good is one of these rare species. Her achievements need to be publicized so that others may follow in her footsteps. Mary is the only woman to have served as Chairman of the Board of the American Chemical Society (1978, 1980) and to receive the American Institute of Chemists Gold Medal. She is also one of the few women in this country to direct industrial research.

Mary was born on June 20, 1931, at Grapevine, Texas, which is not far from the present Dallas-Fort Worth International Airport. Her parents, John W. and Winnie (Mercer) Lowe, were teachers. Her grandfather and father had been semi-pro baseball players.   Mary, a self-confessed "bookaholic," graduated from Kirby, Arkansas, high school where her parents were teaching.

At the suggestion of her father, the bright young lady enrolled in a practical course at Arkansas State Teachers College at Conway, her first choice for a major being home economics.   Following her introduction to chemistry under Professor E. E. Cordrey, she became a "chemaholic."   She rationalized her change of majors by saying that a good cook could also be a good chemist. Mary attended college year-round, surviving by teaching laboratory courses in chemistry and physics for a mere $15 monthly.

After receiving her B.S. in 1950, she accepted a graduate teaching fellowship at the University of Arkansas, where she claimed to have been in "hog's heaven" with an annual stipend of $1,000.   (Coincidentally, she worked as a waitress off campus in a restaurant named "Hog's Heaven.")   Mary received the M.S. and Ph.D. degrees in 1953 and 1955 and an honorary L.D.D. in 1979 from the University of Arkansas.

Mary became a chemistry instructor at Louisiana State University at Baton Rouge in 1954.   She was later promoted to the rank of Associate Professor.   In 1958, she transferred to LSU in New Orleans.   Sixteen years later she was designated as a Boyd Professor, the highest faculty rank in the LSU system.   In this capacity, she returned to the Baton Rouge campus in 1979.   The next year she accepted a position as Vice President and Director of Research at UOP in Des Plaines, Illinois.   Thanks to Mary, the UOP Research Center is considered the leading research organization for the entire Signal Companies.

Dr. Good was elected President of ACS in 1987.   She

has also served as Chairman of the Amelia Earhart Fellowship Committee of Zonta International and was a member of the Board of Directors of Oak Ridge Associated Universities. She is President of the Inorganic Division of the International Union of Pure and Applied Chemistry (IUPAC), member of the Board of Directors of the Industrial Research Institute and of the National Institute for Petroleum and Energy Research, member of the Board of Trustees of Rensselaer Polytechnic Institute, and past vice president of the National Science Board, She is also a fellow of AIC, a member of the American Chemical Society, Chemical Society (London), Phi Beta Kappa, Sigma Xi, Iota Sigma Pi and past president of the Zonta Club in New Orleans.

Mary has authored a book and written over one hundred articles for scientific journals. Her research interests have been in Mœssbauer spectroscopy, antifouling marine coatings, transition metal complexes, including those of ruthenium, and catalysts based on this element.

Other honors include: the only woman of sixteen recipients to be named Scientist of the Year by *Industrial Research and Development* (1982); recipient of the ACS Garvan Award (1979), Herty Medal (1975), and Florida Section ACS Award (1979). She was also awarded an honorary degree from the University of Illinois at Chicago in 1983 and from Clarkson University in 1984, and was elected to membership in the National Academy of Engineering in 1987.

Two sons were born to Mary and Dr. Billy Jewel Good, whom she married in 1952. Husband Bill Good was a professor of physics for twenty-five years and Dean of Science for twelve at LSU in New Orleans. He is now retired from teaching and is a successful professional artist.

Their older boy Billy is working towards his doctorate in Marine Biology at LSU. Their younger son James graduated from Tulane with a major in architecture. He and his wife spent some time in the Philippines where they were working on water systems for the Peace Corps.

(Photograph courtesy E. I. du Pont de Nemours & Co.)

CRAWFORD HALLOCK GREENEWALT

In that Crawford Greenewalt not only married Margaretta du Pont but spent his entire career with E. I. du Pont de Nemours and Company, it seems fitting to include a brief sketch of the Du Pont history in his profile.

Antoine Laurent Lavoisier (1743-1794) was charged with defrauding the French nation of a considerable sum and was condemned to death on the guillotine. One of his students, Pierre Samuel du Pont de Nemours, escaped turmoil-torn France in 1800 and came to the United States. His son Eleuthère Irenée du Pont, using Lavoisier's techniques, founded the powder works that formed the beginning of the present-day Du Pont Company. The company established its Eastern Research Laboratory at Repauno, New Jersey, in 1902 for explosives research and in 1903 its Experimental Station, near the site of Irenée's original powder mill, for cellulose research. In the early 1920's, Du Pont began the production of rayon and cellophane, lacquers and photographic films.

Crawford joined the Du Pont organization as a control chemist in 1922. Two years later he was transferred to the Experimental Station's Control Research Department. The year before Wallace Carothers joined Du Pont, Crawford was promoted to group leader. While serving as a research supervisor, he applied for eighteen patents, some of which were related to Dr. Carothers' research on nylon.

During the early War years, Crawford was elected a director of Du Pont and subsequently named Chemical Director of the Grasselli Chemicals Department. Crawford, who was present when Enrico Fermi's first sustained fission chain reaction was demonstrated under the football stands at the University of Chicago on December 2, 1942, was named technical director of Du Pont's plutonium plant at Hanford, Washington. At war's end, he returned to Wilmington to become Assistant Director of the Development Department and subsequently Assistant General Manager of the Pigments Department. In 1946, he was named Vice President, in 1947 Vice Chairman of the Executive Committee, and in 1948 President of Du Pont. The next year Du Pont, having produced acrylic (Orlon) and polyester fibers (Dacron) in 1948 and 1950, respectively, became the first chemical company with more than one billion dollars in sales.

In 1950 the U. S. Government requested Du Pont to design, build and operate a plant for making hydrogen bombs near Aiken, South Carolina - now known as the

Savannah River Plant - and this became one of Crawford's responsibilities. As a result, the first hydrogen bomb, which required tritium ($_1H^3$) and deuterium ($_1H^2$) and was produced by the neutron bombardment of lithium ($_3Li^6$), was succesfully exploded in the MIKE test at Enetewok Atoll on November 1, 1952.

Crawford Greenewalt was named chairman of the board of directors in 1962. Five years later he became head of the finance committee, resuming board membership in 1973.

In addition to being a fellow of AIC, Crawford is a member of the National Academy of Science, American Chemical Society, American Association for the Advancement of Science, Chemical Society of London, Society of Industrial Chemists, American Institute of Chemical Engineers, American Philosophy Society, American Academy of Arts and Sciences, and Audubon Society. He has also served as a director of the Boeing Company, Morgan Guaranty Trust Company, National Bureau of Economic Research, Family Service of Northern Delaware, and as director and president of the Wilmington Music School. He is a trustee of the Wilmington Medical Center, Longwood Gardens, Carnegie Institute of Washington, American Museum of Natural History, National Geographic Society, and the Henry Francis du Pont Witherthur Museum; a regent of the Smithsonian Institute; a member of the Business Council and a life member of the MIT Corporation. He co-chaired the Committee on Regional Development for Pennsylvania, New Jersey and Delaware.

Mr. Greenewalt received honorary degrees from the University of Delaware, Northeastern University, Williams College, Austin University, Philadelphia College of Pharmacy, Rensselear Polytechnic Institute, Polytechnic

Institute of Brooklyn, Columbia University, New York University, Jefferson Medical School, Kenyon College, Kansas State University, Temple University, University of Pennsylvania, Swarthmore College, Drexel University, University of Notre Dame, and Bowdoin College.

He received the Gold Medal of Merit from the Wharton School Alumni Association (1952), Chemical Industry Medal from the Society of Chemical Industry (1952), Wilbur Procter Prize for Scientific Achievement from the Scientific Research Society of America (1957), Medal for Advancement of Research from the American Society of Metals (1958), AIC Gold Medal (1959), Gold Medal of Achievement from the Poor Richard Club (1959), Gold Medal Award from the Economics Club (1961), John F. Lewis Prize from the American Philosophical Society (1961), John Fritz Medal from the American Institute of Chemical Engineers (1962), Society Medal from the Society of Chemical Industry (1963), Robert E. Wilson Award from the American Institute of Chemical Engineers (1967), U. S. Camera Achievement Award (1967), and the Rosenberg Medal from the University of Chicago (1971).

As well as the author of several scientific publications, Crawford has written three books: *The Uncommon Man* (1959), *Hummingbirds* (1960), and *Bird Song: Acoustics and Physiology* (1968). In addition to his eighteen U. S. patents, he has been granted thirty-seven patents in foreign countries.

Crawford was born in Cummington, Massachusetts, on August 16, 1902, to Dr. Frank Lindsay, a resident physician at Girard College, and Mary (Hallock) Greenewalt, a concert pianist. After graduating from William Penn Charter School in Philadelphia, he enrolled at Massachusetts Institute of Technology where he received a B.S. degree in chemical engineering in 1922. At MIT, he served as manager of the boxing and basketball teams, was a member of the Tech Show Chorus and sang in the Tech Glee Club. He inherited his appreciation for music from his mother and, while in school, played the clarinet and the cello. In addition to his amateur status of tennis player, his other hobbies of machinist, photographer, horticulturist and ornithologist are on a professional basis, i.e., he equipped his Greenville home with a complete machine shop, made time lapse photographic equipment for studying flooring and birds in flight, and became proficient at raising orchids. He has traveled more than 100,000 miles in numerous trips to Latin America and the Caribbeans to photograph hummingbirds in flight and is known to have photographed more different species of hummingbirds than any other man in history.

The Greenewalts are parents of Mrs. Nancy Frederick, Crawford H., Jr. and David.

(Photograph courtesy of Rice University.)

NORMAN HACKERMAN

Norman was born on March 2, 1912, in Baltimore, Maryland, the son of Jacob and Anna (Raffel) Hackerman. After graduating from Baltimore City College, he enrolled in Johns Hopkins University where he received his A.B. and Ph.D. degrees in 1932 and 1935, respectively. The next five years he was Assistant Professor of Chemistry at Loyola College, part-time chemist for Colloid Corporation, and assistant chemist with the U.S. Coast Guard. In 1941 he became assistant professor of chemistry at Virginia Polytechnic Institute. Two years later he accepted a position as research chemist with Kellex Corporation. Dr. Hackerman joined the faculty of the University of Texas at Austin in 1945; after serving as assistant professor (1945-46) and associate professor (1946-50) and while serving as Professor of Chemistry (1950-70), he was named Director of the Corrosion Research Laboratory (1948-61), Director of Research and Sponsored Programs (1960-610, Vice President and Provost (1961-63), Vice Chancellor for Academic Affairs (1963-67) and President (1967-70). Since 1970 he has served as President and Professor of Chemistry at Rice University.

In addition to being an honorary fellow of AIC, Professor Hackerman is a fellow of the American Association for the Advancement of Science, New York Academy of Sciences and the American Academy of Arts and Sciences. He is a member of the National Academy of Sciences, Philosophical Society, The Faraday Society,* Sigma Xi, Alpha Chi Sigma, Phi Kappa Phi, Phi Lambda Upsilon, International Society of Electrochemistry, National Association of Corrosion Engineers, Electrochemical Society and American Chemical Society. He has served as president of the Electrochemical Society and as editor of that society's journal. He was chairman of the ACS Council Committee on Chemistry and Public Affairs, and on the editorial boards of the ACS monograph series and *Corrosion Science.* He was Chairman of the Board for Argonne National Laboratories, the University Research Association, National Research Council, National Science Board, and Intersociety Corrosion Committee. He served on the Board of Directors of the American Council on Education, Mitre Corporation, Oak Ridge Associated Universities, and the Gordon Research Conferences, being Chairman of the Conferences on Corrosion and Chemistry and Interfaces. He has served on several committees for the National Academy of Science, on the Governor's Task Force for Higher Education in Texas, and as Chairman of the Texas Independent Colleges and Universities.

*Now the Faraday Division of the Royal Society of Chemistry.

Norman received AIC's Honor Scroll in 1945 and Gold Medal in 1978. He was a Joseph L. Mattiello Lecturer in 1964, recipient of the Whitney Award of NACE (1956), Palladium Medal of the Electrochemical Society (1965), Southwestern ACS Regional Award (1965), Mirabeau B. Lamar Award of the Association of Texas Colleges and Universities (1981), Distinguished Alumni Award from Johns Hopkins University (1982), Edward Acheson Award of the Electrochemical Society (1984), and the Alumni Gold Medal for distinguished service to Rice University (1984). He has received honorary doctoral degrees from Austin College, Texas Christian University, St. Edwards University, and Abilene Christian University. He has been awarded several patents by the U. S. Patent Office and is the author or co-author of over 200 articles in technical journals.

In addition to his other activities, Norman is an accomplished squash player. He also finds time to serve as chairman of the Scientific Advisory Board of the Robert A. Welch Foundation, which foundation funds a prestigious and lucrative biennial chemist award and supports chemical research in almost every institution of higher learning in the state of Texas.

Hackerman's 1940 marriage to Gene Allison Coulbourne resulted in the birth of four children: Patricia Gale, Stephen Miles, Sally Griffith and Katherine Elizabeth. Pat Hackerman Berry is Office Manager with Gilpin, Maynard, Parson, Pohl and Bennett in Houston, Texas. Steve is a partner in the law firm of Gaker & Botts in Houston. Sally Hackerman Myer and her physician husband and family live in Temple, Texas, where he is with Scott White Clinic. Kathy Hackerman Gaffney is co-owner with her husband of RoyCorp in Manhattan Beach, California.

VLADIMIR HAENSEL

Vladimir was born in Freiburg, Germany, September 1, 1914. He received precollege education in Moscow before emigrating to Germany in 1928 and to the United States in 1930. Five years following his arrival in this country, he received his B.S. from Northwestern University; then in 1937 his M.S. from Massachusetts Institute of Technology under V. N. Ipatieff. Haensel returned to Northwestern to obtain his Ph.D. in 1941.

While a graduate student, Vladimir worked for Universal Oil Products. Following receipt of his doctorate, he returned to UOP, to become Vice President and Director of Research in 1964 and Vice President of Science and Technology in 1972. After retiring from UOP, he joined the faculty of Chemical Engineering at the

University of Massachusetts.

Dr. Haensel made many contributions to the conversion processes of gasoline, such as catalytic cracking and platforming, which in turn has increased the supply and quality of gasoline. This was necessary because the development of the automobile combustion engine required more volatile hydrocarbons. While the supply of this so-called "straight run" gasoline was adequate when automobiles were still considered a luxury, there was not enough straight run gasoline once Americans fell in love with automobiles. Haensel's hydrocarbons were achieved by separating "shell-still" topping and other hydrocarbon fractions from crude oil; the platforming process uses a dual function catalyst consisting of platinum gamma alumina support. High octane lead-free gasoline was obtained when petroleum and hydrogen were heated at high temperatures in the presence of this dual catalyst system. This process, which requires alumina produced from aluminum halides, operates at temperatures that are high enough to permit the use of sulfur-containing crudes. Aliphatic hydrocarbons are converted to aromatic hydrocarbons in the platforming process. The first commercial platforming unit was installed at the Old Dutch Refining Company in Muskegon, Michigan, in 1929. Many additional units were then installed and platforming has become a standard practice in petroleum refining.

For his work, Vladimir received AIC's Pioneer Award in 1967. He is also recipient of the Precision Scientific Company Award (1952), Progress Award of the American Institute of Chemical Engineers (1957), and ACS Industrial and Engineering Chemistry Award (1965). Dr. Haensel has published 150 reports in scientific journals and has been awarded 145 patents by the U. S. Patent Office. He is a fellow of AIC, a member of the American Chemical Society, National Academy of Science, National Academy of Engineering, the American Institute of Chemical Engineers, and a past president of the Catalyst Society.

Dr. Haensel became a United States citizen and was married in 1939. He and his wife have two children.

(Photograph courtesy of Brigham Young University.)

HOWARD TRACY HALL

The diamond, which is one of earth's most important minerals, is simply a closely packed cubic arrangement of carbon atoms. In spite of its chemical simplicity, the synthesis of diamonds was not achieved until the late 1950's when Howard Tracy Hall patented the synthesis of industrial diamonds, using his patented high pressure/high temperature "belt" apparatus, which can maintain a pressure of a million psi at a temperature of 2000°C. Over two hundred tons of industrial diamonds have been made worldwide as a result of Dr. Hall's invention.

In that the "belt" patent was assigned to General

Electric and could not be used by Tracy after he left, he invented and patented a tetrahedral press. He was also instrumental in starting Megadiamond Industries which produces sintered diamonds using his process.

Tracy was born in Ogden, Utah, on October 20, 1919, to Howard and Florence (Tracy) Hall. After high school, he enrolled in Weber College. He then transferred to the University of Utah where he received B.S., M.S. and Ph.D. degrees in 1942, 1943 and 1948, respectively. During World War Two he served for two years as an Ensign in the U.S. Navy, working in electronics.

While in school, Tracy worked as a photographer, an analyst for Sperry Flour Mills and for the U. S. Bureau of Mines Research Laboratory at Salt Lake City. From 1948 to 1955 he was a research associate with General Electric in Schenectady, New York. Thereafter he joined the faculty of Brigham Young University and in 1980 was made Professor of Chemistry and Chemical Engineering Emeritus. During his tenure he received over $1.3 million in grants from national funding agencies. These twenty-five years with Brigham Young also saw his investigation of fundamentals of high pressure processes, which included: the first melting curve of germanium under high pressure and temperature; the first high pressure, high temperature X-ray diffraction apparatus; induced phase change of ytterbium from close-packed to a non-close-packed structure; determination of the "resistance cusp" in cesium; and the synthesis of over one hundred rare earth compounds and polymorphs.

Dr. Hall has published close to one hundred articles in scientific journals and has been awarded nineteen patents by the U. S. Patent Office. He has also been awarded patents in seventeen foreign countries. He was awarded an honorary doctoral degree by Brigham Young

University in 1971. In 1980, he was admitted to practice patent law before the U. S. Patent and Trademark Office.

Tracy received the AIC Pioneer Award in 1970. He is also recipient of the Research Medal from the American Society of Tool and Manufacturing Engineers (1962), Modern Pioneers in Creative Industry Award from the National Association of Manufacturers (1965), James E. Talmage Scientific Achievement Award from BYU (1965), Outstanding Manhood Award from BYU (1971), ACS Gold Medal Award for Creative Invention (1972), Engineering Materials Achievement Award from the American Society for Metals (1973), IR-100 Industrial Research Magazine Award for invention of indexible sintered diamond cutting tools (1974), Distinguished Alumni Award from Weber State University (1975), International Prize for New Materials from the American Physical Society (1977), Willard Gardner Prize of the Utah Academy of Science, Arts and Letters (1977), and Karl G. Maeser Research Award from BYU (1978). He is a lifetime fellow of AIC and a member of the American Chemical Society, American Association for the Advancement of Science, American Physical Society, Sigma Xi, Phi Kappa Phi, Utah Academy of Science, Arts and Letters, and Timbanogos Club of Utah.

Dr. Hall has been very active in the Church of Jesus Christ of Latter Day Saints. He held the office of bishop from 1976 to 1981. He and his wife spent the following two years as missionaries in Zimbabwe and South Africa. In addition to photography, he is a draftsman, bookkeeper, typist, machinist, welder, electrician, mechanic and "old time" piano player. In fact, he served as priesthood organist for Ogden's 18th Ward from 1936 to 1938 and was the leader of the city's "High Hatter's Dance Band" from 1937 to 1939.

Tracy's 1941 marriage to Ida-Rose Langford resulted in the birth of seven children: Sherlene (Bartholomew), Howard Tracy, Jr., David Richard, Elizabeth (Neil), Virginia (Wood), Charlotte (Weight), and Nancy (Mecham).

WILLIAM EDWARD HANFORD

Many of those selected as delegates to the Gibson Island Conferences in the 1930's and early 1940's would later become recipients of the Chemical Pioneer Award. Dr. William Edward Hanford, better known as "Butch," was no exception.

The second of three boys, Butch was born in Bristol, Pennsylvania, on December 9, 1908. He is a direct descendent of Thomas Cook Hanford who arrived in Massachusetts in 1643 and Irene Laing (Hanford) who was a member of an old Pennsylvania Quaker family. On both sides of the family, Dr. Hanford's progeny can trace their "colony" roots back to the seventeenth century, for Butch's wife (Lorraine H. Eason) was a descendent of James Harwood who arrived in America in 1643.

Butch enrolled in the Philadelphia College of Pharmacy and Science, receiving his B.S. degree in 1930. After working a year for Rohm and Haas, he enrolled in the University of Illinois where he received his M.S. and Ph.D. degrees in 1932 and 1935, respectively. Thereafter he accepted a position as research chemist for Du Pont where he and his associates, D. F. Holmes and B. E. Christ, produced some of the first polyurethanes in America by the reaction of diisocyanates with polyesters and polyesteramides. In conjunction with Robert M. Joyce, he produced telomers (the term coined from the Greek word for terminal body) from ethylene and carbon tetrachloride. He and Joyce also produced ionomers by the copolymerization of ethylene and acrylic acid, copolymers of ethylene and vinyl acetate, and useful products from Roy Plunkett's PTFE and commercial diketenes.

In 1942 Hanford became Director of Research for GAF. With A. L. Fox, J. M. Cross, O. A. Zoss, and C. Z. Schildknecht, he developed the first household liquid detergent and an isotactic polymer of methyl vinyl ether, the first isotactic polymer on record. Four years later, he joined M. W. Kellogg Company. As Vice-President of Research, he directed the development of the Sassol process for the production of hydrocarbons from coal and the now widely used process for the production of ammonia from methane. In 1957 he became Director of Research for Olin and revived his interest in polyurethane chemistry, i.e., developing a process for making diisocyanates from carbon monoxide and dinitro compounds and producing new flame retardant polyols for polyurethane manufacture. In 1967 he left Olin to assume the position of Director of Research for World Water Resources, Inc. There he designed equipment for water treatment in developing countries.

Butch has been granted more than 120 patents by the U.S. Patent Office and over 100 foreign patents. He has published numerous scientific reports and is co-author (with J. C. Sauer) of a chapter on "Chemistry of Ketenes" in *Organic Reactions* (1942) and co-author (with Donald R. Sargent) of a chapter in *Organic Chemistry: An Advanced Treatise* (1943).

He has served on the board of directors of M. W. Kellogg, Pullman, Trailmobile Corporation, Pedlow & Nease and World Water Resources, Inc. He is past president and director of AIC; member, national councilor and past director of ACS; past president and director of the Industrial Research Institute; chairman and director of the American Section of the Society of Chemical Industry; and Director of RESA, the industrial branch of Sigma Xi. He is also a member of the New York Academy of Sciences, National Research Council, American Institute of Chemical Engineers, Society of History and Technology, Phi Beta Kappa, Alpha Chi Sigma, Kappa Phi, Chemists Club, Cosmos Club, New York Athletic Club, and Baltustrol and Canoe Brook Golf Club.

Butch was named a Pioneer in Polymer Science by *Polymer News* in 1934. He was recipient of the AIC's Pioneer Award in 1967 and Gold Medal in 1974 and also received the Chemical Industry Medal in 1961. He holds honorary doctoral degrees from Alfred University and Philadelphia College of Pharmacy and Science.

The Hanfords lost their daughter Ruth Harwood in 1948. Their son, William Jr., who holds a Doctor of Juris Prudence from Vanderbilt, is Vice President of Cemcon, a venture research corporation. He and his wife Mona are parents of William Bruce Hanford III and Tania Ruth.

NORMAN BRUCE HANNAY

Norman Bruce was born in Mt. Vernon, Washington, on February 9, 1921, to Norman Bond and Winnie (Evans) Hannay.   After graduating from Swarthmore College, where he received his B.A. in 1942, he entered Princeton to achieve the M.A. (1943) and Ph.D. (1944). During these latter two years he was also associated with the Manhattan Project. Graduate research was in the field of dipole moments and molecular structure. His industrial research has involved such fields as thermionic emission, electron attachment and ionization phenomena, mass spectrographic analysis of trace impurities in solids, semiconductors,   solid   state   chemistry,   and superconductors. He has been associated with research programs leading to single crystals of silicon and the silicon transistor as well as intercalation (layered) superconductors.

Bruce's employment with Bell Laboratories in 1944 resulted in his being a member of Bell's technical staff for thirty-eight years, his positions including Vice President of Research (1973-1982). At the time he accepted the AIC Gold Medal (1986), this modest gentleman made the statement that he was only one among many at Bell Laboratories and he recognized that it was the work of many outstanding colleagues that gave substance to what he might have contributed.

Dr. Hannay is a fellow of American Institute of Chemists. In addition to AIC's Gold Medal, he has also received the Acheson Medal of the Electrochemical Society, Industrial Research Institute Medal, Berkeley Citation of the University of California at Berkeley and Perkin Medal of the Society of Chemical Industry. In addition, he has been awarded honorary doctoral degrees from Tel Aviv University, Swarthmore College and the Polytechnic Institute of New York. He was a Regent's Professor at UCLA and at the University of California at San Diego.

A former foreign secretary of the National Academy of Engineering, he is also a member of the National Academy of Sciences, a corresponding member of the Mexican Academy of Engineering, and a fellow of the American Academy of Arts and Sciences and the American Physical Society. He served as president of the Electrochemical Society and the Industrial Research Institute, is an honorary member of the Electrochemical Society, past chairman of the Directors of Industrial Research, past member of the Board of Directors of the American Society for Testing Materials, and a member of Phi Beta Kappa and Sigma Xi. He has served on numerous editorial boards and extensively in government and university advisory roles.   The author of approximately ninety scientific articles and of *Solid State Chemistry**, he is also editor or co-editor of three books and editor of seven volumes of *Treatise on Solid State Chemistry*.

Hannay married Joan Anderson in 1943.   Their children are Robin and Brooke.

*Prentice Hall, 1967.

ROWLAND CURTIS HANSFORD

The need for high grade gasoline and the desire to obtain the maximum amount of gasoline from a barrel of crude oil was responsible for Rowland Curtis Hansford being named recipient of AIC's Pioneer Award in 1976. It was Rowland who invented a catalyst conversion process to improve hydrocracking. This process, known as "Unicracking," employs crystalline aluminosilicate (molecular sieves) as the catalysts. It is capable of converting low grade crude oil to high grade gasoline, so that over 500,000 barrels of petroleum feedstock are refined annually via this unique cracking process. It is also used in the production of petrochemical naphtha. The first Unicracking plant was installed in 1964. As a result of new catalyst regeneration processes, the pioneer plant continues to use some of the original catalyst.

Rowland was born in Belington, West Virginia, on January 26, 1912. He received his B.S. from Davis and Elkins College in 1933. For the next two years he was employed by E. I. du Pont de Nemours. He then returned to school to obtain his M.S. from George Washington University in 1937. Thereafter he joined Socony Vacuum Oil Company.* In 1952 he went to work for Union Oil Company of California, retiring from Union Oil twenty-five years later.

Rowland is a fellow of the American Institute of Chemists and a member of the American Chemical Society and American Association for the Advancement of Science. He was a founding member of the Philadelphia Catalysis Club from which the Catalysis Society and its twelve local sections evolved. He was also a founding member of the California Catalysis Society, one of the affiliates of the national society.

In addition to AIC's Pioneer Award, Rowland has received the ACS (Southern California Section) Tolman Medal, The Catalysis Club of Philadelphia Award, and an honorary D.Sc. degree from his alma mater.

He married Frances Rogers of New York in 1953. Rowland, who now resides in semi-retirement in Leisure World in Laguna Hills, California, is still active as a consultant in the field of catalysis.

*Now Mobil Oil.

(Photograph courtesy of George de Vincent.)

MILTON HARRIS

The name *Babylon* means *the land of wool,* and wool garments were worn in Babylon as early as 4000 B.C. Moreover, there is evidence that the spinning and weaving of linen and cotton were practiced in Egypt and Pakistan in 3400 and 3000 B.C., respectively.* But why would a bright young man spend a lifetime investigating fibers that have been used for over 6000 years? This question was asked of Milton Harris on the occasion of a symposium honoring his seventy-fifth birthday. Milton's response, that his

*From C. H. Fisher's chapter in *History of Polymer Science and Technology* (1982).

acceptance of a lucrative Cheney Brothers scholarship on protein fibers while a graduate student at Yale had sparked his interest in fibers, was appended with the statement, "It just shows on what flimsy threads our lives are run." The words contained on the scroll he received on this occasion summarize his achievements:

> "The friends and colleagues of Milton Harris, cognizant of his many contributions to the advancement of chemistry, in all of its branches, noting especially his work in natural and synthetic polymers, fiber and textile science, and chemical information systems, and grateful for his leadership in strengthening scientific and technical society, while encouraging more productive interaction of the scientific community and the public, now join in expressing their esteem to the Milton Harris 75th Anniversary Symposium, on April 27-28, 1981, in Washington, D.C."

Milton was born in Portland, Oregon, on March 21, 1906. As a boy, his parents ran a "Mom and Pop" grocery store and he delivered the groceries. The reason he did not follow in his parents' footsteps was that he often passed a library as he made his deliveries. When he had the time, he would browse in the library's technical book section. To this day, he can remember as a lad reading Slosson's *Creative Chemistry*. Once in high school, he took chemistry - the only science course available - and his teacher was able to generate fun and excitement in the subject which exists for Milton to this day.

When Milton entered Oregon Agricultural College*
in 1922, he was forced to major in chemical engineering, as
chemistry as a major was nonexistent.   After he had
completed all the available chemistry courses, his
professor Floyd Rowland advised him to take a four-week
summer course at the University of Washington.
Following receipt of his B.S. in 1929, Milton was persuaded
to attend Yale where Tom Hawley, also of State, was
enrolled. Milton received his Ph.D. from Yale in 1929 and
accepted a position in the Cheney Brothers silk mill where
Tom Hawley was also employed. One day two years later
Milton received a telephone call from his research
professor at Yale (T. B. Johnson) advising him of a textile
program being initiated by the National Bureau of
Standards. Milton accepted the position and was named
Director of Textile Research on Cellulose, Silk and Wool.
When the Textile Foundation moved to Princeton, Milton
was faced with the choice of heading the institute at
Princeton, accepting a professorship in chemistry at
"starvation wages," or starting his own research laboratory.
He opted for the latter and founded the Harris
Laboratories, acquired by the Gillette Company in 1956.
Milton not only retained presidency of Harris until 1961
but also took on the responsibility of director of research
for Gillette.   He continued as Gillette's vice-president until
1966.

Dr. Harris made tremendous contributions to our
fundamental knowledge of natural fibers; he also
contributed greatly to the American Chemical Society. He
joined ACS in 1931,   was Chairman of the Cellulose
Division in 1954, national councilor from 1959 to 1964,
treasurer from 1974 to 1975, and served as chairman of the
board from 1966 to 1972.

*Now Oregon State University.

Milton was also director of six other organizations. Moreover, he served on the President's Science Advisory Committee, National Research Council, Advisory Committee of the National Science Foundation, Central Committee of the International Council of Scientific Unions and United Nations Educational, Scientific and Cultural Organizations, and on the Executive Committee of the Environmental Protection Agency. Milton is a fellow of AIC and a member of the National Academy of Engineering, American Association for the Advancement of Science, American Society of Biological Chemists, The Chemists Club, The Cosmos Club, Directors of Industrial Research, The Fiber Society, Industrial Research Institute, New York Academy of Science, Society of Chemical Industry, Society of Cosmetic Chemists, Society for the History of Technology, Society of Engineering Science, Sigma Xi, Textile Institute (England), Washington Academy of Sciences, Yale Chemists Association, and the Yale Club of Washington, D.C.

Dr. Harris has been awarded many U. S. and foreign patents and has published over 200 scientific reports. He served as editor or co-editor of *Harris' Handbook of Textile Fibers, Natural and Synthetic Fibers* and *Chemistry in the Economy*. He was also section editor of *Chemical Abstracts*, a member of the advisory board of *Science* and on the advisory boards of the *Journal of Polymer Science, Textile Research Journal, Advances in Chemistry Series,* and *Chemical & Engineering News*.

Milton was awarded AIC's Honor Scroll in 1957 and Gold Medal in 1982. He has also received the Washington Academy of Sciences Award (1943), Olney Medal for Research in the Field of Textile Chemistry from the American Association of Textile Chemists and Colorists (1945), War Department and Navy Department Citation for Outstanding Service to the Office of Scientific Research and

Development during World War Two, Naval Ordinance Development Award; Honorary Degree, Doctor of Textile Science of the Philadelphia College of Textiles and Science (1955); Harold DeWitt Smith Memorial Medal Award of the American Society for Testing Materials (1966); Perkin Medal of the Society of Chemical Industry (1970); Yale's Wilbur Lucius Cross (1974); and ACS Priestley Medal (1980). He was selected a Pioneer in Polymer Science by *Polymer News* in 1982.

Milton married Carolyn Wolf in 1934. Their two sons, John and Barney, both successful businessmen, have given them seven grandchilren.

PAUL HARTECK

1979's Chemical Pioneer Paul Harteck started his postdoctoral work with Lord Rutherford by preparing heavy water made by sequential electrolysis. He was able to use this deuterium-enriched water for original thermofusion studies. Bombarding a solid deuterium compound with deuterons, he produced tritium by the nuclear reaction: $_1H^2 + _1H^2 \rightarrow _1H^3 + _1H^1$. He used the deuterium counterpart of ammonium sulfate $(ND_4)_2SO_4$ to meet the requirement of low vapor pressure for this reaction which produced tritium. The tritium from the thermofusion provided an opportunity for the characterization and subsequent identification of tritium in the atmosphere. Throughout his illustrious career, Dr. Harteck undoubtedly worked with more Nobel Laureates than any other Pioneer.

Paul was born in Vienna on July 20, 1902. He attended the University of Vienna and the University of Berlin, where he received his Ph.D. in 1926. He served as assistant to Professor Eucken at Breslau from 1926 to 1928 and as an assistant to Nobel Laureate *Geheimrat* Haber at Kaiser Wilhelm Institute from 1928 to 1933. The next year he was a Rockefeller Fellow at Cavendish Laboratory before accepting a position as Professor of Physical Chemistry and Director of the Institute of Physical Chemistry. In 1951 he was made Distinguished Research Professor at Rensselaer Polytech.

Dr. Harteck is a member of the American Chemical Society, the German Chemical Society and the Belgium Chemical Society. He was married in 1948 and is the father of three children.

HENRY BOHN HASS

There's an erudite chemist named Hass
Who can turn out the limericks en masse
He recites them aloud
To the AIC crowd
And then he sits down on his chair.*

The word *limerick* was derived from the name of a county in Munster Province in Southwestern Ireland. Limericks in verse form were first used by Edward Lear in the 1840's. Often baudy and nonsensical, limericks consist of five lines of basically anapectic meter in which lines 1, 2 and 5 as well as lines 3 and 4 rhyme. Although Lear wrote

*Composed with an aabbc meter by David Roethel, Executive Secretary of AIC.

many of these verses in his *Book of Nonsense*, they were not called limericks until the end of the nineteenth century.

Henry Bohn Hass, who is credited with the discovery of gas chromatography, one of chemistry's most powerful analytical tools, was also the author of many limericks, some of which were published in his book *Collected Poems*, dedicated to his daughter Charlotte and son-in-law Donald Hudgin. Henry claimed that what are now called limericks were written in Sanskrit in the Bhagavad Gita over 1700 years ago. He was quick to point out that there are only twenty limericks in the book *A Thousand Limericks* because most of the poems do not have the rhyming sequence aabba, noted above.

The second child and only son, Henry was born on January 15, 1902, in Huntington, Ohio, to Frederick W. Hass, a Methodist minister, and Alma Marie (Bohn) Hass. Alma's father, Henry Bohn, emigrated to the United States in 1852 after failing in his attempt to change Germany's form of government to democracy. Henry Bohn died when Alma was sixteen years and she was determined to name her first son after him. According to family legend, Henry Bohn Hass was "Henry the Eighth".

Reverend Hass encouraged his two children to skip grades in school. Accordingly, Henry passed his high school entrance examination while in the seventh grade and caught up with his sister already in high school. Not to be denied, however, she received her B.A. at the age of eighteen; Henry was nineteen when he graduated from Ohio Weslyan University Magna Cum Laude in 1921. His father had hoped Henry would follow him in the ministry, and Henry did serve as an assistant in Bible classes during his junior year in college; but his vocation was to be chemistry.

Henry accepted a graduate assistantship at Ohio State University under Professor William Lloyd Evans. Upon receiving his doctorate in 1924, he accepted a summer position at Baltimore Engineering Corporation in West Virginia. Because he could read German, he was able to focus on a pertinent matter in the literature, thus he settled a controversy on the use of activated charcoal as an absorbent for recovering gasoline from natural gas.

In 1928, Dr. Hass became a member of the faculty of Purdue University. There, with the support of a small unrestricted research grant from Josiah K. Lilly, he and Earl T. McBee investigated the chlorination of ethane. This research resulted in the invention of a successful "heat and mix" chlorination technique, which allows hot compressed hydrocarbon to become readily chlorinated without soot formation. This process was adopted by the Ethyl Corporation to produce tetraethyllead.

Before Dr. Hass joined Purdue's staff, the university had not granted a single doctorate in chemistry. Henry introduced the concept of industry-supported graduate research and Purdue soon became famous for its practical doctoral graduates. Henry was made head of the chemistry department in 1937. Two years later, he accepted appointments to the National Research Committee and the Manhattan Project. His successful vapor phase chlorination process led to production of C_8F_{16} for the gaseous diffusion plant of Manhattan's Oak Ridge project. This process replaced the more expensive direct perfluorination of hydrocarbons involving the chlorination of methyl groups of xylenes and conversion of hexachlorides to hexafluorides by reaction with hydrogen fluoride, followed by perfluorination to C_8F_{16}. Moreover, Drs. Hass and McBee received documents complimenting them for "research which contributed to the successful conclusion of World War II."

Hass, et al. then developed the vapor phase process for the nitration of alkanes. Chlorination studies led to the discovery of the chain reaction mechanism involved in vapor phase chlorination. The production of nitromethane, nitroethane and 1- and 2-nitropropane by the vapor phase nitration of propane is explained by the formation of OH. and $\cdot NO_2$ radicals formed by the dissociation of nitric acid. The OH. radical abstract a hydrogen atom from the propane and the residual promply couples with the $\cdot NO_2$ radical. Both nitroalkanes and alkyl nitrites were produced, but the latter were cleaved to produce NO. and RO. radical. The RO. radical then decomposed to produce an aldehyde or ketone and a lower molecular weight alkyl radical; the process was then repeated. Nitroalkanes provided new solvents for the chemical industry and were later used as fuel for racing cars and as propellants for the Polaris missile.

In 1949, Dr. Hass became manager of research for GAF's Eastern Pennsylvania facility. Three years later he accepted a position as president of the Sugar Research Foundation where he developed monofatty acid esters of sucrose and a process for the hydrogenolysis of molasses for the production of glycerol. The fatty acid esters were patented and produced in Japan, but the U. S. Food and Drug Administration did not approve production in this country until some time later, at which time the Japanese patents had expired. In 1961, Fidel Castro seized the sugar industry in Cuba, reducing the income of the Sugar Research Foundation. Henry, however, stayed on as consultant. Thereafter, he became Director of Research for M. W. Kellogg Company, retiring from this position at the age of sixty-eight.

Henry was recipient of AIC's Gold Medal and Chemical Pioneer Award, the Perkin Medal, Modern Pioneer Award from the National Association of Manufacturers, and the Cuban Honor of Merit. He was granted honorary degrees from his alma mater and the universities of Chattanooga, Long Island, Ohio and Purdue. A lifetime fellow of AIC and a member of the American Chemical Society, American Association for the Advancement of Science and Society of Chemistry Industry, he was awarded fifty U. S. patents and published over one hundred scientific articles.

Dr. Hass' 1921 marriage to Georgianna Herancourt gave them three children. Daughter Charlotte was the first recipient of the Charlotte Hudgin award for superior teaching. Her husband, Dr. Donald E. Hudgin, president of Princeton's Polymer Laboratories, received his doctorate under the direction of his father-in-law. The Hass' son Thomas is an obstetrician and gynecologist. Son Robert is a computer scientist at Standard of Indiana. Henry and Georgianna have thirteen grandchildren and eight great grandchildren.

Henry Hass died of pneumonia February 13, 1987, in Manhasset, New York. He was eighty-five.

ALLAN STUART HAY

There have been some conservative chemists who have failed to accept the chemistry of macromolecules because of the "goo and gunk" connotation of polymers. While it is true that many of the original synthetic polymers were not crystalline and could not be characterized by classical melting and boiling point techniques, the "goo and gunk" concept is truly in the eye of the beholder. Modern organic chemists recognize that polymer chemistry provides better examples than pre-twentieth century organic chemistry and unique reactions which were unknown before the advent of the macromolecular age.

One of the new reactions, polymerization by oxidative coupling, was discovered by Chemical Pioneer

Allan Stuart Hay in 1956.* He showed that halogen-free 2,6-disubstituted phenols with small groups substituted in the 2 and 6 positions could be coupled through carbon and oxygen atoms when oxygen was bubbled through a solution of the substituted phenol at room temperature in the presence of an amine and a copper(I) salt. He and coworkers also showed that this radical coupling polymerization occurs when the reactant is 4-chloro or 4-bromo-2,6-dimethylphenol. The oxidative coupling polymerization reaction has also been used to produce polyacetylenes and polyazo compounds. Poly (2,6-dimethylphenyl) 1,4 ether (PPO) was one of the first of the high performance polymers. The commercial product (Noryl®) is usually a blend of polystyrene (PS) and PPO. Alloying with PS approves processibility but the high performance properties of PPO are maintained in the blend. The heat deflection temperature varies as the ratios of the two components are changed. Noryl is an engineering thermoplastic, one of the class of plastics that is replacing metals in many applications.

Allan was born on July 23, 1929, in Edmonton, Alberta, Canada. After completing Eastwood High School in 1946, he enrolled in the University of Alberta to study chemistry. His choice of organic chemistry can be attributed to the excellent teaching of Dr. Reuben B. Sandin. Upon receipt of his M.Sc. degree in 1952, he became an instructor and conducted graduate research under Sandin's direction. He obtained summer employment with the National Research Council of Canada and Du Pont. In 1955, he received his doctorate from the University of Illinois. Thereafter, he accepted a position with General Electric Research Laboratories in

*Described in 1959 in an article in the *Journal of the American Chemical Society,* coauthored by H. S. Blanchard, G. F. Endres, and J. W. Eustance.

Schenectady, New York, where he is now Research and Development Manager of the Chemical Laboratories in charge of 200 scientists and engineers.

Dr. Hay is a member of the American Institute of Chemists, American Chemical Society, American Association for the Advancement of Science, Alpha Chi Sigma, Phi Lambda Upsilon, Sigma Xi, and a fellow of the Royal Society of Chemistry and the New York Academy of Sciences. Awardee of 55 U. S. patents, he received the Chemical Pioneer Award in 1985, Carothers Award in 1984, Achievement Award of the Industrial Research Institute in 1981, Society of Plastics Engineers International Award in 1975; and, for the development of PPO, IR Award of the Industrial Research Magazine and Kirkpatrick Chemical Engineering Award in 1965 and 1967, respectively.

Allan married Janet Keck in 1956. They have four children. Susan is a graduate of Brown University (1985), Lauren a graduate student in hydrology at the University of Arizona, Bruce received a doctorate in chemistry from the University of Minnesota (1986), and Randy received a doctorate in Geophysics at Princeton (1986).

The Hays spend part of the summer months at their home in Lake George where they water ski, sail and swim. Allan collects Canadian postage stamps, specializing in those which contain a G.E. phosphor which glows green under ultraviolet light - thereby speeding up the postage service.

(Photograph courtesy of Wadsworth Laboratories/Photo Unit
New York State Department of Health.)

ELIZABETH LEE HAZEN

The Elizabeth Lee Hazen Microbiology Laboratories
at Mississippi University for Women in Columbus were
dedicated in 1977 in honor of Dr. Hazen, who - with Rachel
Brown - discovered Nystatin.   Dr. Hazen's will provided
funds to support microbiological research at her alma
mater.

At the time Dr. Hazen became involved in research
that led to the discovery of Nystatin, widespread research
was underway to find new antibiotics to supplement the
recently discovered "wonder drug" penicillin. There was
no known substance that was effective against fungal

infections in the way that penicillin affected bacteria. In 1946, Gilbert Dalldorf, Director of New York's Division of Laboratories and Research, assigned Drs. Hazen and Brown the task of finding and isolating an effective anti-fungal substance. Two years later, Dr. Hazen obtained a soil sample from a friend's farm in Virginia that led to the discovery of a new stremptomycete and eventually the world's first safe, effective antifungal antibiotic. Chemist Rachel Brown worked on the isolation and purification of the active substances they produced. Elizabeth grew the cultures from which Rachel's group extracted and purified the active agents. Each step of the way, Dr. Hazen thoroughly tested samples for antifungal activity; as purification progressed, she added tests for toxicity and protective action in mice. The discovery of Nystatin resulted from the fruitful union of these two dedicated scientists, and on October 10, 1950, they were able to report their findings to the National Academy of Sciences.

Squibb and Sons' commercial development of Nystatin, marketed as Mycostatin, made available the first antibiotic effective against fungi. This drug, which is still one of the most widely used anti-fungal agents available, is used to combat infections such as thrush. In veterinary practice, it is applied to prevent fatal fungal infection in turkeys. Nonmedical uses include treating bananas before shipping. Following flood damage in Florence, Italy, in 1966, it was used to prevent moldy growths on priceless art treasures. It has also been used successfully in this country to treat elm trees infected with Dutch elm diseases.

The patents on Nystatin were assigned to the Research Corporation of New York. The more than $13 million in royalties have been used to support the Brown-Hazen program of research and training to combat fungal diseases and for philanthropic endeavors of the

Corporation. These royalties have furthered the education of and launched many young scientists, supported publications, remodeled laboratories, and so on.

Dr. Hazen was an accomplished medical mycologist in every respect. She made many notable contributions to science, including the publication of valuable data. Her most significant publication was an authoritative reference book for clinical mycologists entitled *Laboratory Identification of Pathogenic Fungi Simplified*, now in its second edition. Among the many honors bestowed upon her were the Sara Benham Award of the Mycological Society of the Americas, Squibb Award in Chemotherapy, and honorary degrees (D.Sc.) from Hobart and William Smith Colleges. In 1975, Drs. Hazen and Brown were awarded the prestigious Chemical Pioneer Award, the first time in the Institute's then fifty-year history to present the award to women.

Born on a farm near Lula, Mississippi, in 1885, Elizabeth Hazen was orphaned at an early age. She was raised by an aunt and uncle, Mr. and Mrs. Robert Henry Hazen. She attended Coahoma County public schools before enrolling at Mississippi Industrial Institute and College.* After graduating in 1910, she taught science for a number of years before working as an Army diagnostic laboratory technician during World War I. In 1927, Elizabeth completed her doctorate at Columbia. For the next four years, she continued at Columbia as resident bacteriologist and instructor. She then began her long and productive association with New York's Department of Health. She was responsible for establishing the Division's mycology laboratory in New York City in 1944. A part of her work at that time involved screening human serums for evidence of fungal infections.

*Now the Mississippi University for Women.

Following her retirement in 1960, she became Guest Investigator in Dermatology at Columbia's College of Physicians until 1973. Dr. Hazen passed away on June 24, 1975.

(Photograph courtesy of U. S. Department of Agriculture.)

STERLING BROWN HENDRICKS

Sterling Hendricks is best known for creative and economically-important research on soils, plant growth, and other phenomena in agricultural chemistry. For his years of investigation and discovery into these aspects of chemistry he received the ACS Hillebrand Prize (1938), Honorary LLD from the University of Arkansas (1946), Geological Society of America's Day Medal (1952), USDA Distinguished Service Award (1953), President's Distinguished Service Award (1958), Rockefeller Public Service Award (1961), (with H. A. Borthwick) Texas Research Foundation's Hoblitzelle National Award (1962), American Society of Plant Physiologists' Stephen Hales

Prize (1962), and honorary D.Sc. from Kansas State University (1963). It was "for pioneering discoveries in photoperiodism, for the discovery and isolation of phytochrome and for a lifetime of distinguished service to this nation" that he was made AIC Chemical Pioneer in 1971. He was elected to the National Academy of Sciences in 1952 and listed in the *World's Who's Who in Science* in 1968 as one of the greatest scientists of all time.

Dr. Hendricks' researches also included the investigation of properties of clays and the relation of clay characteristics to atomic arrangements and crystal structures. He studied ion-exchange phenomena, the capacities of clay to absorb water through hydrogen bonding, and the retention of salts. He established the compositions, mineral groupings, crystal structures, ways of identifications, analysis of amounts, and extents of occurrences of clays in soils. In this latter work, water films were shown to be held in molecular layers by the surface of the clays through hydrogen bonding to oxygen atoms of the layered silicate structures. The surface termination of clay crystals was found to leave an excess negative charge on the crystal lattice that was compensated by external positive charges, cations; the type of soil and its fertility were found to depend on these phenomena.

Moreover, he studied the effect of day length on plant flowering by measuring the spectral region and radiant energy required to counterbalance the effect of night on the flowering. These investigations led him to discover that low energies of red radiation were adequate to control flowering and that the effect could be reversed by radiation near the limit of the visible spectrum. This striking reversible effect of light was also shown to control germination of many seeds, lengthening of plant stems, night movement of leaves, and many other growth responses, as well as flowering; and that this effect was caused by a blue pigment present in very small amounts in leaves and stems. This he explained as follows: The pigment, a protein, is changed by red radiation, as is shown by physiological methods, to an enzymatically active form that can be changed back to the inactive form through its enzymatic action or by the light at the red limit of the visible spectrum. Isolated through use of a spectroscopic assay and methods of protein chemistry, the pigment shows all of the spectroscopic properties established by the physiological studies.

Sterling was born on April 13, 1902, in Elysian Fields, Texas, to James G. and Daisy (Gamlin) Hendricks. His father's medical profession without doubt influenced his son's interest in science. Sterling earned a degree in chemical engineering at the University of Arkansas in 1922, an M.S. at Kansas State University in 1924, and a Ph.D. in physical chemistry at the California Institute of Technology in 1926. He was an instructor at Kansas State College from 1923-24; a research associate, Geophysics Laboratory, Carnegie Institute in 1926; research associate, Rockefeller Institute, from 1927-28; chemist, USDA's Bureau of Chemistry and Soils, 1928-40; Chemist, Bureau of Plant Industry, 1940-43; Chief Scientist, Mineral Nutrition Laboratory, Agricultural Research Service, 1943-67. He retired from his long career with the U. S. Department of Agriculture in 1970.

His professional affiliations included the National Academy of Sciences, American Chemical Society, American Society of Agronomy, American Mineral Society (president, 1954), and Geological Society. He was the author of more than 200 publications. He was, moreover, an active mountaineer and a member of the third party to conquer Mount McKinley, North America's highest mountain.

He and Edith Ochiltree were married in 1931. Seven weeks before they were to celebrate their fiftieth anniversary, Sterling passed away in Novato, California.

(Photograph courtesy of North Carolina Collection,
UNC Library at Chapel Hill.)

CHARLES HOLMES HERTY

*"The spark of his genius and energy
touched Georgia pines, and forests of
smoke-stacks began growing in the South."**

The Herty Medal, presented annually by the Georgia
section of the American Chemical Society to a deserving
chemist working in the South, was named for Charles
Holmes Herty.

*Notation on the memorial tablet in the Capitol at Atlanta,
Georgia.

Charles was born on December 4, 1867, in Milledgeville, Georgia, to Bernard Herty and his wife. Bernard enlisted in the Confederate Army at the age of seventeen years and advanced to the rank of caption. Following the war, he became a druggist. He and his wife died when Charles was eleven, leaving him and his younger sister in the care of an aunt.

Herty's education was varied and involved different schools in this country and abroad. He graduated from Georgia Military Academy to complete his Ph.B. requirements from the University of Georgia in 1886. Thereafter, he entered Johns Hopkins University where his extracurricular activities included glee club and baseball. His doctoral thesis in 1890 was entitled "The Double Halides of Lead and the Alkali Metals."

Following a brief period as assistant chemist at the Georgia Experiment Station, Herty, his wife, and two young children went to Berlin. There he attended the lectures of the great synthetic dye chemist Otto N. Witt. The next year he studied in Zürich with Alfred Werner, whose work, which was concerned with complex inorganic compounds, was related to that described in Herty's doctoral thesis. Charles' work with Werner resulted in a publication in 1901, the first publication of an American with Werner.

When in 1901 Herty heard criticism of the methods used in Georgia and nearby states to collect turpentine and gum from pine trees, he consulted with the U. S. Bureau of Forestry and visited pine-growing states to learn that the turpentine and naval stores industry was declining. As a remedial measure, he invented the "cup." From 1904 to 1905, he was with the Chattanooga Pottery Company developing and manufactuirng his turpentine cup. This invention not only made money for the pine industry, but it made Herty financially secure.

In September 1919, President Wilson sent Herty abroad to arrange for the purchase of impounded dyes. This trip helped found the Textile Foundation. Herty also helped promote the Ransdell bill of 1930 that established the National Institute of Health. With help from the Chemical Foundation and the State of Georgia, he established the Savannah Pulp and Paper Laboratory to conduct research on ways to make newsprint from southern pines, which grow much faster than the Canadian spruce used theretofore for newsprint. The effort was successful and on March 31, 1933, *The Soperton News* was printed on paper from Herty's mill. He did not undertake this venture for personal reward, but, in his own words, "so that people living in the midst of the finest paper material might not longer endure the bitterest sort of poverty."

Charles was also successful in the academic field. In 1891, he became instructor at his alma mater, the University of Georgia. He advanced to adjunct professor in 1894 and held the appointment until 1902. Three years later, he accepted the position as head of the chemistry department of the University of North Carolina and served as dean of the School of Applied Science from 1908 to 1911. He received many honors, including AIC's Gold Medal in 1932 and honorary fellow in 1949, man of the year for Georgia and the South in 1938, and seven honorary degrees.

Herty was president of the Synthetic Organic Chemical Manufacturers Association from 1921 until 1926, when he became advisor to the Chemical Foundation headed by Francis P. Garvan. He remained in this position until 1935. He also served as president of the American Chemical Society in 1915 and 1916 and was active in the society's affairs. Further, he was editor of *Industrial and Engineering Chemistry* from 1916 to 1921 and helped organize essay contests for high school and college freshmen financed by the Garvans.

Charles Herty has been described as a man of singularly warm and attractive personality, who, gifted with a brilliant mind, had received superb scientific training. He believed science to be truly worthwhile when related to human affairs. During his entire life he turned his scientific work toward the improvement of existing conditions, whether by eliminating the waste of turpentine resources, or by working to establish the National Institute of Health, or by developing a paper industry for the South. Dr. Herty's sincerity, honesty, and devotion to his profession won the admiration of the many who knew him. He will long be remembered as a truly great man who served his people to the best of his scientific ability.

Charles died on July 28, 1938, in a Savannah hospital after three weeks of illness, at which time he was director of the Pulp and Paper Laboratory of the Industrial Commission of Savannah. He was survived by two sons and a daughter and by the aunt who had cared for him as a boy. Son Charles Holmes Herty, Jr., who was born in 1896 (deceased 1953), became distinguished in his own right as a chemical engineer and metallurgist.

CHARLES CLIFTON HOBBS

The petroleum oxidation processes pioneered by Celanese attracted the attention of Charles Hobbs when he was a graduate student at the University of Oklahoma. His interest in hydrocarbon oxidation grew out of his graduate research on a variation of the Etard reaction in which hexanes were oxidized by chromyl chloride. Charlie joined Celanese in 1952 and has spent his career at its Technical Center in Corpus Christi working on liquid phase oxidation (LPO) processes. He was made Research Associate in 1958, Group Leader in 1963, and Senior Research Associate in 1967.

Charlie and his associates developed and applied a novel relative kinetic approach, supplemented by carbon-14 tracer techniques, to sort out the pathways of intermediates in the LPO of butane. This research led to sufficient understanding of the system to permit development of a mathematical model which has had a variety of applications. Among the achievements of this work is a fourfold increase in the production of methyl . ethyl ketone as a coproduct. Hobbs and his group have also developed a catalyst which gives improved yields of acids from aldehyde oxidation. Dr. Hobbs anticipates that continued improvement of catalytic oxidation processes can permit greater utilization of our limited hydrocarbon resources as well as assist in the inevitable development of alternative feedstocks.

Charlie was born in Wewoka, Oklahoma, on March 23, 1927. His family moved several times during his childhood and finally settled in the small town of Ryan, Oklahoma. There he completed his junior year in high school. Ryan High School offered no math or science courses, however, so Charlie was compelled to complete his senior year at Classen High School in Oklahoma City. Following his graduation in 1944, he spent one semester at the University of Oklahoma. He then enlisted in what was at that time the Army Air Force and spent two quarters of his military service studying at Louisiana State University. Once his service was completed, he returned to the University of Oklahoma where he received the B.S., M.S., and Ph.D. degrees in 1949, 1951 and 1953, respectively.

Dr. Hobbs received the Chemical Pioneer Award in 1974. He is a lifetime fellow of the American Institute of Chemists, a member of the American Chemical Society - past chairman of the South Texas Section, Sigma Xi, Phi Lambda Upsilon and Pi Mu Epsilon. He has been awarded twenty patents by the U. S. Patent Office and has published several research articles. He authored the section on "Hydrocarbon Oxidation" in the third edition of Kirk-Othmer's *Encyclopedia of Chemical Technology* and co-authored the article on "Acetic Acid" in the fifth edition of Ullmann's *Encyclopedia of Industrial Chemistry*.

In 1950 Charlie married Hsiao-Hsia Tsai, whom he met in graduate school. They have three children - all of whom are graduates of the University of Texas at Austin, which can lead to some interesting partisan discussions during football season. Hsiao-Hsia received her Masters in Fine Arts and is a well known painter and sculptor. She has exhibited her art widely in this country and in Europe. The Hobbs children continue to live in Austin where Jeff is an engineer with IBM, Jenny is a teacher, and John is a project analyst with Advanced Micro Devices.

JOHN PAUL HOGAN

Engraved in stone over the lintel of Entrance 12 of the Department of Commerce Building in our nation's capital are words spoken by Abraham Lincoln after he received his first and only patent on May 22, 1849. They are: "The Patent System added the fuel of interest to fire of Genius." One of these geniuses is John Paul Hogan.

Hogan, with colleague Robert Banks, developed the most widely used processes for making high density polyethylene (HDPE). Together they were granted a patent for the production of polypropylene (PP). The significance of these discoveries can be realized when one notes that Giulio Natta and Karl Ziegler received the Nobel Prize in 1963 for discoveries in chemistry and technology of high polymers, the latter being HDPE and PP.

Paul, the third of four children, was born on August 7, 1919, on a farm in Graves County, one mile north of Lowes, Kentucky. Since scientists are seldom considered celebrities, the town of Lowes is recognized instead as the birthplace of its favorite son - Alben W. Barkley, Vice President during Franklin Roosevelt's second term. Paul's father, Charles, and Barkley were schoolmates. Paul's mother was Alma Wyman Hogan.

After completing high school, where he played basketball, in 1936, Paul entered Murray State University to major in chemistry and physics. He spent one semester (1941) studying engineering at the University of Redlands, California, but it was Murray State which granted him his B.S. degree in 1942.

Dr. Hogan began his career as a teacher at Mayfield, Kentucky, High School in 1942. The next school year found him at Oklahoma State University where, among other things, he taught intensive eight-week courses in physics to Army Air Corps preflight students. He also enrolled in graduate chemistry courses taught by Professor O. C. Derner. With the closure of the preflight training school in 1944, Paul accepted a position as research chemist at Phillips Petroleum Company. His investigations during his forty years with Phillips have been primarily in the field of catalysis.

Together with Bob Banks, Paul worked for four years on the Fischer-Tropsch process, eventually abandoned because of a sharp increase in the cost of natural gas. Consequently, they investigated the catalytic conversion of gaseous olefins to higher boiling liquid hydrocarbons and ultimately were able to obtain solid crystalline PP along with other polymeric products. This same catalyst was then used to produce HDPE and poly(4-

methyl-1-pentene). The commercial production of these new polyolefins was new, but polyolefins had been known for many years. Polymethylene, a linear polymer, which is essentially the same as HDPE, was produced by E. Hindermann in 1897 by decomposition of diazomethane. A small amount of low density polyethylene (LDPE), a highly branched polymer, was produced accidentally in 1933 by E. W. Faucett and R. O. Gibson. A larger amount (8g) of LDPE was produced in 1935. LDPE, produced commercially using this extremely high pressure process (2,000 atm) during World War II, was used for radar coaxial cable. HDPE was produced by the catalytic polymerization of ethylene at moderate pressures (6-12 atm) by Zletz of Standard Oil of Indiana in 1950, by Hogan and Banks in 1951, and by Ziegler, Breil, Martin and Holzkamp in late 1953. Hogan and Banks used a hexavalent chromium oxide on silica as the catalyst system and Ziegler and co-workers used aluminumalkyl and titanium tetrachloride. PP was produced commercially in the late 1950's.

Dr. Hogan was awarded the ACS Award for Creative Invention in 1969, was recipient of the Chemical Pioneer Award in 1971, received the Inventor of the Year Award by the Oklahoma Bar Association in 1976, and was named Man of the Year by the Society of Plastics Engineers in 1981. He was awarded an honorary D.Sc. degree and Distinguished Alumnus Award by Murray State University in 1971 and 1972, respectively, and was named a Pioneer in Polymer Science by *Polymer News* in 1982. Paul and his co-inventor Bob Banks were awarded the Perkin Medal in 1987.

In 1943, Paul married Glenda M. Moultrie, a schoolmate at Murray State. He and Glenda have three children. Daughter Fay is the wife of R. Wayne Sweney, an attorney; she teaches literature in the Coeur d'Alene,

Idaho, high school. Son Kenneth, who married Linda Hahn, now an accountant, is a mathematics teacher at Moore High School located in a suburb of Oklahoma City; Ken and Linda have two children. Daughter Susan, a supervising accountant, is married to Randall C. Lair, an aeronautical engineer in Wichita, Kansas; she and her husband have two children.

At the time Paul received the Pioneer Award, his inventions were cited as "one of the great technological accomplishments of this century."

HARRY NICHOLLS HOLMES

The 1951 recipient of AIC's Gold Medal was Harry Holmes.

Harry obtained his B.S. and M.S. degrees from Westminster College in 1899 and 1904, respectively. As a graduate student at Johns Hopkins, he caught the research spirit of Ira Remson and developed clearness in thinking and writing and received his Ph.D. degree in chemistry in 1907.

Dr. Holmes was head of the Chemistry Department at Earlham College from 1907 to 1914, when he became professor and head of the Chemistry Department at Oberlin. In 1918, he served with the United States Army. Thereafter, he returned to Oberlin where he remained until his retirement in 1945. Under his leadership Oberlin became the leading liberal arts college in chemical research in the United States.

Holmes was widely known for his work in colloid chemistry, physical chemistry, emulsions, and vitamins, which involved dialysis, gels, catalysts, adsorption, and biochemistry. In 1937, he and Ruth E. Corbet were the first to isolate crystalline vitamin A. With co-workers he isolated butanol from bone marrow. It was Holmes who introduced the laboratory technique of chromatography into the United States. Moroever, he conducted the first laboratory class in this country on colloid chemistry in 1910, wrote the first laboratory manual of colloid chemistry used in this country in 1921, and with J. H. Matthews organized the first colloid symposium in 1923.

Harry wrote excellent books for both chemists and laymen, contributed extensively to scientific and technical journals, lectured widely in America and Europe, and published valuable articles on the history of aluminum and the life and work of Charles Martin Hall. His two series of general chemistry textbooks, with accompanying laboratory manuals, were published in several editions. One popular book on science entitled *Out of the Test Tube* went through five editions. He was the author of *Strategic Materials and National Strength* (1943).

In addition to AIC's Gold Medal, Holmes' other tokens of esteem included an honorary LL.D. degree from Westminster College in 1941, the Oberlin alumni medal in 1945, AIC honorary fellowship in 1951, ACS Kendall Company award in colloid chemistry in 1954, James F. Norris Award of the ACS Northeastern Section (for outstanding performance in teaching chemistry) in 1955, and the Westminster alumni award in 1957. His former students established the Holmes Prize Fund in his honor.

Holmes served on the Executive Committee (chemistry) of the National Research Council for several years; he chaired the NRC subcommittee on colloid chemistry from 1919 to 1925. He was chairman of the Cleveland Section of the American Chemical Society in 1924, secretary of the Division of Physical and Inorganic Chemistry in 1919, and chairman of the Division in 1921. He was president of the American Chemical Society in 1942, consultant to the National Defense Research Council and a member of the War Production Board in 1942, and a civilian with the Office of Scientific Research and Development in 1944. His professional affiliations included the American Association for the Advancement of Science, American Institute of Chemists, Sigma Xi, Alpha Chi Sigma, and Phi Lambda Upsilon. Holmes took a vital interest in athletics and his versatility was further demonstrated by his skill in painting. He also enjoyed gardening and golf.

Born on July 10, 1879, at Fay in Lawrence County, Pennsylvania, to John Pattison and Eliza (Nicholls) Holmes, he married Mary Shively on July 15, 1909. Two children resulted from this union: Charles S. and Richard R.

Dr. Holmes died on July 1, 1958, in Oberlin.

SAMUEL EMMETT HORNE, JR.

Since Hevea rubber is a cis-1,4-polyisoprene, this specific elastomer - which occurs in over 200 species of plants - has been known for many centuries. As a result of investigations in the early part of the nineteenth century, Michael Faraday showed that natural rubber was a polymer consisting of isoprene units. In the early part of this century, Mathews and Strange and Harries produced polyisoprene by polymerizing isoprene by means of a sodium metal initiator. The first synthetic rubber, produced in Germany during World War I, was a polymer of 2,3-dimethylbutadiene. The principal synthetic rubber produced during World War II was a copolymer of butadiene and styrene. This was called Buna S by Tschunkur and Bock who patented it in Germany in 1933. The U. S. Rubber Reserve Corporation named this elastomer Government Rubber-Styrene; it is now known as SBR. SBR is the most widely used elastomer today.

In 1954, Nobel Laureate K. Ziegler used a coordination catalyst (titanium tetrachloride) and trialkylaluminum to produce linear polyethylene (HDPE). Shortly thereafter, Samual Horne used this Ziegler catalyst to produce cis-polyisoprene. This unique elastomer was produced by B. F. Goodrich under the trade name Ameripol-SN. Isoprene can be polymerized to 4 different isomers, viz., cis-1,4, trans-1,4, 3,4 and 1,2-polyisoprene. The original product obtained by Horne and co-workers consisted primarily (98 percent) of cis-poly 1,4-isoprene. Horne used a modified Ziegler catalyst to produce trans-1,4 polyisoprene. This hard resin, whose structure is identical to balata and gutta percha, is used for golf ball covers. Both NR and IR as well as 1,4-polybutadiene are used in radial pneumatic tires.

Dr. Horne joined Goodrich's Brecksville, Ohio, plant in 1950. He was a senior research associate at the time of his retirement in 1982. Since then, he has served as science advisor for Polysar Inc. at the Rubber Technical Center in Stow, Ohio.

Born in Jacksonville, Florida, on July 26, 1924, to Samuel Emmett and Pearle Lovett Horne, Samuel Emmett Horne, Jr., attended grade school in Tampa. Following high school graduation in 1942, he served as a lieutenant (JG) in the U. S. Navy (1943-46). Thereafter, he returned to Emory University to receive his A.B., M.A., and Ph.D. degrees in 1947, 1948, and 1950, respectively. As a Coca Cola Research Fellow, he conducted graduate research in terpene chemistry under the direction of Professor Royals. Emory conferred an honorary Sc.D. degree upon Dr. Horne in 1982.

Dr. Horne was recipient of AIC's Pioneer Award in 1974, Midgeley Medal of the Detroit ACS Section in 1978, and the Goodyear Medal of the ACS Rubber Division in 1980. He chaired a Gordon Conference on hydrocarbon chemistry in 1969. A lifetime fellow of the American Institute of Chemists, he is a member of the American Chemical Society, American Association for the Advancement of Science, Sigma Xi, and the New York and Ohio Academies of Science. Sam, whose scientific investigations have been widely published, has been awarded many patents by the U. S. Patent Office, is an ACS tour speaker, and has presented seminars at the Universities of Akron, New Hampshire, Minnesota, Iowa and Malaysia and at Pensacola Junior College and the New York Academy of Sciences.

Four children resulted from Sam's 1949 marriage to Matilda Sue Ross: Vicki, Peggy, Melanie and Sam III. Herself an Emory graduate, Mrs. Horne was a psychiatric nurse with the Veteran's Administration until her retirement in 1983. Son Sam is an aeronautical engineer. Dr. and Mrs. Horne have one grandchild.

Dr. Horne's hobbies include acting, stamp and coin collecting, and comparative religions. He and his wife have been very active in community and summer stock theater in the greater Cleveland area - acting, producing plays, building sets, and so on. Each has received acting awards for their efforts in the theater. Sam also teaches comparative religions and the Old Testament. His interest in comparative religions became avid during World War II when he realized the way to understand people of other cultures was to understand their faiths.

(Photograph courtesy of The Standard Oil Company of Ohio.)

EVERETT CLARK HUGHES

"For pioneering discoveries in petroleum chemistry and petrochemicals resulting in 132 patents and for being the kind of research director who is beloved by both scientists and stockholders." *

Everett was born in Wadena, Minnesota, on November 22, 1904, to Albert B. and Pearl Sylpha (Moses) Hughes. After graduating from Worthington High School, he enrolled at Carleton College where he received his A.B.

*Citation of Dr. Hughes' AIC Chemical Pioneer Award.

Heckshor Research Fellowship at Cornell University, where he conducted research under the direction of Professor John R. Johnson. Upon receipt of his doctorate from Cornell, he accepted a position as a research chemist with Standard Oil of Ohio (Sohio). In 1944 he was promoted to Chief of Chemical and Physical Research, ten years later became Research Manager, and in 1961 Vice President in charge of Research. His major discoveries while with Sohio included Boron gasoline, catalysts for the ammoxidation of propylene for the production of acrylonitrile and the barrier polymer Barex. Sohio's royalties from these inventions exceed $250 million. Hughes also developed oils for machinery alloys, chromia-alumina catalysts for reforming heavy naphtha, the use of microballoons for reducing evaporation of crude oil in storage tanks, boron compounds for increasing the octane number of gasoline, bismuth phosphomolybdate catalysts for the production of AN by the ammoxidation of propylene, and butadiene-acrylonitrile-ethyl acrylate terpolymer barrier containers (Barex).

In 1970, Dr. Hughes retired from Sohio to join the faculty of the University of California School of Medicine, where he is now Director of Research of Otolaryngology.

Everett, who was recipient of AIC's Pioneer Award in 1971, has been presented the Gordon Research Conferences Chair, the IR 100 Award, and the ACS Morley Medal. In addition to being an AIC fellow, he is also a fellow of the American Association for the Advancement of Science and a member of the American Chemical Society, American Petroleum Institute, Cleveland Association of Research Directors, Society of Plastics Engineers, Society of Chemical Industry, Alpha Chi Sigma, Sigma Xi, and the Industrial Research Institute, Inc. He has served ACS as chairman and councilor of the Cleveland Section, chairman of the Petroleum Division, and chairman of the Gordon Research Conferences Management Board. He has been awarded several patents by the U. S. Patent Office and numerous foreign patents.

Everett married Ruth Scherer on June 20, 1931. Their five children are: Dr. Mary A. Allen, a psychiatrist in Menlo Park, California; Mrs. Kathleen Barker, an attorney in Torrance, California; Robert Clark Hughes, a chemical physicist at Sandia National Laboratories; Bruce Albert Hughes, a mechanical engineer at General Electric in Evandale, Ohio; and Ralph Scherer Hughes, an industrial engineer with American Protective Industries in Pomona, California. The Hughes also have fifteen grandchildren.

JAMES DANIEL IDOL, JR.

Lexicographers define the word *idol* as an object of passionate devotion. Marilyn Thorn Randall may well agree to this definition as it applies to James Daniel Idol, whom she married in 1977. His talents have also been duly recognized by the American Institute of Chemists - Pioneer Award, and by the National Association of Manufacturers - Modern Pioneer Medal. Moreover, he was recipient of the Joseph P. Stewart Distinguished Service Award in 1975, ACS Creative Invention Award in 1975, Perkin Medal in 1979, and was cited as a polymer science pioneer in *Polymer News* in 1983.

Jim was born in Harrisonville, Missouri, on August 7, 1928, to James Daniel and Gladys Rosita Lile Idol. After completing high school in 1945, he enrolled in William

Jewell College where he received his B.S. degree in chemistry in 1949. He was a Westinghouse and Hooker Chemical Fellow at Purdue where he worked under the direction of Professor Earl McBee.   Upon receiving his doctorate in 1955, Dr. Idol joined Standard Oil of Ohio. Ten years later he was promoted to Research Manager. Following the advice of Henry Hass, Jim discovered the single step ammoxidation of propylene process - now used almost exclusively for the production of acrylonitrile. Not content with this major discovery, Jim developed acrylonitrile-based "Barex" barrier plastics, which are still used for packaging a wide variety of processed meats, foodstuffs, drugs, household products and personal care items.   These two major developments are not only of great commercial importance, but they are classic examples of the advantage of disregarding negative attitudes in research.   Prior to Jim's discoveries, most organic chemists maintained that a one-step ammoxidation of propylene was not possible and that a high acrylonitrile content copolymer would be thermally unstable.

Dr. Idol left Sohio in 1977 to become Director of Venture Research at Ashland Chemical Company.

A lifetime fellow of AIC, he is a member of the American Chemical Society, Society of the Plastics Industry, American Institute of Chemical Engineers, Society of Plastics Engineers, Industrial Research Institute, Society of Chemical Industry, Plastics Pioneers Association, Council of Chemical Research, Indiana Academy of Science, American Association for the Advancement of Science, Alpha Chi Sigma, Sigma Xi, Theta Chi Delta, Kappa Mu Epsilon, Alpha Phi Omega, Phi Gamma Omega, and Worthington Hills Country Club.

Jim is an accomplished pianist, singer, fisherman and bridge player.   Always active in chemical society affairs, it was his chairmanship of the ACS Industrial and Engineering Division which provided the catalyst for him to meet his future wife at a Valentine's Day cocktail party in Washington in 1976.

Because he was born into a newspaper family, it was believed that Jim was predestined to become a member of the "Fourth Estate."   The fact that he became instead one of the nation's top industrial chemists must have resulted from a chemistry seed having been sewn while he was a student at William Jewell.

ROBERT MICHAEL JOYCE

Bob Joyce, who was among the 184 Ph.D. chemists trained by Roger Adams at the University of Illinois, spent his entire forty-year career with Du Pont.

Born in Lincoln, Nebraska, on September 19, 1915, Bob attended Lincoln High School and Phillips Exeter Academy. He then entered the University of Nebraska where in 1935 he received his B.S. in chemistry and in 1936 M.S. in organic chemistry (Organic Arsenicals). Under Adams, he researched the stereochemistry of substituted biphenyls to receive his doctorate in 1938.

As a research chemist at Du Pont's Central Research Department, he first studied nylon-6 (polycaprolactam). Later, while working with Butch Hanford, he discovered the chain transfer reaction of carbon tetrachloride and chloroform in ethylene polymerization to give low-molecular-weight chlorine-containing products, or "telomerization," which principle has since become widely used to control molecular weight ranges and to put specific end groups on addition polymers. In 1941, Bob began to follow up on a study of the inadvertent polymerization of tetrafluoroethylene made two years earlier by Roy Plunkett. Bob found methods for polymerizing this monomer and for fabricating the non-melting polymer into films and solid shapes, which work led to the commercial development of "Teflon" polytetrafluoroethylene by Du Pont's Plastics Department. Incidentally, the first large-scale use of Teflon, launched during World War II, was in nose cones for proximity fuses.

Promoted to Research Supervisor (1945) and Laboratory Director (1950), Bob expanded his research interests to include reactions at high pressure, carbonylation, reactions in supercritical water, polymer synthesis, and solid state physics. From 1955 to 1963, he was Assistant Director and from 1963 to 1965 Director of the Central Research Department. The next seven years he was Director of Research for the Film Department, followed by Director of Research for the Pharmaceuticals Division of the Biochemicals Department from 1972 until his retirement in 1978.

In addition to being a fellow of AIC, Bob is a member of the American Chemical Society and the American Association for the Advancement of Science. The recipient of a number of U. S. patents, he is the author of the National Academy of Sciences Biographical Memoir on Elmer K. Bolton, former director of Du Pont's Chemical Department; he edited the article *Frontiers in Chemistry* for the centennial issue of *SCIENCE*; served as editorial consultant in the preparation of *Prudent Practices for Disposal of Chemicals from Laboratories*, published by the National Academy Press in 1983; and has authored numerous technical papers. He is secretary-treasurer and editorial consultant for *Organic Reactions* and a consultant for the Board on Chemical Sciences and Technology of the National Research Council.

Bob's 1941 marriage to Dorothy M. Ross (now deceased) of Wilmington, Delaware, produced two children: Daughter (Mrs.) Kathleen Joyce Lofstedt of Bremerton, Washington, and son (Dr.) Richard R. Joyce, an infrared astronomer at the Kitt Peak National Observatory in Tucson, Arizona. Bob married Mrs. Nedra E. Karrer of Sun City Center, Florida, in 1985.

(Photograph courtesy of DePauw University Archives.)

PERCY LAVON JULIAN

"For pioneering research in the chemistry of indole derivatives and related alkaloids, including the total synthesis of the drug, physostigmine; for significant advances in the chemistry and manufacture of sterols, progesterone and other sex hormones, hydrocortisone and related anti-inflammatory steroids; for creative inventions leading to practical methods for manufacturing phosphatides, protein products, emulsifiers, adhesives, protective coatings, and other products from soybeans; and for exemplary leadership in science,

*education and civic affairs, bringing major
benefits to mankind.*[*]

Dr. Julian was an internationally renowned chemist
and humanitarian. By his synthesis of the alkaloid
physostigmine and authentic d,l-eserethole, he
demonstrated the previously alleged synthesis of the latter
compound to be incorrect.

Named by the *World's Who's Who in Science* in
1968 as one of the most distinguished scientists in all
history in all the world, Percy was born on April 11, 1899,
in Montgomery, Alabama, to James S. and Elizabeth Lena
(Adams) Julian. He received his early education in
Montgomery and graduated from DePauw University in
1920 as the top student in his class and with Phi Beta Kappa
honors. After teaching for two years at Fisk University, he
received his M.S. at Harvard. Further graduate studies
under Dr. E. P. Kohler at Harvard were interrupted by
brief teaching careers at West Virginia State College and
Howard University. Upon receipt of a Rockefeller
Foundation Fellowship, he resumed his doctoral studies at
the University of Vienna with Professor Ernst Spaeth, the
famous alkaloidal chemist, and received his Ph.D. degree in
1931.

When he became director of research for the
Glidden Company's Soya Products Division, Julian had to
transform himself into a protein chemist, an engineer, a
paper coating and paper sizing specialist, salesman, cost
accountant, and recruiter of helpers. His first task at
Glidden was to develop a method and to build a plant for
manufacturing large quantities of relatively pure protein
from soybeans. The proteins which resulted coat books,
magazine paper and labels for good printing, increase the

---

[*]Citation of Dr. Julian's Chemical Pioneer Award.

wet strength of paper; and led to the creation of emulsion paints. Morever, an edible variety of protein led to many food products and similar studies on the nutritive value of soy protein, the result of which the annual soy bean harvest in this country had grown from a million bushels in 1929 to almost a billion bushels in 1967. Dr. Julian's other successes include commercialization of the female hormone progesterone and the adrenal steroid cortexolone - cortexolone became the raw material for making hydrocortisone - and the isolation of sterols from soybean oil and their manufacture.

In late 1953 the Glidden Company abandoned the steroid field because they thought soya sterols were no longer a competitive raw material. Dr. Julian then established the Julian Laboratories, Inc; Laboratorios Julian de México, S.A. in Mexico City; and Empresa Agro-Química Guatemalteca, S.A. in Guatemala. He later established the Julian Research Institute and Julian Associates, Inc. In Relateleheu (Guatemala), he began domestication of the so-called "wild-growing yam," a project he later sold to the Upjohn Company, which has been one of the successful domestications of this raw material. In early 1961, Laboratorios Julian de México, S.A. and Julian Laboratories, Inc. were acquired by Smith Kline and French Laboratories of Philadelphia; thus, in a seven-year period, Dr. Julian converted a few thousand dollars of original capital into a few million.

Dr. Julian's competent and successful researches led to many honors: Harvard's Austin Fellow (1922-23), Research Fellow in Biophysics (1923-24), Derby Scholar (1924-25), and University Fellow (1925-26); Sigma Xi, Northwestern University (1945); Spingarn Medal (1947); Distinguished Service Award for 1949-50, Phi Beta Kappa Association, Chicago (1949); Chicagoan of the Year Award from *Chicago Sun-Times* (1950); Honor Scroll Award,

American Institute of Chemists (1964); and AIC Chemical Pioneer Award (1968). His honorary degrees included DePauw University (1947), Fisk University (1947), West Virginia State College (1948), Northeastern University (1948), Morgan State College (1950), Lincoln (Pennsylvania) University (1954), Roosevelt University (1961), Virginia State College (1962), Morehouse College (1963), and Oberlin College (1964). What is more, the new mathematics-science center at DePauw was named in memory of Dr. Julian and the MacMurray College chemistry building was named "The Percy Lavon Julian Hall of Chemistry."

Percy Julian was a member, director, or president of many organizations, such as Provident Hospital, Boy Scouts, Public Welfare Commission of Illinois, Urban League, Fund for the Republic, and Rotary Club. His membership on educational and religious boards is equally impressive: boards of trustees or directors of Howard, Fisk, and Roosevelt Universities, Southern Union College, Chicago Theological Seminary, and the First Congregational Church of Oak Park. This great humanitarian once said that he spent as much of his time "building bridges within the human family" as he did to science. He drew upon his knowledge of history, upon his study of the humanities, and upon his many personal experiences in his efforts to provide a better world for all humankind.

Dr. Julian married Anna Johnson on December 24, 1935, and became the father of Percy L., Jr., and Faith Roselle. His wife, who received her doctorate in sociology from the University of Pennsylvania, was a trustee of MacMurray College. Dr. Julian, who fancied farming as a hobby and loved the outdoors and fine animals, owned a 500-acre farm in Indiana. He passed away on April 19, 1980.

ISABELLA LUGOSKI KARLE

Isabella was named AIC's Chemical Pioneer in 1984. She and her husband, Jerome Karle, have the distinction of being two of the few husband and wife Ph.D. scientists with biographies in *Who's Who in America*. Jerome was recipient of the Nobel Prize in Chemistry in 1985. Moreover, the Karles' three children are also scientists. Daughter Louis Hansen, Ph.D., is a theoretical chemist at Brookhaven National Laboratory. Daughter Jean Marianne Karle, Ph.D., is a research scientist at Walter Reed Institute of Research. Daughter Madeline Karle Tawney, M.S., is employed in the Director's Office of the Natural History Museum of the Smithsonian Institute. Over the years, Jerome and Isabella have attended scientific meetings around the world. The fact that their children usually accompanied their parents presumably led them to also choose careers in science.

Isabella and Jerome were married in 1942 while graduate students at the University of Michigan. Upon receipt of their doctorates (Isabella, 1944; Jerome, 1943), they both accepted positions with the Manhattan Project of the University of Chicago. Isabella then returned to her alma mater where she served as instructor while Jerome worked on a project for the U. S. Navy at Ann Arbor. In 1946, they joined the Naval Research Laboratory in Washington, D.C., and have often collaborated scientifically on x-ray diffraction studies. She has been head of the x-ray diffraction section since 1959; he was head of the electron diffraction section from 1946 to 1958.

Isabella has published over two hundred articles in scientific journals and been granted several patents by the U. S. Patent Office. She has the distinction of being one of the 1000 most cited contemporary scientists by the Institute for Scientific Information (ISI). She and her husband have co-authored several publications, one of which, first cited by ISI in *Comments* No. 50 (December 1980), has been cited 300 times. This paper, originally appearing in *Acta Crystallographia* in 1963, described a new phase determination procedure for the structure of cyclo (hexaglycl) hemihydrate and contained the first example of the folding of the backbone in a cyclic monopeptide.

At the time she accepted the Chemical Pioneer Award, Isabella described the conformation of endogenous enkephalin in her report *From Xray Reflection to a Complete Molecular Structure*. This linear pentapeptide, which functions as a natural analgesic with opiate-like activity, similar to morphine, occurs naturally in the brain, gut and spinal cord. The four different conformations of [Leu^5] enkephalin illustrate the complexity of structures that can be solved by direct phase determination. In addition to studies of organic compounds, structure analysis by direct phase determination from x-ray intensive data can also be used for metal clusters, polyions, metalloorganic complexes, inorganic substances, minerals and alloys.

Dr. Karle received honorary doctoral degrees from her alma mater (1976) and Wayne State University (1979). She and her husband received the honorary degree Doctor of Humane Letters from Georgetown University (1984) and an honorary D.Sc. degree from the University of Maryland (1986). In addition to the Pioneer Award, Isabella has received the Lifetime Achievement Award from Women in Science and Engineering (1986), Dexter Conrad Award from the Office of Naval Research (1980), ACS Garvan Award (1976), Federal Women's Award from the U. S. Government (1973), ACS Hillebrand Award (1970), Annual Achievement Award from the Society of Women Engineers (1968), and Superior Civilian Service Award from the U. S. Navy Department (1965). She is a fellow of AIC and a member of the National Academy of Sciences, American Chemical Society, and American Biochemical Society. President of the American Crystallographic Association in 1976, she is a member of the editorial board of *Polymers, International Journal of Peptide and Protein Research,* and *Chemical and Engineering News.*

This extraordinary woman is the daughter of Polish immigrants, Zygmunt Apolonaris and Elizabeth Graczyk Lugoski.

(Photograph courtesy of American Institute of Chemists.)

FREDERICK J. KAROL

Frederick Karol, whose entire professional career has been with Union Carbide Corporation in New Jersey, was named Chemical Pioneer in 1988. The award was made primarily for his pioneering work in basic chemistry or organotransition metal catalysts for use in fluidized bed reactors, and the development of linear, low density polyethylene resins leading to the commercial success of the UNIPOL polyethylene process.

Dr. Karol has been a principal inventor and investigator in catalyst research and development programs for producing low and high density polyethylenes by the low pressure, fluid bed UNIPOL process.   This process is the basis for the technology licensing program in polyethylene and for Union Carbide's future in the business.   Some fifty UNIPOL reactors totaling more than five million metric tons of annual capacity are in operation around the world. Currently Dr. Karol manages the total Union Carbide research and development effort in polyolefin catalysis.

Frederick's awards include the 1982 Thomas Edison Patent Award of the Research and Development Council of New Jersey and the 1987 Excellence in Catalysis Award by the Catalysis Society of Metropolitan New York.

Born in Norton, Massachusetts, on February 28, 1933, Frederick received his B.A. in chemistry from Boston University (1954) and doctorate in organic chemistry from Massachusetts Institute of Technology (1962).

Dr. Karol was married in 1958 and is the father of three children.

PERCIVAL CLEVELAND KEITH

"P. C." or "Dobie," as Percival Keith was known to his friends, was an expert in the chemistry of coal and petroleum and an advocate of the conversion of natural gas to gasoline. He received his early education from a private tutor and graduated from Austin College in Sherman, Texas. Thereafter he studied electrochemical engineering at the Massachusetts Institute of Technology.

As a dynamic young Texan, Keith began his career at the research laboratory of the Texas Company. He conducted field research for Universal Oil Products in 1923-24; the following year he was president of Keith, Winkler, and Koch. From 1925 to 1927 he was vice president in charge of the operations for Cross Engineering Company. In 1929 he became vice president in charge of engineering and research for M. W. Kellogg Company of New York City; and in 1942 was elected president of Kellex Corporation, a Kellogg subsidiary, which was specially created as a part of the Manhattan Engineer District (later part of the Atomic Energy Commision) during World War II. Kellex built the uranium gaseous diffusion plant at Oak Ridge and Keith was in charge of construction. He played a major role in the design and construction of the gas diffusion plant for the separation and production of uranium-235. For his work on the Manhattan Project, in 1946 the War Department cited him for "brilliant accomplishments involving grave responsibility and technical administrative ability in connection with the development of the greatest weapon of all time, the atomic bomb." The citation further hailed his "rare technical ability, his initiative, his exceptional capacity as an executive and his inspiring devotion to duty." That same year, *Time* magazine described him as "the red-faced, hurry-up man who bossed the construction of the famed atom bomb plant at Oak Ridge."

From 1943 to his retirement twenty years later, he was president of Hydrocarbon Research, Inc., of New York City. Keith was so convinced that gasoline could be produced from natural gas that Hydrocarbon Research, Inc. built a $15 million plant at Brownsville, Texas. This method eventually proved too expensive, however. After retiring, Keith was active in developing ways to recover crude oil from depleted fields. He obtained many patents related to the oil refining industry and contributed articles to various professional journals.

Keith received AIC's prestigious Pioneer Award in 1973 "for brilliant leadership in the design and erection of the Oak Ridge gaseous diffusion plant, which provided materials for bringing World War II to a successful conclusion, and whose processes are the source of U-235 for present commercial power plants using atomic energy."

Dobie was a member or fellow of the National Academy of Sciences, National Academy of Engineering, American Chemical Society, American Institute of Mechanical Engineers, and American Petroleum Institute. He was also a member of the Union League, Chemist's Club, Down Town Association of New York City, Somerset Hills Country Club of Bernardsville, New Jersey, and Essex Fox Hounds of Peapack, New Jersey. A Roman Catholic and Republican, he enjoyed preparing gourmet meals and playing golf.

He was born in Tyler, Texas, on September 24, 1900, to Percival Cleveland and Mac (Johnston) Keith; his father was a pharmacist. Keith was twice a widower. In 1927 he married Martha MacDonald; born to them were Percival Cleveland, who married Patricia Gravelle; Christopher, who married Margaret Frahn; and Martha, who married Peter Dane. In 1941 Dobie married Ann Barlow; their two children are Mac Johnston, who married Benjamin Griswold IV; and Dennis, who married Anne Brown. In 1976 he married Elizabeth (Miller) Vila. Dobie passed away in Peapack on July 9, 1976.

KARL KLAGER

The first artificial earth satellite, launched by the Russians from the Baikonur Cosmodrome on October 4, 1957, was simply a test payload containing a radio beacon and a thermometer.   This 84 kg satellite, christened *Sputnik*, meaning *traveler*, orbited the earth once every 96 minutes in an elliptical trajectory until early in 1958 when it re-entered the earth's atmosphere and burned up.   On November 3, 1957, *Sputnik II* (weight 519 kg), carrying a dog called "Laika" and a week's supply of dog food, was launched.   Laika's ten days in space proved that life could survive the weightlessness of outer space.   The United States' first attempt to place a satellite in earth's orbit on December 6, 1956, ended with an explosion of the Vanguard rocket booster on the launch pad.   Our first successful satellite, *Explorer I*, was launched by a group led by Dr. Wernher von Braun on January 31, 1958; the second, *Vanguard I,* was launched on March 17, 1958. In spite of the moderate success of these small satellites, greater thrust was needed.

Karl Klager was one of 450 German scientists who, in 1949, was shipped to this country from Stuttgart as a voluntary prisoner of war in "Operation Paperclip." Some years later, he became prominent as one of the men responsible for providing the thrust required by our launch vehicles to send satellites into space. In fact, much of the progress made since that first *beep beep* was heard from outer space has been because of the research and development efforts of Dr. Klager and his associates.

While working for IG Farbenindustrie during World War II, Karl had developed a rocket and torpedo fuel, but he was scarcely a rocket expert. At the time he arrived in this country, he knew little about life here, even less about the economy, and could not speak English.   The Navy offered him six dollars a day plus an allowance for his family. After studying the prices in a Sears Roebuck catalog, he decided they could live on this stipend.   Nine months later, he and his family were transported to Pasadena so that he could demonstrate his skill as a "rocket expert."   After submitting eleven disclosures on the production of nitropolymer intermediates, he was ready to join Aerojet General. But he was not allowed to do so because he was not a legal immigrant. To overcome this, he walked across the Mexican border and back again to be welcomed as an immigrant. He then went to work for Aerojet as a research chemist.   In 1973, he retired as Vice President of Science for the Solid Rocket Plant, which employed 20,000 workers. Since then, he has served as a consultant.

Dr. Klager is credited with the invention of an

economical process for the production of unsymmetrical dimethylhydrazine (UDMH) rocket fuel for the Bomarc missiles. The UDMH liquid propellant, produced by a catalytic hydrogenation process, was used in the Titan, Gemini and upper Apollo missiles. Karl is also credited with the co-invention and development of a polyurethane solid propellant binder used with aluminum powder and an ammonium perchlorate oxidizer for the Minuteman and Polaris missiles.

Born in Vienna, Austria, in 1908, Karl attended the famous Benedictine Monastery and then entered the university as a pre-med student. His decision to become a chemist was catalyzed by a phobia of cadavers used in medical studies - he had to be carried out of the cadaver-filled laboratory on a stretcher! After graduating as a Diploma Chemist in 1931, he conducted doctoral research under Professor Ernst Spaeth at the University of Vienna, receiving his doctorate in 1934. The next two years he worked as a chemist for firms in Arad, Rumania; the next three, in Budapest. In 1939, he accepted a position with Farben at Ludwigshafen where, under the direction of Dr. Walter Reppe, he worked on acetylene chemistry, propargyl alcohol, cyclooctatraene, dyestuffs and plastics. He became an American citizen in 1955.

Dr. Klager has been awarded seventy-one patents by the U. S. Patent Office and sixteen by the German Patent Office. Dr. Reppe is co-patentee of several of the German patents. Karl is a lifetime fellow of AIC, and a member of the American Institute for Aeronautics and Astronautics, American Chemical Society, and Sigma Xi. He served as chairman of the Sacramento Chapter of ACS and counselor for the Sacramento Chapter of AIAA. He has published over fifty articles in professional journals and was co-author of the 1970 ACS monograph *Propellant Manufacture, Hazards and Testing*. He has presented seminars at the University of Tokyo (1952), Kentron, South Africa (1980), and Chung Shan Institute of Science and Technology in Taiwan (1981). He was recipient of the Chemical Pioneer Award (1978), Inventor of the Year Award from the Patent Lawyers Association of Northern California (1978), AIAA's Jones H. Wyld Propulsion Award (1972), and the U. S. Navy's Distinguished Public Service Award (1958).

Karl and Elizabeth Ramona, whom he married in 1938, are parents of Peter, now a dentist in the U. S. Army. Peter and his wife have one daughter. Karl and Peter were model train enthusiasts. He and Elizabeth enjoy flower gardening and traveling; their interest in Mayan Indian lore resulted from their travels to Mexico and Peru.

(Photograph courtesy of University of Wyoming.)

HENRY GRANGER KNIGHT

*". . . a capsule review of his life reads like
the abstract of an up-dated story by Horatio Alger.
The ten-year old boy who promised his dying
mother he would 'be somebody'; his struggle for a
formal education, complete with Ph.D.; progress in
teaching from a one-room rural school to the
deanship of important agricultural colleges; and
finally the growth of the new chief of a bureau in
the U. S. Department of Agriculture into the director
of the world's largest research organization."**

*Written by Florence E. Wall, early member of the American
Institute of Chemists.

By virtue of hard work and an attractive and cooperative personality, Henry Knight advanced during his career to positions of increasing responsibility. At the University of Washington, he was first an assistant and then an instructor in chemistry prior to earning his B.A. in 1902. He studied and taught for one year at the University of Chicago and then returned to Washington, where he received his M.A. degree in 1904. For the next six years, he was professor of chemistry and state chemist at the University of Wyoming. The following eight years he was director of the Wyoming Experiment Station and Farmers' Institute; in 1912 he also became dean of the College of Agriculture. Following a year at the University of Illinois, where he received his Ph.D. degree in 1917, Knight returned to Wyoming as the director of the State Council for Defense. He then became dean and director of Oklahoma Agricultural College (1918-21). Following a year as honorary fellow at Cornell, he was made director of the University of West Virginia Experiment Station and dean of the College of Agriculture (1926-27).

Henry became chief of the new Bureau of Chemistry and Soils, which included the Fixed Nitrogen Laboratory, in the U. S. Department of Agriculture in 1927. Six years later, Congress appropriated several million dollars for the construction of four large regional research laboratories (now Centers) to be located in Philadelphia, Peoria, Berkeley and New Orleans, their principal purpose being to develop new products and new and expanded uses of farm crops. Dr. Knight and some of his associates had the privilege and responsibility of planning, building, and operating these laboratories. Henry was well equipped for this major undertaking because of his rare gift for organization and administration and his ability to win the cooperation and devotion of those who worked with him. His prediction that the four regional Centers would do great things for agriculture and society has long been realized.

Dr. Knight was awarded AIC's Gold Medal in 1941, at which time he was chief of the Department of Agriculture's Bureau of Agricultural Chemistry and Engineering. The award was made in recognition of his outstanding accomplishments in the field of agricultural chemistry, and his executive and creative ability as administrator of the four regional research laboratories. An honorary fellow of AIC, he served as its fifth president from 1932 to 1934. He was also active in the American Chemical Society.

Henry enjoyed the outdoors and outdoor activities, including hunting, fishing, motoring, and golf. He also enjoyed music and dancing, was an excellent amateur photographer, and a delightful raconteur with a keen sense of humor.

Born July 21, 1878, on a farm near Bennington, Kansas, the son of Pony Express Rider Edwin R. and Elva (Edwards) Knight, Henry died on July 13, 1942, in Washington, D.C., where he had lived more than a decade of his life. The day following his death, his obituaries were published in *The New York Herald Tribune* and in the *New York Times*. Henry was survived by his wife and a son, Richard D. Knight.

WILLIAM STANDISH KNOWLES

While St. Louis is well known today as the home of world class scientists and a thriving chemical industry, there were neither chemists nor a chemical industry in the city at the time of the Louisiana Purchase. It was in 1901 that John F. Queeney founded the Monsanto Company for the production of saccharin. Forty-one years later, William Standish Knowles joined Monsanto and has spent his entire career with them. Promoted to senior scientist in 1965 and to a Distinguished Monsanto Fellow in 1970, he was recipient of the American Institute of Chemists' Pioneer Award in 1983.

Bill's most important contribution to science was the invention and development of a homogeneous catalytic asymmetric hydrogenation process (patented in

1974), which has been widely acclaimed as the most outstanding achievement to date in catalytic selectivity. While Louis Pasteur separated optical isomers by physical means, Bill used a catalytic hydrogenation process to convert olefins to optically active isomers, such as L-amino acids. This catalyst, a coordination complex of rhodium and an optically active phosphine ligand, such as Rh (COD) (bisphosphine) +,BF_4−, can be used to produce either L or D isomers. The ligand is the chiral 1,2-bis (o-anisylphenyl phosphine) ethene. Bill's technique is used for the large-scale production of L-DOPA, used in the treatment of Parkinson's disease. Dr. Knowles' research not only proved that the challenge of asymmetric synthesis could be met, but he actually achieved direct synthesis of D- and L-amino acid intermediates with stereospecificity theretofore observed only in enzymatic processes. The practical formation of one or the other of two enantiomorphs with optical purity in excess of 95 percent is the mark of an elegant process.

This Chemical Pioneer has also contributed to the development of the total synthesis of steroids, such as cortisone and tolowin to a process for the synthesis of chloramphenicol, and to catalytic hydrogenation.

Born in Taunton, Massachusetts, on June 1, 1917, Bill majored in chemistry at Harvard where he received the B.S. degree in 1939. Graduate research on lactones at Columbia, under the direction of Professor Robert C. Elderfield, gave him his doctorate in 1942. During 1951-52, he returned as a post-doctoral fellow to Harvard where he conducted research with Professor R. B. Woodward.

Bill was recipient of the ACS Award for Creative Invention in 1982, the St. Louis ACS Award in 1978, and the IR-100 Award in 1974. He is a member of the American Institute of Chemists, American Chemical Society,

American Association for the Advancement of Science, Chemical Society of London, Sigma Xi, New York Academy of Science, Association of Harvard Chemists and Society of Chemical Industry. His many publications, fourteen of which are related to catalytic asymmetric hydrogenation, include three papers with Elderfield in 1942 in *Journal of Organic Chemistry*. He has also been awarded thirty-two patents by the U. S. Patent Office.

Bill married Lesley Ann Charbonnier in 1945. They are parents of four children and have three grandchildren. In recent years, family activities have centered around a cabin in Jackson Hole, Wyoming, where there is a continual flow of guests throughout the summer.

JOHN KOLLAR

In 1859, Charles Adolph Wurtz prepared ethylene glycol by the saponification of its acetate which he obtained by the reaction of silver acetate and ethylene iodide. Because it had a sweet taste like glycerol, he named it glycol. Ethylene glycol was produced as a byproduct in the Mellon Institute's Prest-o-lite research project in 1922. The object of this investigation was the production of actylene by the thermal cracking of natural gases. The byproduct ethylene was converted to ethylene chlorohydrin by the addition of aqueous chlorine. The ethylene chlorohydrin was then converted to ethylene oxide by heating with a lime slurry and the ethylene oxide was hydrolyzed at 300°C to ethylene glycol (Prestone). Although there was little demand at that time for this petrochemical, ethylene glycol was used commercially as an antifreeze for automobile radiators in 1925. Today, about fifty percent of the 400,000 tons of ethylene glycol produced annually is used as an antifreeze and coolant for automobile and airplane motors; almost thirty percent of this dihyric alcohol is used for the production of polyesters, such as polyethylene terephthalate (PET).

It was John Kollar who developed a highly selective process for the direct oxidation of ethylene in an acetic acid solvent using a dual catalyst of tellurium and a bromide. John also developed processes for the production of propylene oxide, tertiary butyl alcohol and styrene which are now produced at annual rates of 900,000 tons, 850,000 tons and 850,000 tons, respectively, in plants in Texas, The Netherlands, Japan and Spain. Dr. Kollar has been awarded sixty U. S. patents and approximately one thousand foreign patents for processes involving selective electrophilic oxidation and acetoxylation of olefins. He also discovered processes which utilize hydroperoxides in the presence of metal catalysts for the epoxidation of olefins, oxidation of secondary amines to oximes, oxidation of tertiary amines to amine oxides as well as the oxidation of olefins to glycols; ditertiary butyl peroxide for the oxidative dehydrodimerization of methanol to produce glycol, which was used to produce propylene glycol, glycerol and 1,3-propanediol. His innovative processes are used to produce adipic acid, caprolactone, terephthalic acid, ethylbenzene, isoprene, adiponitrile and hexamethylenediamine.

John was born in Duquesne, Pennsylvania, on April 22, 1935, to Andrew and Mary (Brinck) Kollar. He accepted an athletic scholarship to Columbia where he received his A.B. in 1957. While an undergraduate, he worked during the summers at Gulf Research and Development Company. For the next four years, he completed graduate chemistry work by attending Carnegie

Institute in the evenings while working full time at Gulf during the day. He then joined Halcon International; nine years later he became Director of Chemical Research. He is now president of Redox Technologies, Inc., formed by a group of entrepreneurs in 1974.

Recipient of the American Institute of Chemists' Pioneer Award in 1977, Dr. Kollar is a lifetime fellow of AIC and a member of the American Chemical Society. He has published several articles on hydroperoxide epoxidation in scientific journals.

John's 1959 marriage to Patricia Ann Weber produced four children. Son J. Christopher is completing medical studies at the College of Medicine and Dentistry of New Jersey. Son David Mark is a practicing psychologist at St. Joseph's Hospital. Daughter Melissa Ann is aspiring to a career in physical education. Daughter Linda Rebecca is a middle school student at Wyckoff's Eisenhower School.

WAYNE EDWARD KUHN

Chaucer's *good felawe*, Shakespeare's *king of good fellows*, and Swift's *hail fellow, well met* apply perfectly to Wayne Edward Kuhn, AIC's 1967 Gold Medalist. Not only is Wayne a good fellow, but he has the distinction of being a fellow of AIC, of the American Institute of Chemical Engineers and of the Society of Automotive Engineers. In addition to serving as president of AIC, he was president and councilor of the Petroleum Division of ACS and president of the Commercial Development Association. He is also a member of the American Society of Testing Materials, American Association for the Advancement of Science, American Rocket Society, American Institute of Astronautics and Aeronautics, Chemical Society of London, Society of Automotive Engineers, Farm Chemurgy, Business Advisory Council on Federal Reports,

Research Society of America, Alpha Chi Sigma, Acacia Fraternity of Cornell, Foster Scholz Club of Reed, a former Reed Trustee, Cosmos Club, Chemists Club of New York, International Club of Portland, Aero Club of Portland, and Admirals Club. Moreover, he has been a member of the same Masonic lodge for over fifty years and is a registered professional engineer in Oregon and California. He has published over 100 scientific reports and been granted numerous U. S. patents.

Born in Oshkosh, Wisconsin, on October 25, 1903, to Edward John and Emma G. Kuhn, he was raised in the Pacific Northwest. Following high school, he enrolled in Reed College (B.A., 1925). He served as a graduate assistant at Cornell, where he received his Ph.D. degree n 1929. Harvard bestowed the AMP degree upon him in 1956.

Prior to his retirement, Wayne spent thirty-six years (1929-1965) with Texaco in various positions in Bayonne, New Jersey, Port Arthur, Texas, and New York City. From the early 1940's to the present day, Wayne has demonstrated his managerial talents by working with the Business Advisory Council on Federal Reports, which council serves as a liaison between business and government to minimize paperwork and assure meaningful reporting programs in the public interest. He returned to Portland in 1965 and continues to regularly attend meetings of the Council in Washington, D.C. This youthful octogenarian plans to continue to serve the Council until he is too old to stand for re-election. Dr. Kuhn is also a director for five companies in the Northwest.

In addition to the Gold Medal, Dr. Kuhn was awarded the Honor Scroll by the American Institute of Chemists. He has also been recipient of the following awards: American Petroleum Industry, National Honor

Award of the Commercial Chemical Development Association, and Foster Scholz Distinguished Award; and was recognized as a Pioneer of the American Institute of Astronautics and Aeronautics. Citations have been bestowed upon him by the Office of Scientific Research and Development, Army Ordinance, Navy Bureau of Ships, Defense Science Board, and National Science Foundation.

Wayne aptly demonstrates his belief that one of the most important ingredients for personal satisfaction are one's friends and associates. His *Fish for Dinner - Just Catch It* was described in a four-column story in the *New York Times* in 1970 by Jean Hewitt, Food Editor and wife of Dr. Eric J. Hewitt, a former fellow of AIC. According to the *Times* story, Wayne's guests trolled for salmon in the Pacific and cooked the fish, Indian style, on stakes near an outdoor fire near the Kuhn's beach house.

Wayne married Agnes Lakie in 1929. Their son, William E. Kuhn, is head of Kuhn Management Consultants of Denver, Colorado.

STEPHANIE LOUISE KWOLEK

"For her creative work in the
preparation of liquid crystalline solutions of
an aromatic polyamide for the production of
high strength, high modulus fibers used in
passenger car tires."

When cotton was king a few decades ago, there was much romance associated with natural fibers. There was also, in the mid 1930's, some romance associated with regenerated cellulose (rayon) when the strength of cordura viscose rayon was increased to a 6g/denier and the strength of   regenerated fibers produced by the

---

*Citation on the Chemical Pioneer Award.

saponification of steam-stretched cellulose acetate fiber (Fortisan) was increased to 7g/denier. However, these strong cellulosic fibers were displaced, to a large extent, by nylon and polyester cord with tenacities as high as 10g/denier. Subsequent research by Stephanie Louise Kwolek in the mid 1960's resulted in the discovery of liquid crystalline solutions of aromatic polyamides which could be spun directly to highly oriented fibers with tenacities as high as 30g/denier. A plant for the production of these aramid fibers with an annual capacity of 7000 tons was built by Du Pont in 1971 and expanded to 40 thousand tons in 1983.

Stephanie's discoveriess have made possible a host of new products based on Kevlar® aramid fiber which contributes to our quality of life. Included in this list of products are reinforced belts in radial tires, ballistic and flack vests, safety work apparel, inflatable boats and fiber-reinforced composites for aircraft, marine and recreational equipment.

Stephanie was born in New Kensington, Pennsylvania, on July 31, 1923, to John and Nellie Kwolek. After graduating from D. T. Watson High School in 1942, she enrolled in Carnegie Mellon University where she majored in chemistry (B.S. 1946). She was awarded an honorary D.Sc. degree by Worcester Polytechnic Institute in 1981 and was inducted into the University of Akron Polymer Processing Hall of Fame in 1985.

Recipient of the AIC Chemical Pioneer Award in 1980, she also received the ACS Delaware Section Publication Award (1959); Franklin Institute of Philadelphia, Howard N. Potts Medal (1976); American Society for Metals Award (1978); ACS Award for Creative Invention (1980); Carnegie Mellon University Association Merit Award (1983); and Society of Plastics

Engineering/Technology Award (1985). A fellow of the American Institute of Chemists and a member of the American Chemical Society, Franklin Institute, Sigma Xi and Phi Kappa Phi, she has authored twenty-five scientific articles and been awarded sixteen U. S. patents.

(Photograph courtesy of Pach Bros., New York.)

RALPH LOUIS LANDAU

Ralph Landau was one of twelve individuals presented with the first National Medal of Technology by President Reagan in February 1985.

Recognized as one of America's most successful "entrepreneurs" by the Economists of London, Dr. Landau has been responsible for many major developments in the chemical industry, to wit: 1951, production of ethylene oxide by the fixed bed-silver catalytic oxidation of ethylene; 1955, production of maleic anhydride by the oxidation of benzene; 1956, production of terephthalic acid by the oxidation of p-xylene; 1960, production of cyclohexanol and cyclohexanone by the boric acid-catalyzed oxidation of cyclohexane; 1966, production of propylene oxide by the hydroperoxidation of isobutane and the production of styrene by the hydroperoxidation of ethylbenzene; 1980, production of acetic acid by the carbonylation of methanol obtained from coal. Moreover, one of the companies he founded, Halcon, has been the world's major source of new petrochemical processes during the last twenty-five years. More than forty plants have been constructed worldwide to use technology developed by Halcon.

Ralph was born in Philadelphia, Pennsylvania, on May 19, 1916, to Samuel and Deanna Landau. He received his B.S. degree in chemical engineering in 1937 from the University of Pennsylvania. Four years later, he was granted a doctor of science degree in chemical engineering from Massachusetts Institute of Technology. Thereafter, he accepted employment with M. W. Kellogg Company. As head of the chemistry department for Kellex Corporation, from 1943-45 he worked on the Manhattan Project at Oak Ridge. The following year he cofounded Scientific Design Company, which became Halcon International in 1963. In 1966, Halcon joined with ARCO Chemical Company to form Oxirane. Dr. Landau served as Halcon's president and chairman of the board until 1975. In 1980, Halcon sold its half interest in Oxirane to ARCO. Dr. Landau is now associated with Listowel Inc. and the Department of Economics of Stanford University.

A fellow of the American Institute of Chemists and the American Institute of Chemical Engineers, Ralph is also a member of the National Academy of Engineers, American Academy of Arts and Sciences, American Association for the Advancement of Science, and Electrochemical Society. He has published two books, approximately one hundred scientific reports, and has been granted several patents by the U. S. Patent Office.

Dr. Landau was the 1981 recipient of AIC's Chemical Pioneer Award. His other honors include the American Institute of Chemical Engineers Founders Award and Petroleum and Petrochemical Division Award, Chemical Industry Medal, Perkin Medal, Hugh Otto Wolff Prize of the University of Pennsylvania, Winthrop-Sears Award for Chemical Entrepreneurship, Third Mason Lectureship at Stanford, Distinguished Award in Technology of the Association of Consulting Chemists and Chemical Engineers, and the Second Warren K. Lewis Lectureship at MIT. He has received honorary D.Sc. degrees from Polytechnic Institute of New York, Ohio State University, and Clarkson College.

He and his wife, Claire Sackler, whom he married in 1940, have one child.

Ralph includes among his hobbies people, sailing and music.

(Photograph courtesy of the American Institute of Chemists.)

WALTER SAVAGE LANDIS

Walter Landis was presented AIC's Gold Medal Award in 1943 " . . . in recognition not only of Dr. Landis' outstanding contributions to engineering and development work, largely in the field of nitrogen derivatives, but also for his services to the professional side of chemistry as an able executive, and for his contributions of time and effort toward raising the professional standard of chemists."

The Gold Medal was only one of the many honors received by Landis. Other tokens of esteem include the honorary D.Sc. from Lehigh University (1922), Chemical Industry Medal of the American Section of the Society of

Chemical Industry (1936), Joseph W. Richards Memorial Lecturer (1936), Perkin Medal (1939), and honorary fellowship in the AIC (1945).

Landis was unusually talented in research, invention and management. He established American Cyanamid Company's first research laboratory in 1913. He received more than fifty patents and played a major role in the development of several important processes and manufacturing plants, which included the production of sodium cyanide from cyanamid, marketed as early as 1916; and the development of processes for making ferrocyanide, dicyandiamid, urea, hydrocyanic acid, argon, ammonium phosphate, and explosives. During World War I he participated in building the first American plant to produce ammonia from cyanamid and to oxidize ammonia to nitric acid, designed a portable hydrogen generator for the United States Army, and was consultant to many industrial groups faced with the problems of producing munitions. In the early 1930's, he worked on improvements in the DeLaval electrothermic process at Trolhatten, Sweden, and Sorpsborg, Norway, and on the electrothermic process for magnesium at Radentheim, Austria. His versatility is further evidenced in his hundreds of articles on financial and economic subjects as well as professional phases of chemistry.

Landis attended public schools in Pottstown, Pennsylvania, and Orlando, Florida; the Bethlehem Preparatory School; and Lehigh University, where he received the degree of metallurgical engineer in 1902. He studied further and taught as an assistant in Lehigh's Department of Metallurgy to receive his M.S. in 1906. From 1905 to 1906, he also studied crystallography and mineralogy at Heidelberg, Germany, and worked at Krupp Institute in Aachen, Germany. His consulting relationship with American Cyanamid began in 1909 when he was an assistant professor of metallurgy at Lehigh. The next year he became associate professor at Lehigh. Two years later, a major career change occurred when he left Lehigh and distinguished himself while working as chief technologist for American Cyanamid. In 1923, he became vice president, a position he held for the rest of his life. He was also a director of five other companies.

Active in several professional organizations, Walter was the seventeenth president (1920) of the American Electrochemical Society, chairman of the New York Section of the American Chemical Society (1932), and president of the Chemists Club of New York. He was a member of the American Institute of Chemical Engineers, American Institute of Mining and Metallurgical Engineers, Chemist Advisory Council, Tau Beta Pi, Sigma Xi, and Epsilon Chi.

Landis, who was born in Pottstown, on July 5, 1891, to Daniel and Clara (Savage) Landis, died at the age of fifty-three at his home in Old Greenwich, Connecticut.

IRVING ENGLANDER LEVINE

Because of the limited availability of coal tar byproduct naphthalene and the need for more phthalic anhydride for the production of alkyd resins and phthalic ester plasticizers, Irving Levine began his investigations of the use of petroleum fractions containing naphthalene derivatives as a source of phthalic anhydride. Although he obtained low yields of phthalic anhydride from these fractions, he still encountered many purification problems. His observations that relatively large amounts of C_8 aromatics, such as ortho, metal and para-xylene and ethylbenzene, were being produced in the primitive catalytic cracking then in use caused him to investigate the possibility of separating ortho-xylene from the C_8 aromatic fraction obtained. Thus, he was able to obtain a C_8 aromatic mixture containing 85 percent ortho-xylene by use of the distillation columns then available. Fortunately, the 15 percent C_8 isomers in the mixture were oxidized selectively to carbon dioxide and water and a satisfactory yield of phthalic anhydride was obtained in the vanadium oxide-catalyzed oxidation process.

Levine's process was scaled up from laboratory to production scale by substituting the 85 percent ortho-xylene C_8 aromatic fraction for naphthalene in Reichhold's phthalic anhydride production facility. As a result of this successful experiment, Standard Oil of California* built a phthalic anhydride production plant with an annual capacity of 3000 tons at Richmond, California. Today more than a million tons are produced yearly by this process, which accounts for more than 85 percent of the world's production of this chemical.

Levine also investigated synthetic detergents, polymerization, fibers, films, surface coatings, single cell proteins, and the solvent treatment of foods; and was involved in the development of commercial processes for the production of polyisobutylene, alpha olefins, and dimethyl terephthalate.

Recipient of the 1969 Chemical Pioneer Award, Irving is an AIC fellow and a member of the American Chemical Society. He has published many reports in scientific journals and has been awarded several patents by the U. S. Patent Office.

Irving was born in Cincinnati on October 18, 1909. He received his B.A., M.A., and Ph.D. degrees (1934, 1936 and 1937, respectively) from the University of Cincinnati, where he was a Laws Fellow in graduate school. Thereafter, he accepted a position of research chemist

*Now Chevron Research Company.

with Standard Oil of California at Richmond. He was promoted to senior research chemist (1945), manager of the chemical division (1954), vice president of the chemicals department (1959), and vice president of special products (1960).

Dr. Levine married Venona Gregory in 1952. They have two sons, John and Eric.

(Photograph courtesy of The MIT Museum.)

WARREN KENDALL LEWIS

Warren was born on a farm near Laurel, Delaware, on August 21, 1882. At the age of twelve, he went to live with a family in Boston to take advantage of the educational opportunities Boston afforded for future enrollment at the Massachusetts Institute of Technology. In 1905, he received his B.S. degree from MIT. His career as an MIT research associate came to an end when he left this country to study at the University of Breslau, Germany, where he received his doctorate in 1908. Upon his return, he was employed for one year as a chemist for the W. H. McElwain Company. He then returned to MIT. In 1914, he was promoted to the rank of professor; from 1920 through 1929, he was head of the Department of Chemical

Engineering; he became emeritus professor in 1947.

During the Second World War, Dr. Lewis served as acting executive officer of MIT's Department of Chemical Engineering and handled all administrative work in connection with war research projects and his department's war training courses. He was also consultant with the National Defense Research Committee of the Office of Scientific Research and Development on chemical warfare problems and served on special committees for the Manhattan Project. Through the years, he was an active consultant for industry, with the full realization that such activity contributed breadth and background to his teaching.

With fellow professors W. H. McAdams and William H. Walker, Lewis wrote *Principles of Chemical Engineering,* one of the most important textbooks in its field. He also wrote numerous articles on chemical engineering for technical journals, many of which were concerned with research in the fields of petroleum, leather manufacture, distillation and heat flow.

Dr. Lewis was made an honorary doctor of science by the University of Delaware in 1937 and an honorary doctor of engineering by Princeton in 1947. He received the Perkin Medal for valuable work in applied chemistry in 1936, Priestley Medal in 1947, President's Medal for Merit in 1948, and AIC's Gold Medal in 1949. That same year he was also named AIC honorary fellow. According to a 1947 reader poll by the *Chemical Bulletin,* official organ of the Chicago Section of the American Chemical Society, Dr. Lewis was named one of the "ablest chemists and chemical engineers working in the United States."

Doc Lewis' most important contributions to our country were not things you could see - like World War I gas masks or aviation fuel from fluid bed cracking in World War II - but in the realm of the intangible: Teaching men how to think for themselves and defend their ideas. Former students - many now executives in the petrochemical industries - have printed a booklet "A Dollar to a Doughnut"* to illustrate the stimulating atmosphere of his classes. His influence as a teacher has left his indelible stamp on them.

Hiking and mountain-climbing were Lewis' principal modes of relaxation. On one occasion, the then sexegenarian joined a group planning to take a new and unexplored trek over the White Mountains. As they were about to start, the guide, a very husky young man, turned to Lewis and said that he felt a man of his advanced age was exceedingly foodhardy to attempt the very strenuous assignment ahead of them and recommended strongly that Lewis give up the thought of going along; that if he did insist on going, he would undertake no responsibility for the consequences. Lewis pooh-poohed the young man and proceeded to lead the expedition over the trail and back to camp, at which time the guide praised, "Well, Doc Lewis, when a man of your age can climb mountains the way you did today, and talk all the time while he is doing it, that's something!"

This plucky gentleman married Rosalind D. Kenway in 1909 to become the father of four children. A daughter, Mrs. George L. McFarland, Jr., lives in Salem, Virginia.

*Published by the American Institute of Chemical Engineers.

(Photograph courtesy of Karl Gene.)

WILLARD FRANK LIBBY

Nobel Laureate Willard Libby received many honors for his valuable researches in several fields. He earned the award for discovering carbon-14 (or radiocarbon) and finding a way to use it to determine the age of prehistoric plant and animal remains; that is, he correlated the concentration of carbon-14 in various organic materials with age and developed a dating method that is effective in determining ages up to approximately 50,000 years and a second based on the concentration of tritium. His dating methods proved valuable, particularly in archeology. His book *Radiocarbon Dating*, published in 1952, was followed by a second edition in 1955.

Willard Frank was born on December 17, 1908, at Grand Valley, Colorado, to Edward Ora and Eva May (Rivers) Libby. After completing graduate school at the University of California at Berkeley (B.S., 1931; Ph.D., 1933), he continued on as a professor until such time as the Second World War interrupted his teaching. During this intervening period, he worked under Harold Urey in the War Research Division at Columbia University on the development of the gaseous-diffusion process for separating the isotopes of uranium. In 1945 he became professor of chemistry at the Institute for Nuclear Studies at the University of Chicago. Nine years later, President Dwight D. Eisenhower appointed him to the U. S. Atomic Energy Commission. After serving as a member of the commission for four years, he rejoined the faculty at the University of California - in Los Angeles.

In the late 1950's, he - with Edward Teller - strongly opposed Linus Pauling's petition that radioactive testing be banned. Like Teller, Libby was ideologically committed to the Cold War and one of the chief defenders of nuclear testing. Consequently, ignoring the potential horrors of a nuclear war, the two men set out to prove the world could easily survive if such should occur. To substantiate this contention, with great fanfare Libby built a cheap fallout shelter at his home. A few weeks later, it burned to the ground. This caused nuclear critic Leo Szilard to quip, "This proves not only that there is a God but that he has a sense of humor."

In spite of the great controversy existing between the two nuclear-minded schools of thought, Dr. Libby received many awards and honors in addition to the Nobel Prize. These included: Research Corporation Award, 1951; Chandler Medal, 1954; American Chemical Society Award, 1956; Remsen Memorial lecture award, 1955; City College of New York Bicentennial lecture award, 1956; Elliott

Cresson Medal award, 1957; Willard Gibbs medal, 1958; Albert Einstein award, 1959; Priestley Award, 1959; Day Medal, 1961; California Alumnus of Year award, 1963; Gold Medal, American Institute of Chemists, 1970; and Lehman award, 1971. He was elected to the National Academy of Sciences in 1950 and made a Guggenheim Memorial Foundation fellow in 1941 and 1952. Honorary degrees included Wesleyan University, 1955; University of Dublin, 1957; Syracuse University, 1957; Trinity College, 1957; Carnegie Institute of Technology, 1959; Georgetown University, 1962; Manhattan College, 1963; Newcastle-Upon-Tyne, 1965; Gustavas Adolphus College, 1970; University of South Florida, 1975; and University of Colorado, 1977. He was a member of the American Association for the Advancement of Science, American Chemical Society, American Institute of Chemists, American Institute of Aeronautics and Astronautics, American Physical Society, Phi Beta Kappa, Pi Mu Epsilon, Sigma Xi, and Alpha Chi Sigma.

Daughters Susan Charlotte and Janet Eva are the result of Libby's 1940 marriage to Leonor Hickey. Death came to this great man on September 8, 1980, at Los Angeles.

ROBERT DEAN LUNDBERG

In that almost half of all industrial chemists and chemical engineers work in some phase of the polymer industry, it is not surprising to note that many of AIC's Pioneers have been polymer scientists. So it is with Robert D. Lundberg, 1986 awardee, who was cited for his pioneering studies of ionically associating polymers and for the discovery of the unique properties of sulfonated ethylene propylene terpolymers (EPDM).

Robert was born in Valley City, North Dakota, on May 30, 1928. After serving his country in the U. S. Marines from 1946 to 1948, he returned to school to graduate in 1950. Thereafter, he entered Harvard, where he received his B.A., M.S. and Ph.D. degrees under the guidance of Paul M. Doty. He then joined Union Carbide Chemical

Company, where he held positions as group leader of exploratory polymer research (1957-1967) and the next two years as group head of polymer research. In 1969 he accepted a position as group head of polymer science for Exxon Research Engineering Company, where he is now group head of dispersants and polymer science of Exxon's Paramins Technical Division. With coworkers at Exxon, he sulfonated EPDM and produced a new type of ionic elastomer.

Dr. Lundberg has co-authored four papers with Professor Doty and three with Fred E. Bailey. He and E. F. Cox co-authored a chapter in a book published by Marcel Dekker which describes the commercialization of polycaprolactone at Union Carbide. Of his more than sixty-five technical articles, five deal with polylactones. Dr. Lundberg has also been awarded over one hundred fifty patents by the U. S. Patent Office.

Robert is a fellow of the American Institute of Chemical Engineers, and a member of the American Chemical Society and the New York Academy of Science. He and wife Patricia, whom he married in 1953, have two children, Michael and Barbara.

ROBERT V. MacALLISTER

The most abundant of the ketoses is D-fructose, which occurs naturally in fruit juices and honey and may be obtained by the hydrolysis of inulin from Jerusalem artichokes, golden rod, dandelions, dahlias and chicory. Invert sugar, a mixture containing equal quantities of D-fructose and D-glucose, is obtained when cane or beet sugar (sucrose) is hydrolyzed by acids or invertase (sucrase). Prior to 1957, sucrose, glucose, corn syrup and invert sugar were the dominant nutritive sweeteners in this country and attempts to convert glucose to fructose by base-catalyzed isomerization produced inferior products. Then in 1971, Takasaki and Tanabe patented the use of a specific strain of *streptomyces* as an enzyme for the isomerization of D-xylose (aldopentose) to D-xylulose (a ketopentose). Under the direction of Robert MacAllister, the Clinton Corn Processing Company learned how to efficiently use this enzyme to convert corn syrup to very high quality fructose corn syrup.

Original high fructose corn syrup contained about thirty percent fructose. Under MacAllister's direction, fructose was increased to forty-two percent by using an enzyme absorbed on a solid. He was able to increase the fructose content of his high fructose corn syrup to ninety percent by elution in a column containing a calcium-form ion-exchange resin. The largest demand, nevertheless, is for a high fructose corn syrup containing fifty-five percent fructose, which product accounts for over thirty percent of the U.S. nutritive sweetener market - and this percentage is increasing.

Robert was born in Clinton, Iowa, on Valentine's Day 1913 to Wallace A. and Jessimum M. (Gray) MacAllister. He attended Clinton public schools and enrolled in Wartburg College (B.A. chemistry, 1934). After graduating, he spent eight years as a research chemist at the Clinton Corn Processing Company. He then went on to obtain his doctorate in chemistry-chemical engineering from the California Institute of Technology (1949). For the next twelve years, he worked as a research chemist and director of chemical research for General Foods Corporation at Tarrytown, New York. In 1961, he returned to Clinton as research director. Since his retirement in 1978, he has been a consultant and a mathematics instructor at Mt. St. Clare College.

Dr. MacAllister, who was awarded the AIC Chemical Pioneer Award in 1984, is a fellow of the American Institute of Chemists and a member of the American Chemical Society, Sigma Xi, the Iowa Academy of Sciences, and Rotary International. His other honors include the Putnam Food Award (1971) and the Poverello

Award from Mt. St. Clare College (1984). He has published many scientific reports and been awarded twelve patents by the U. S. Patent Office.

Bob married Alice Chekal in 1939.

ALAN GRAHAM MacDIARMID

It was Philadelphian Benjamin Franklin who in 1747 developed the principle of conservation of charge, i.e., the theory that the total quantity of electricity in amber or other insulators is constant. More recently, another Philadelphian - Alan Graham MacDiarmid - investigated the conductivity of polymers of sulfur nitride, acetylene and aniline to find that these polymers - now called "synthetic metals" - are good conductors of electricity.

Dr. MacDiarmid has shown that the conductivity of conjugated polymers such as polyacetylene is dependent on intra and interchain charge transport proceses and that the conductivity of trans polyacetylene is increased when it is partially oxidized (p-doped) or partially reduced (n-doped). He has used sodium and potassium as n-dopants and arsenic pentofluoride as a p-dopant.

Alan has also made rechargeable batteries from "polyaniline" produced by the oxidation of aniline; the conductivity of this conductor is increased by simple acid-base interactions as dopants.   He has proposed the production of rechargeable flashlight batteries by replacing the conventional manganese dioxide by "polyaniline."

Born in Masterton, New Zealand, on April 14, 1927, Alan received his B.S. (1948) and M.S. (1950) degrees from the University of New Zealand. He continued graduate studies as a Fulbright Scholar at the University of Wisconsin to receive a second M.S. (1952) and Ph.D. (1953). Acceptance of a Shell fellowship at the University of Cambridge earned him a second Ph.D. (1955). For the next six months, he served as assistant lecturer at the University of St. Andrews in Scotland. Thereafter, he accepted a faculty position at the University of Pennsylvania where he has been a full professor since 1964.

Dr. MacDiarmid was made AIC's Chemical Pioneer in 1984. Other tokens of esteem include the Centenary Medal of the Royal Society of Chemistry, England (1983), Madison Marshall Award of the North Alabama ACS Section (1982), Arthur K. Doolittle Award for best paper (1982), ACS Frederich Stanley Kipping Award (1970), and Philadelphia ACS Section Award (1967); an honorary D.Sc. from Pennsylvania's Elizabethtown College (1983) and an honorary M.A. from the University of Pennsylvania (1972). He has served as a guest lecturer at the University of Karlsruhe (1972), Kyoto University (1975), and Hebrew University of Jerusalem (1983); and was a Robert A. Welch Foundation Lecturer in 1981 and an ASEA Centenary Lecturer in Sweden in 1983.

This AIC fellow is also a member of Alpha Chi Sigma, Phi Lambda Upsilon, Sigma Xi, the Chemical Society and American Chemical Society. He served as chairman of ACS's Inorganic Division (1975), as its national councilor from the Philadlephia Section (1979-81), and on advisory committees for the National Research Council. Editor-in-chief of a four-volume monograph series on *Organometallic Compounds of Group IV Elements* and of *Inorganic Syntheses,* he has also served on the editorial boards or editorial advisory boards of *Synthesis in Inorganic and Metal-Organic Chemistry, Journal of Inorganic and Nuclear Chemistry, Inorganic Methods and Reactions,* and *Monatshefte für Chemie.* Moreover, he has authored or co-authored approximately 270 scientific reports and been awarded numerous U. S. patents.

Alan and Marian, whom he married in 1954, have four children: Heather S., Dawn F., Duncan C., and Gail R.

(Photograph courtesy of State of Florida, Department of Citrus.)

LOUIS GARDNER MacDOWELL

Orange juice, which has been called the Cinderella product of the Florida citrus industry, is unique. Unlike juices such as tomato, pineapple and grape, which are consumed as canned or bottled juices, orange juice is usually consumed as fresh juice and the consumer is well aware of its unique flavor. The first attempts by the U. S. Department of Agriculture to produce frozen concentrated orange juice by a low temperature vacuum evaporation process were only moderately successful; the color and flavor were satisfactory, but the reconstituted juice lacked the aroma and zip associated with fresh orange juice. Hence, attempts to export frozen orange juice in the 1930's were unsuccessful because the consumer knew the true taste of fresh orange juice. Likewise, concentrated orange juice, consumed by expectant and nursing mothers as a source of Vitamin C during the second world war, served more as a medicine than a beverage.

We who live in northern climates of this country can thank Louis Gardner MacDowell for the opportunity to enjoy an abundant supply of fresh or concentrated orange juice. Because of MacDowell's ingenuity in over-concentrating orange juice and then diluting it with fresh juice to a preselected concentration before freezing, frozen orange juice is now widely accepted.

Louis was born in Asbury Park, New Jersey, on July 29, 1912, to Louis G. and Emma B. MacDowell. After completing high school in Melbourne, Florida, he entered the University of Florida where he received his B.S. (1933) and Ph.D. (1936) degrees in chemistry. For the next six years he was with Union Carbide. He was a consultant for the U. S. Quartermaster Corps (1942-1945) and became the Research Director for the Florida Citrus Commission in 1942.

A life fellow of the American Institute of Chemists, Dr. MacDowell was named Chemical Pioneer in 1978. He was a member of the American Chemical Society and Institute of Food Technologists.

MacDowell, who is now deceased, married Helen Gartelman in 1936. Their children are: Sheila, Julie, and Kathleen. His hobbies were gardening, hunting and fishing.

HERMAN FRANCIS MARK

"Mark, the perfect man and behold the upright."
This Biblical verse* could be paraphrased to describe
nonagenarian Herman Mark, who is still upright and not far
from perfect. Moreover, he continues to work at a pace
which would tire many younger men. According to Dr.
Eric S. Proskauer, editor-in-chief of Interscience
Publishers, Inc., "Mark's secret is that he is such a skillful
juggler of projects that he can keep a dozen projects going
at once without seeming to bear the full weight of any one
of them." Herman is also blessed with the faculty of total
recall so that he does not have to waste time looking up
what he has previously read or heard. He can also read and

*Psalm XIX, verse 37.

listen simultaneously and remember both the written and the spoken word.

Dr. Mark, who played a major role in the development of polymer science, has the rare ability to make the complex appear simple and to reduce confusion in fields of adolescent sciences. This uncanny ability was demonstrated in his plenary lecture "Degradation of Polymers in Hostile Environments" before the 1982 Kansas City ACS symposium. Those who listened to Professor Mark's lecture could not help but conclude that the science of polymer degradation in the presence of corrosives is a mature science and one in which most problems would be solved in the near future.

The title *Geheimrat* (meaning *privy councilor*) was jokingly bestowed upon Herman on the occasion of his sixtieth birthday (in 1955). Herman's son, Hans, stated "Our Geheimrat is just the opposite" of the official title, which was formerly given to distinguished professors, usually "stuffed shirts," by Germany's Kaisers.

The eldest of three children, Herman was born in Vienna on May 3, 1895. His father Herman Carl was a physician; his mother was Lili Mueller. Son Herman was an outstanding athlete. He played tennis and soccer at the Theresienische Academie and often would run ten times around the cinder track before running the two miles to his family's five-room apartment. His interest in chemistry was kindled at the age of ten when he was given a tour of the laboratories at the University of Vienna by a playmate whose father was a professor of chemical technology. Later the two boys set up a chemical laboratory in Herman's bedroom.

At the age of eighteen, Herman volunteered for the Kaiserschutzen Regiment, an elite Alpine unit. He was shipped to South Tyrol where he enjoyed skiing, mountain climbing and other phases of army life. He survived the first battles of his unit at Lbon and Przemyst on the Russian front where eighty-five percent of his unit was killed, wounded or taken prisoner. Later, he was wounded in the ankle by shrapnel; after receiving a chestful of decorations for bravery, he was shipped back to a hospital in Vienna. Following his recovery, he was sent to the Italian front. Promoted to the rank of lieutenant, he led his 300 men in a successful counterattack of a ridge known as Zugna Torta, for which he was awarded the Leopold Order. Later forced to surrender at Acquanina, he was interned in a requisitioned convent at Monopoli where he became fluent in Italian, French and English. Herman escaped from the camp to return to Vienna to visit his seriously ill father.

Following the war, Herman commenced studies at the University of Vienna and two years later received his doctorate Summa Cum Laude under the direction of Professor W. Schlenk. Thereafter, he spent one year as chemistry instructor at the University of Berlin and four years as a research fellow at the Kaiser Wilhelm Institut für Faserstoff-Chemie in Berlin-Dahlem. He then accepted a position with I. G. Farben Industrie in Ludwigshafen, simultaneously holding an associate professorship at the Technical University in Karlsruhe.

Herman married Marie (Mimi) Schramek in 1922. Because of his Jewish lineage, in 1938 he and his family escaped from Germany through Switzerland. He joined Brooklyn's Polytechnic Institute* as "advanced professor" in 1940 and two years later was made full professor. In 1961 he was promoted to Dean of Faculty and is now Dean and Professor Emeritus.

*Now Polytechnic Institute of New York.

Dr. Mark is a fellow of AIC and the American Academy of Arts and Sciences, a member of the National Academy of Sciences and over fifty other academies and societies. He was named a Pioneer in Polymer Science by *Polymer News*, received AIC's Honor Scroll and made Chemical Pioneer in 1972. His other honors include: the Harrison Howe Award, Nichols Medal, Polymer Chemistry Award, Willard Gibbs Medal, Borden Plastics and Coatings Award from the ACS, Perkin Medal from the Society of Chemical Industry, International Award from the Society of Plastics Engineers, and the National Medal of Science. His more than twenty honorary doctoral degrees include those by the University of Vienna and the Polytechnic Institute of Brooklyn.

Herman has authored at least five hundred publications and more than twenty books. He initiated the *Journal of Polymer Science* and related journals and still serves as their editor. He was also founder and editor of the *Encyclopedia of Polymer Science and Technology*.

Herman lost his wife in 1980. They had two sons. Peter, a Ph.D. physicist, passed away in 1975. Son Hans, also a Ph.D. physicist, formerly with the Massachusetts Institute of Technology, is serving as chancellor of the University of Texas at Austin. Hans and his wife, Marion G. (Thorpe), whom he married in 1951, are parents of Jane H. and James P.

CARL SHIPP MARVEL

Carl Shipp Marvel, who is affectionately known as "Speed," has touched the lives of numerous chemists, both in their collegiate and industrial careers.

Carl was advised by his uncle to study chemistry if he intended to continue the family farming tradition. Accordingly, Carl enrolled at Illinois Wesleyan University. There Carl was fortunate in having an inspirational and dedicated Professor Homberger who emphasized descriptive chemistry and even questioned the usefulness of some chemical theories being taught to other graduate students. During his junior year, Carl synthesized sixty-five organic compounds by developing a "library of smells"; in other words, his nose was his "spectroscope" to record the odor of every available organic compound.

Professor Homberger was responsible for Carl's sidelining his farming career. For once he had obtained his B.S. and M.S. degrees, he was awarded a $250.00 yearly scholarship at the University of Illinois. With his background in chemistry and his "library of smells," it seems reasonable to expect that Carl would have been on firm ground. Such was not the case, however. The dean of the graduate school, Dr. David Kinley, was shocked at the young man's deficiency in chemistry and assigned him an overload of chemistry courses so that he might "make the grade." Carl managed to keep up with his colleagues by working in the laboratory until late in the evening and returning to the laboratory in the morning before the 7:30 breakfast deadline, which meant he had to run from the laboratory to the dining hall to get there before the doors closed. Some say that was the origin of his nickname.

Carl's professor of qualitative organic analysis, Oliver Kamm, who wrote the book used in quality organic analysis, was impressed by the short cuts the young man was able to make through the use of his library of smells. But it was Roger Adams who, rightly impressed with Carl's abilities, was responsible for Carl remaining in graduate school. After receipt of his doctorate in 1920, Carl stayed on at the university, retiring as full professor of chemistry in 1961. He then joined the faculty at the University of Arizona where he was active until his death in January of 1988 at the age of 93.

During his career at Illinois, Carl synthesized amino acids and organic metallic compounds, which investigations were described in his first seventy publications. He became a polymer chemist through a series of unpredictable events. In 1929, under Carl's direction, one of his graduate students, M. E. P. Friedrich, investigated arsenic compounds. Friedrich reacted lithiumalkyl with an arsonium compound and obtained a solid instead of the expected gaseous ethylene. Dr. Marvel then attempted to characterize what he would discover to be linear polyethylene (HDPE).

Not only did Carl supply his former student Wallace Carothers with a more economical adipic acid, but in the early 1930's he also investigated the copolymer of alpha olefins and sulfur dioxide, the structure of vinyl polymers, and (during the second world war) studied the effect of chain transfer agents on emulsion polymerization of butadiene and styrene. In the late 1950's, he turned his attention to heat resistant polymers which were needed for the space age. His seven decades of research efforts resulted in over five hundred scientific articles, four books and fifty-two U. S. patents. Morever, he directed the research of over one hundred seventy-five doctoral candidates who are now numbered among the nations leading polymer chemists.

Dr. Marvel was awarded AIC's Gold Medal in 1955 and Chemical Pioneer Award in 1970 and was named a Pioneer in Polymer Science by *Polymer News* in 1979. His other tokens of esteem are: Nichols Medal from the New York Section of ACS (1944), Willard Gibbs Medal from the Chicago Section of ACS (1950), Priestley Medal (1956), ACS Award in Polymer Chemistry (1964), Society of Plastics Engineers International Award in Plastics Science and Engineering (1964), Perkin Medal of the Society of the Chemical Industry (1965), Madison Marshall Award from the North Alabama Section of ACS (1966), Air Force Materials Laboratory Distinguished Service Award (1966), Air Force Systems Command Award for Outstanding Achievement (1966), John R. Kuebler Award from Alpha Chi Sigma (1970), ACS Award in Chemistry and Plastics Coatings (1973), Alumni Achievement Award from the University of Illinois (1976), Certificate of

Honorary Membership in the Illinois State Academy of Science (1977), University of Arizona Foundation for Creative Science Award (1978); ACS Division of Chemistry Award (1978), and ACS San Francisco Recognition Award for forty years of service as a council member. He has also been awarded honorary degrees by his alma mater (1946), University of Louvain (Belgium) (1970), University of Illinois (1963), and Polytechnic Institute of New York (1983).

In addition to the many seminars he has presented, he has given the following name lectures: Foster Lecture, University of Buffalo (1937); Edgar Fahs Smith Memorial Lecture, Philadelphia Section ACS (1948); Frank Burnett Dains Memorial Lecture at the University of Kansas (1949); American Swiss Foundation Lectures in Basel, Zürich, Geneva and Bern (1951); S. C. Lind Lectureship Series of the Eastern Tennessee Section of ACS (1985); and Julius Stieglitz Memorial Lecture, Chicago Section ACS (1973).

Dr. Marvel was a fellow of the American Institute of Chemists, New York Academy and American Association for the Advancement of Science, and a member of the National Academy of Science, American Academy of Arts and Sciences, American Chemical Society, American Philosophical Society, Phi Beta Kappa, Phi Lambda Upsilon, Phi Kappa Phi, Gamma Alpha, Alpha Chi Sigma, Omega Beta Pi, and Tau Kappa Epsilon.

Carl married Alberta Hughes in 1933. They have two children, Mary Katherine and John Hughes. John, who has shared the prestigious Charles A. Thomas and Carroll A. Hochwalt Awards* with Melvin L. Rueppel, is General Manager of the Research Division of Monsanto's

*These awards, which carry $25,000 and a silver medallion, were named to honor Hochwalt and AIC Medallist Thomas.

Agricultural Products Company. His development of analytical techniques to quantify metabolites resulting from herbicide applications make possible the determination of the structure of these metabolites using extremely small doses of pesticides.

Dr. Marvel's books *Unusual Feeding Habits of a Cape May Warbler* (1928) and *The Blue Grossbeck in Western Ontario* (1950) are just as well accepted by the 400,000 members of the Audubon Society as have been his articles on chemistry. Not only was Carl a leader for the ornithologists, but he will continue to be a leader for all polymer research scientists.

ORVILLE EDWARD MAY

*"One Sunday morning at daylight, he
arrived at Rocky Creek Public Golf Course in
Washington. After the usual two hour wait,
his foursome teed off. The third hole is a par
three. Orville took a mighty swing. The ball
went high and true, landed on the green and
rolled into the hole. Orville left the ball in
the hole, picked up his clubs and went
home. He has never played (golf) since. He
had done his best. He had seen the top of
the mountain as he had done so many times
in so many different ways before and since."**

*William J. Sparks in describing May's experience with golf.

Some scientists are blessed with attractive personalities, good will and love for their friends and colleagues. Some scientists are talented and creative in research. A few scientists are skilled in motivating others and in organizing and managing large organizations. In that Orville May had all of these talents and good qualities, he was admired and loved by his many, many friends and associates.

May started his research career in 1923 as a chemist for the U. S. Department of Agriculture in the Bureau of Chemistry and Soils near Washington, D.C., that is, across the Potomac River in Arlington, Virginia. Working days, he studied for his advanced degrees at night. At the Bureau, he was the leader of a group that worked, with emphasis on fermentations, to find new industrial uses for farm crops. His principal areas of expertise were mold fermentations; biochemistry of molds; submerged mold fermentations; processing and utilization of agricultural products; flavors and beverages; and organization, direction, and administration of research and development. Unusually successful in selecting and training scientists, Dr. May surrounded himself with competent scientists, which was fortunate for him since competent scientists and research managers were in particular demand at the time the four USDA Regional Research Centers were established.

Some of the scientists in May's Arlington Farm Laboratory helped plan the programs of the four new research centers, and many of these men were given important positions in them. It is appropriate to mention that Dr. Percy A. Wells, because of his outstanding work at the Arlington laboratory, was selected at the age of thirty-four to be Director of the Eastern Regional Research Center in Philadelphia. At Arlington, under Wells' immediate supervision and May's general direction, a group of microbiologists had developed valuable new techniques and conducted research that led to several commercialized developments, such as "steep liquor," a byproduct of corn wet-milling, which is an inexpensive and highly effective nutrient for fermentations in general.

May's sterling performance as a scientist and research administrator at the Arlington laboratory did not go unnoticed. In 1936 he was made director of the new Regional Soybean Industrial Products Laboratory in Urbana, Illinois, in which position he remained until 1939 when he was appointed Director of the new and large Northern Regional Research Center in Peoria. With May at the helm, his microbiologists used steep liquor, Arlington Farm techniques, and a microorganism found in a rotten Peoria cantelope to develop the first feasible method for manufacturing penicillin. In 1942, May was made research coordinator for the USDA's Agricultural Research Administration in Washington, D.C. Two years later, he was promoted Chief of the Bureau of Agricultural and Industrial Chemistry, in which position he administered all the post harvest research for the USDA.

Having served the USDA with distinction for twenty-three years, May joined the Coca-Cola Company in Atlanta, Georgia. In this position of vice president, which he held until his retirement in 1966, May was in charge of research, quality control, and the development of new commercial products. As "keeper of the secret" composition of Coca-Cola, his photograph and responsibilities were reported in *FORTUNE* magazine. During the May era in Atlanta, new and successful products were manufactured and the Coca-Cola Company grew in both size and profitability.

Dr. May received AIC's prestigious Gold Medal in 1968 and was made an honorary fellow. With the following words, the late and great Senator Everett M. Dirkson commented on these honors in a letter to one of May's friends: "I know personally that this high honor to Orville May is well deserved and I find great pleasure in recalling our collaboration in developing the Northern Regional Laboratory dedicated to making science useful to people."

May was a member of many organizations, including the American Chemical Society, American Oil Chemists Society, American Institute of Chemists, Institute of Food Technology, American Public Health Association, American Association for the Advancement of Science, Cosmos Club in Washington, D.C., Capital City Club in Atlanta, Alpha Chi Sigma, Phi Lambda Upsilon, and Sigma Xi.

Born in New Albin, Iowa, on August 22, 1901, to George B. and Frances M. (Dailey) May, Orville was educated at Loras College, University of Minnesota, and George Washington University (A.B., 1924; M.S., 1926; Ph.D., 1929). He married Katherine Marie Barrett in 1926; their two children are Elaine Marie and George Barrett. He and his wife were charming hosts and dispensed delightful hospitality in their home, at the Cosmos Club and at the Capital City Club. Orville's death, which followed that of his wife, occurred in 1981 in Atlanta.

HENRY GEORGE McGRATH, JR.

The use of farmyard manure for its nitrogen content in agriculture is as old as agriculture itself. Man's dependence on manure, which was alleviated to a small extent by the use of sodium and potassium nitrate, led to the neo-Malthusianism movement, which was based on the belief of Thomas Robert Malthus that "the power of population is indefinitely greater than the power of the earth to produce subsistence for Man." Nineteenth century chemists recognized that agricultural needs could be improved by fixation of nitrogen. This was accomplished by Nobel Laureate Fritz Haber, who combined nitrogen and hydrogen under pressure, in the presence of a catalyst to produce ammonia. It was Karl Bosch who "scaled up" this laboratory process to full plant scale. The ammonia, unfortunately, was used by

Germany during the first world war to make munitions - and thereby prolonged the war; its discoverer, Haber, fled Germany in 1933 to escape the anti-Semitic barbarism of the Nazi regime.

Another Nobel Laureate, Friedrich Karl Rudolph Bergius, extended the Haber technique to the high pressure hydrogenation of coal for the production of gasoline. A second process, conducted at a lower pressure, was that of Fischer and Tropsch, i.e., "the gasoline to coal" process; likewise used commercially in Germany for coal conversion to liquid fuel, which process allowed Hitler to prolong the second world war.

Since that time, contributions to both the Haber-Bosch and the Fischer-Tropsch processes were made by Henry George McGrath, Jr., who received the American Institute of Chemists' Pioneer Award in 1977 for his pioneering role in the development of the modern synthetic ammonia process and for the conversion of coal to gasoline.

Henry was born in Lawrence, Massachusetts, on March 30, 1915, to Henry George and Marion (Poore) McGrath. He received his B.S. and M.S. degrees from the Massachusetts Institute of Technology in 1936 and 1937, respectively, under the direction of Professor Edwin R. Gilliland. He then joined the M. W. Kellogg Company where he held positions of increasing responsibility before leaving as Vice President in 1971. From 1972 to 1975, he served as Director of Processes for UOP in Des Plaines, Illinois. From 1976 to 1983, he was Senior Staff Engineer for TRW Systems and Energy Division in McLean, Virginia; he has been a consultant for them since his retirement.

McGrath's initial research efforts at Kellogg were

related to the catalytic conversion of paraffins and naphthenes to aromatics, such as toluene and xylenes. Later he worked on the production of synthetic fuels and chemicals from coal. This investigation resulted in construction of the world's largest synthetic fuel plant (Sassol) near Johannesburg, South Africa, which converts indigenous subbituminous coal to liquid hydrocarbons. Henry also was involved in the development and design of the world's first commercial catalytic reforming plant for the conversion of naphtha to aromatics and the development of plants for the production of ethylene from naphtha and gas-oil feedstocks. His high pressure steam-hydrocarbon reforming process, which was applied to the synthesis of ammonia in 1953, is rated as the most outstanding development in ammonia process technology since the invention of the Haber-Bosch process.

McGrath, who has published several scientific reports and been granted over forty U. S. patents, has presented lectures on his developments in Canada, France, Turkey, Spain, England and the United States. He was editor of *Origin and Refining of Petroleum*, published by the American Chemical Society in its Symposium series.

A life fellow of the American Institute of Chemists, he is a member of the American Institute of Chemical Engineers, The American Petroleum Institute, Chemical Marketing Research Association, and American Chemical Society. He served as president and secretary of the World Congress of the American section of Société de Chimie Industrielle. A licensed professional engineer in the state of New York, he was also president of the MIT Club of New Jersey.

Henry married Mildred Ragan in 1940. They have two daughters, Caroline and Sallie.

ANDREW WILLIAM MELLON

Andrew, elder son of Judge Thomas and Sarah Jane (Negley) Mellon, was born in Pittsburgh on March 24, 1855. The future financier, industrialist, public official, and philanthropist, received his formal education at the Western University of Pennsylvania* as a member of the class of 1873. On leaving college, he organized a lumber business with his brother Richard. Soon the two men were working with their father to build a huge and successful industrial empire based largely on coal, coke, iron, oil and aluminum enterprises.

In 1911, the late Dr. Robert Kennedy Duncan inaugurated his now famous research procedure - the

*Now the University of Pittsburgh.

industrial fellowship system - in the Department of Industrial Research at the University of Pittsburgh. Andrew and Richard noted the practical success of this educational experiment and saw the soundness of the method of benefiting American industry as a whole by studying manufacturing problems under suitable conditions and by training young scientists for technical service. As a result of this interest, they founded the Mellon Institute of Industrial Research in 1913 and placed the industrial fellowship system on a permanent basis. The affairs of the institution, which was incorporated in 1927, are managed by its board of directors, of which the Mellon brothers were members. Their continued financial support made it possible to develop the industrial fellowship system to a strong position in science and technology.

In 1921 Andrew resigned as President of the Mellon National Bank and as an executive or director of various financial and industrial corporations to become our Secretary of the Treasury. He held this position until 1932 under Presidents Harding, Coolidge and Hoover. While Secretary, Andrew worked to decrease taxes and surtaxes; from 1920 to 1930 he reduced the national debt from $24.298 billions to $16.185. In 1932 he became Ambassador to Great Britain.

The Mellon brothers gave large sums of money in support of health, education and science. Their establishment of the Mellon Institute was representative of their support of research. For their major contributions, the American Institute of Chemists presented them with the Gold Medal in 1931 and honorary fellowship in 1949.

Andrew was trustee of several organizations, including the Carnegie Institute of Pittsburgh, Carnegie Institute of Washington, University of Pittsburgh, and

Pennsylvania College for Women. He was a member of the Council, National Industrial Conference Board; a member of the Board of Managers of the Kingsley Association; and director of the Tuberculosis League of Pittsburgh. During the first world war, he was a member of the Executive Committee in Pennsylvania of the Council of National Defense, a member of the National War Work Finance Committee of the Red Cross, chairman of the War Fund Campaign Committee for Western Pennsylvania, a member of the Advisory Committee of the National Research Council of Washington, a member of the Federal Reserve Board, the Farm Loan Board, and the U. S. Section of the Pan-American High Commission, and director-general of the U. S. Railroad Administration. He had conferred upon him the honorary degree of LL.D. from the Universities of Pittsburgh, Princeton, Columbia, Dartmouth, Rutgers College, and the Pennsylvania Military College. A lifelong art collector, Andrew gave works valued at $35 million, together with $15 million in cash, to found the National Gallery of Art in 1937.

Andrew's 1900 marriage to Nora McMullen produced a son and daughter. Paul, born June 11, 1907, was educated at Yale. Daughter Alisa married David K. E. Bruce of Baltimore. In 1937, at the age of eighty-two, Mellon died in Southampton, New York.

RICHARD BEATTY MELLON

Richard Mellon was president and director of the Mellon National Bank, president and director of the Burrell Improvement Company, president of the Pennsylvania Water Company, president of the Pittsburgh Clearing House Association, president of the Trafford Water Company, vice president of the Union Savings Bank, vice president of the Union Trust Company and president and secretary of the Ligonier Valley Railroad Company. He was a director of the Children's Hospital of Pittsburgh, Federal Reserve Bank of Cleveland, Guaranty Trust Company of New York, National Union Fire Insurance Company, St. Lawrence Securities Company, Tuberculosis League (also treasurer), Union Fidelity and Insurance Company of Pittsburgh, Union Improvement Company (also treasurer and secretary), Union Savings Bank, Union Trust Company of Pittsburgh, Wilkinsburg Bank, Workingman's Savings Bank and Trust Company, and the Allegheny Country Club; a trustee of the University of Pittsburgh, Mellon Institute, Carnegie Institute, and Carnegie Institute of Technology; and a member of the Executive Committee of the Citizen's Committee on City Planning of Pittsburgh. He was also a member of the Duquesne, Union, Pittsburgh Golf, and Allegheny Country Clubs. The University of Pennsylvania conferred the honorary LL.D. degree upon him.

Richard and Andrew were the prime leaders in making successful the development of the Aluminum Company of America, Carborundum Company, Gulf Oil Corporation, Koppers Company, Pittsburgh Coal Company, Pittsburgh Plate Glass Company, and Union Ship Building Company. They were strong supporters of worthy causes, including science. Their establishment of the Mellon Institute for Industrial Research, which is a good example of their support of research, helped to bring them jointly the Gold Medal of the American Institute of Chemists in 1931.

Richard was born on March 19, 1858. He married Jennie King, daughter of Alexander and Sarah Cordelia (Smith) King. Their children are Sarah Cordelia (Mrs. Alan M. Scaife) and Richard King Mellon. Richard passed away on December 1, 1933.

(Photograph courtesy of Dr. Richard W. Jackson)

LAFAYETTE BENEDICT MENDEL

The early researches of the distinguished physiological chemist, Lafayette Mendel, were concerned with the biochemistry of compounds such as creatine, choline, taurine, the purines, nitrogen metabolism, the formation of uric acid, excretion paths of certain inorganic ions, and the metabolism of iodine, allantoin, kynurenic acid, pyrimidines, and purines. He is well known for his research on nutrition, which started in 1905, in collaboration with Thomas B. Osborne. Over one hundred papers describing their joint works were published. Their studies of the proteins of the castor bean, including toxic albumin ricin, proved ricin fatal to rabbits at a dosage of two one-thousands of a milligram per kilogram.   Morover, much new and valuable information was obtained on the relation between diet and health.   Nutrition during Mendel's lifetime was transformed from empiricism into a branch of biochemistry based upon scientific principles.   The practical value of his research has been enormous.

The elder of two boys, Lafayette was born on Febuary 5, 1872, in Delhi, New York, to Benedict, a merchant, and Pauline (Ullman) Mendel, both of whom migrated to this country from Germany.   In 1887 young Mendel obtained a New York State scholarship by competitive examination and entered Yale, where he studied mainly the classics, economics, and humanities. Upon graduation in 1891, he was awarded a fellowship and embarked upon a graduate course in physiological chemistry under Russell H. Chittenden of the Sheffield Scientific School.   Two years later he completed his Ph.D. requirements, his thesis being the proteolyis of the crystalline hempseed protein edestin.   This work aroused his interest in protein chemistry, and especially in the properties of the protein of plant seeds.   In the fall in 1893, Mendel joined the teaching staff of the Sheffield Laboratory of Physiological Chemistry.   In 1895, he took a year's leave of absence to study in Germany: Physiology at Breslau with R. Heidenhain and chemistry at Freiburg im Breisgau with E. Baumann.   In 1897 he was appointed assistant professor at Sheffield; in 1903 he was made a full professor of physiological chemistry.   He left Sheffield in 1921 to become Sterling professor of physiological chemistry at Yale.

Mendel directed the activities of many graduate students, giving special attention to the chemistry and metabolism of fats and to the regulation of blood volume by the supply of fats.   He was frequently invited to give lectures and to serve as a consultant to his medical colleagues and to the food industry. Approachable, kindly and ready with suggestions for the solution of practical problems or with helpful reference to the literature, he was remembered by his students with affection and respect. His influence upon science at Yale and especially upon the medical applications of nutrition was tremendous.

The American Institute of Chemists presented Dr. Mendel with the Gold Medal in 1927 ". . . for meritorious work in academic service."

Lafayette Mendel passed away on December 9, 1935.

EDWIN THEODORE MERTZ

While more than two hundred amino acids have been characterized, less than forty of these are present in proteins.   In 1914, T. B. Osborne and L. B. Mendel demonstrated that the amino acids tryptophan and lysine were essential components of the diet of rats and presumably also of humans.   That another amino acid, histidine, was also an essential component of the diet of animals was demonstrated a few years later by H. Ackroyd, F. G. Hopkins, W. C. Rose and G. J. Cox.   These investigations were continued by Dr. Rose and his students, who fed mixtures of amino acids to rats in order to determine what other amino acids were essential in the diet.   Professor Rose and co-workers, which included Edwin Theodore Mertz, discovered that a new amino acid, threonine, was also essential or indispensible.   This list of amino acids in rats was eventually extended to ten essentials, viz, phenylalanine, arginine, leucine, lysine, tryptophan, threonine, histidine, isoleucine, valine, and methionine. Rose was then able to extend his studies to humans.

Professor Mertz spent much of his career studying the amino acid requirements of animals and humans, the purification of clot-dissolving plasminogens, and the biochemistry of mental retardation. He was the leader of a research team at Purdue that discovered a type of corn with a high lysine content - for it had been discovered that cereal grains, such as wheat, rice and corn, are deficient in lysine, and that small quantities of lysine must be added to these cereals to insure a complete source of essential amino acids. Mertz has also worked on the development of other high lysine cereal grains.

Edwin was born in Missoula, Montana, on December 6, 1909, the third of five children of Reverend Gustav H. Mertz, a Lutheran minister, and his wife Louise (Sain) Mertz. After completing high school in 1927, he entered the University of Montana at Missoula where he earned his tuition by playing the piano in a dance band. He was awarded the B.S. degree in 1931. Graduate research was conducted at the University of Illinois under Professor Rose (M.S., 1933; Ph.D., 1935).

The next two years were spent as a research biochemist for Armour Company in Chicago. He then returned to the University of Illinois to teach for one year as an instructor in biochemistry. From 1938 to 1940 he was a research associate in pathology at the Medical School at the University of Iowa where he investigated the clotting of blood. It was then he became an instructor in agricultural chemistry at the University of Missouri where his research was devoted to investigations of a strain of swine which was afflicted with von Willebrand's disease - a

disease similar to hemophilia.   In 1943 he worked for
Hercules Powder Company as a research chemist and in
1946 accepted a position as Assistant Professor of
Biochemistry at Purdue. He has been a Professor Emeritus
at Purdue since 1976, which was also the year he served as a
Visiting Professor of Chemistry at the University of Notre
Dame.   Since 1977 he has been a consultant in the
Agronomy Department at Purdue, and since 1983 a
consultant to the editor and publisher of *The Saturday
Evening Post.*

The American Institute of Chemists named Dr.
Mertz Chemical Pioneer in 1976. In addition to this award,
he has also received: McCoy Award from Purdue (1967),
John Scott Award in Philadelphia (1967), Hoblitzelle
Award, Texas Research Foundation (1968), Congressional
Medal, Federal Land Banks (1968), ACS Spencer Award
(1970), Osborne-Mendel Award of the American Institute
of Nutrition (1972), and Edward W. Browning Award,
American Society of Agromony (1974).   He was also
awarded the Doctor of Agriculture degree from Purdue in
1976 and received an honorary doctoral degree from his
alma mater in 1979.   He is a fellow of AIC and the
American Association for the Advancement of Science, a
member of the National Academy of Sciences, American
Chemical Society, American Society of Biological
Chemists, American Institute of Nutrition, American
Association of Cereal Chemists, American Society of
Animal Sciences, Sigma Xi and Phi Beta Kappa. Dr. Mertz
has to his credit at least 130 scientific reports and two U. S.
patents.

Edwin's 1936 marriage to Mary Ellen Ruskamp
produced Martha Ellen and Edwin T. Mertz, Jr. His wife
died of cancer in 1982. Daughter Martha Ellen, who has
two girls of her own, teaches French and Spanish to
beginning and advanced high school students. Edwin Jr.,

who is in the diamond business, is married to a registered nurse. Dr. Mertz, who still remains very active in research, is well known as a jazz pianist - a hobby he shares with his younger brother, a retired lawyer and insurance executive. Edwin is proud of the two grand pianos in his living room and enjoys playing duets with visitors.

GEORGE ALEXANDER MILLS

George was born in Saskatoon, Saskatchewan, Canada, on March 20, 1914, to George Robinson and Leafa Johnson Mills. After graduating from high school in 1930, he enrolled in the University of Saskatchewan, where he received his B.S. (1934) and M.S. (1936) degrees. He was awarded his doctorate from Columbia University (1939). The following year he served as instructor in chemistry at Dartmouth. He then joined Houdry Process Company, where he stayed until 1968. The next several years he was with the U. S. Bureau of Mines (1968-75) and the Department of Energy (1975-1981). It was then he joined the faculty of the University of Delaware as Executive Director of the Center of Catalytic Science Technology.

Dr. Mills developed the first synthetic silica-alumina

catalyst, clay catalysts, and made-in-place molecular sieves for petroleum refining; high stability chromia-alumina catalysts for the production of butadiene and aromatic hydrocarbons; and was associated with the development of diazobicyclooctane, a diamino cage structured catalyst (DABCO) used for the production of polyurethanes. He is also credited with the development of a process in which coal is converted catalytically to synthesis gas, then to methanol, and then to high octane gasoline. Further, Dr. Mills and his associates were responsible for fundamental investigations which upgraded the science of catalysis. Included in these developments were dual function catalysts, which combined acidic and metallic functions, the essential acidity of mixed oxide and the theory of variable valency, copper and cobalt homogeneous catalysts for the activation of hydrogen, scissor-type mobile catalysts for gasification of coal, and the modification of platinum group metals used for the conversion of carbon monoxide and hydrogen to alkanes by control of oxidation sites.

Dr. Mills was AIC's Chemical Pioneer in 1982. He has also received ACS's Storch and Murphree awards. In addition to being a lifetime fellow of AIC, George is a member of the National Academy of Engineers, American Chemical Society, American Institute of Chemical Engineers, Sigma Xi, American Ceramics Society, Catalyst Society, and American Association for the Advancement of Science.

George married Roberta Walker in 1940. They are parents of Richard, Sandra, Marilyn and Janice.

ROBERT MITCHELL MILTON

Robert Milton was asked by Professor William Eversole to investigate the use of zeolites for separating air into its components. Bob discovered that naturally occurring zeolites* were not satisfactory for this end use

*Zeolites (derived from the Greek words *zeo,* meaning to boil, and *lithol,* meaning stones), which are naturally occurring minerals, are framework aluminum silicates composed of complex three-dimensional networks of tetrahedral oxides of silicon and aluminum. While these compounds resemble feldspars and feldspathoids, their more open structure contains channels from which ions enter or leave in an ion exchange process. Since large molecules may become entrapped in these open channels, these aluminosilicate hydrates are called molecular sieves. More than thirty different natural zeolites are known. Since they release water vapor but do not disintegrate when heated, zeolites have been used by organic chemists as "boiling stones" for over two centuries.

and proceeded to synthesize zeolites with superior properties by heating sodium silicate, alumina and sodium hydroxide. During his forty-year tenure with Union Carbide, he was able to follow the development of these molecular sieves and to discover their unique activity as catalysts for cracking and their ability to separate linear and branched molecules. X-ray analysis has been used to show the arrangement of the thousand or more atoms in a basic zeolite block. Molecular sieves are now a multi-million dollar business with an unlimited potential.

Dr. Milton also discovered Hi Flux porous boiling tubes and surfaces which have far-reaching implications in the heat exchange field. This invention, which increases the heat transfer coefficient for solids into boiling liquids at low heat fluxes up to 100 times, is used extensively in air conditioning, refrigeration, boilers, and low temperature processing condensers. Bob has directed research and production in cryogenic chemistry, cryobiology, superconductivity, antifreeze formulation, sewage treatment, synthetic emeralds, solid waste disposal, phenolic resins, and genetic engineering.

Bob joined the Linde Company Division of Union Carbide in 1946. He has served Linde as Research Supervisor (1946-54), Development Laboratory Manager (1954-58), and Director of Research (1959-73). He was Executive Vice-President of Showa Unox and Showa Union Gosei in Japan (1973-77) and has been Director of Agricultural Business Developments for Carbide since 1977.

Dr. Milton received the Chemical Pioneer award in 1980. He is also recipient of the ACS Jacob F. Schoellkopf Medal (1963). Moreover, the Sixteenth Kirkpatrick Award for Chemical Engineering Achievement was presented to the Linde Company in 1961 for Bob's development of molecular sieves. A member of the American Chemical Society, American Association for the Advancement of Science, American Institute of Chemical Engineers, Phi Beta Kappa, Sigma Xi, and Gamma Alpha, Bob has published several scientific reports and has been awarded forty-two U. S. patents and over 250 foreign patents.

Robert was born in St. Joseph, Michigan, on November 28, 1928, to Clare Leon and Frances Thornton (Mitchell) Milton. After graduating as class valedictorian from St. Joseph Public High School in 1937, he enrolled in Oberlin College where he received the A.B. degree Magna Cum Laude in 1941. Thereafter he entered into graduate studies in physical chemistry at John Hopkins University (M.A., 1943; Ph.D., 1944). Prior to joining Union Carbide, he served as a research associate at Johns Hopkins and at the end of World War II participated in a U. S. Naval technical mission to investigate cryogenics in Europe.

Bob married Mary Wills Bridge in 1946. They have three children: Mary Gillian Milton Sander of Salt Lake City, Michigan; Suzanne Milton Padilla of Grosse Pointe Park, Michigan; and David Willis Milton, a computer scientist with IBM in Burlington, Vermont. Bob and Mary have seven grandchildren.

Mary is almost as active as her husband. She has been a needlepoint professional and manager of one of suburban New York's leading needlepoint stores, an officer of the Tokyo Women's Club, a licensed realtor, a volunteer nurse, an accomplished horsewoman, chairman of the Bike and Buggy Bridge League, and a figure skater. Bob is also a figure skater, skier and tennis player. Since 1959, the Miltons have vacationed on Mackinac Island, Michigan, where they have a stable of five horses and several carriages.   They are active in revitalizing Wawahkamo Golf Club on Mackinac Island, which, as the oldest continuously operating golf course in Michigan, is registered as a national historic site.

(Photograph courtesy of American Chemical Society.)

WALTER JOSEPH MURPHY

Versatile and talented Walter Murphy contributed importantly to science and society as a chemist, executive, journalist, author, and editor. For these contributions, the AIC honored him in 1950 with its prestigious Gold Medal and honorary fellowship. The AIC periodical *THE CHEMIST* stated: "Dr. Murphy merits the highest praise for the phenomenal growth of the journals and the high standards of technical excellence which distinguish them."

Dr. Murphy also received an honorary D.Sc. degree from the Centre College of Kentucky in 1947, an honor scroll from the American Chemical Society's Division of Industrial and Engineering Chemistry in 1953, and an honor scroll from the American Section of the Société de Chimie Industrielle in 1958.

Walter's career provided him with a wide variety of experience. As a chemist, he worked on the purification and industrial applications of rare gases, particularly neon, and the use of cyanides as insecticides and fumigants. In 1922 he became a sales engineer for the American Cyanamid Company and traveled extensively in Latin America demonstrating how pesticides and fumigants could be used to combat the insects that plagued the citrus-growing industries of Brazil and Cuba and the tobacco industry of Puerto Rico. One of the pioneers in market research and development in the chemical industry, he joined the United States Rubber Company in 1925 and investigated the market potential of heavy industrial chemicals. He became an executive as well as market analyst when he was appointed vice president of George Chemicals, Inc., a marketing organization in New York; thereafter, he became vice president in charge of manufacturing for a subsidiary, Seaboard Crystal Company, and sales assistant to the president of Mutual Chemical Company of America.

Murphy's career turned to editing in 1930 when he became managing editor of *Chemical Marketing*, which later became *Chemical Industries*. Murphy's seventeen-year career with the American Chemical Society began in 1942 when he became editor of the semi-monthly *Chemical and Engineering News* and the monthly *Industrial and Engineering Chemistry* The latter periodical was then published in two editions - industrial and analytical. Under Murphy's management, *Chemical and Engineering News* became a weekly and the analytical edition became a separate monthly, *Analytical Chemistry*. In 1953, the *Journal of Agricultural and Food Chemistry* was established as a new periodical with Murphy as editor.

Two years later, Murphy was made editorial director of the four journals, known as the ACS applied journals. With Murphy at the helm, the applied journals grew into the largest scientific publications program of its kind in the world, the total circulation reaching 165,000. His editorial successes were recognized in 1954 when he was elected president of the Society of Business Magazine Editors.

Convinced that science and technology are important to society as a whole, Murphy helped establish the News Service of the American Chemical Society. With him as its director, the News Service became a well developed public relations group that has helped the general public appreciate the achievements of chemists and chemical engineers. Murphy also maintained relations with academia as a member of the Corporation of Brooklyn Polytechnic Institute of advisory groups of Notre Dame and Fordham. He served on the boards of trustees of the Polytechnic Institute of Brooklyn, Midwest Research Institute, and Southwest Research Institute.

Murphy was sent to Germany after World War II for the Technical Industrial Intelligence Committee of the Joint Chiefs of Staff to investigate wartime developments in the chemical industry. With his encouragement, the Office of Technical Services was established in the U. S. Department of Commerce, the result of which thousands of scientific and technical reports written in Germany during the war were made available in this country.

Murphy lectured widely on scientific and professional subjects and wrote many popular and semi-popular articles. His books include: *I Did Leave Home,* which was concerned with the investigation of the wartime chemical industry; *The Lagoon of Decision* reported his observations of the Bikini atom bomb test; he co-authored *Strategic Materials for Hemisphere*

Defense.

Walter was born on August 20, 1899, to Richard Joseph and Ann (Heath) Murphy. He married Gertrude B. McMahon in 1927; their children are Joan Ann and Walter, Jr. Murphy's hobby was gardening. Cancer took his life on November 26, 1959.

JOHN HENRY NAIR, JR.

John Nair, Jr., the 1966 recipient of the AIC Gold Medal, was a strong supporter of the American Institute of Chemists. He was the first president to visit every chapter, chairman of the board of directors for five years, and honorary fellow. As well as his service to the AIC, his successes in research and development were equalled by his activities in other professional societies: he was elected to several offices in the Syracuse Section of the American Chemical Society, which he served as chairman for two terms and as councilor.

It was Nair who suggested and worked for the establishment of student chapters of the American Chemical Society. The affiliate program, which was initiated in 1937, saw within ten years 3,400 students enrolled in 122 chapters. Nair was also active within the ACS. He served as secretary, chairman, and as a member of the executive committee for the Division of Agricultural and Food Chemistry; represented the National Council of the New York Section, from 1944 to 1962 and served as chairman during 1950-51; he also chaired the organizing committee for the Diamond Jubilee held in New York City in 1951. In 1963, he was elected Director-at-Large and served for three years on the board of directors.

John helped found the Institute of Food Technologists in 1939 and was its president in 1966. He was also president of the Association of Research Directors. In addition, he gave his time and talents to other organizations, including the American Dairy Association, Scientific Research Society of America, Société de Chimie Industrielle, Sigma Xi, Phi Tau Sigma, Delta Sigma Rho, Alpha Chi Sigma, Tau Kappa Epsilon, Summit Civic Association, and The Chemists Club. To every organization, he brought his great energy and enthusiasm.

Nair earned the B.S. degree Cum Laude in 1915 at Beloit College with a thesis, for honors, on electrolytes. He then taught chemistry and coached basketball and track at the Wausau, Wisconsin, high school. Encouraged by his Beloit major professor, a Syracuse University graduate, he enrolled at Syracuse for graduate study where, as a teaching fellow, he studied the miscibility of organic and inorganic liquids under Herman C. Cooper. His studies terminated prematurely in 1917 when he enlisted in the Army Signal Corps. Following the war, he returned to Syracuse. In 1919, he joined Merrell-Soule Company, manufacturers of dried milk, as a research chemist. He became director of the control laboratory and, when Borden acquired Merrell-Soule in 1928, he was appointed assistant director of Borden's Syracuse research laboratories. His research was concerned with various dairy phenomena, e.g., oxidation of butter fat, lipase, dehydration of dairy products and other foods. Ten years later, he was appointed technical advisor to sales management for Borden's Dry Milk Division in Atlanta, in which position he helped solve many problems that plagued ice cream companies in the south.

In 1942, Nair left Borden to become assistant director of research for Continental Foods, a subsidiary of Thomas J. Lipton, Inc. He helped Lipton enter the dehydrated food products division by developing soup mixes and tea extracts. At the same time he was a consultant for Unilever, Ltd.; he continued working for Unilever for several years after retiring from Lipton in 1957. Following retirement, Nair moved to North Carolina and served for a time as a visiting professor at North Carolina State University. He was also a director of Onyx Chemical Corporation and of Avi Publishing Company.

Following his return from an overseas assignment for the International Executive Services Corps. in 1970, he and his wife spent three months in the Philippines working with Reliance Commercial Enterprises, a company which sells coffee, cocoa, chocolate and biscuits to retailers throughout the Philippines.

John was born on February 20, 1893, in Chicago, Illinois, to John Henry and Isabel (Painter) Nair. He grew up in rural Wisconsin except for a period in North Carolina where, following the death of his father, he lived while his mother obtained her medical degree. Once she was established in practice, John became a technician in her office. His mother practiced medicine well into her eighties.

At the age of twenty-seven, John married Claire L. Cook of Syracuse.   His enthusiasm for chemistry influenced their two children to study chemistry, and Janet (Nair) Adams and John Henry III have enjoyed many successes of their own.   Throughout most of his life, the senior Nair was interested in gardening, philately, and golf. He died on a golf course near Syracuse on July 26, 1971.

(Reprinted from THE CHEMIST, with permission.)

ROY CHESTER NEWTON

In 1941, one American farmer produced enough food for twelve people. Despite the dire predictions made early in this century that the world's population will outstrip the food supply, the 1941 ratio continues to improve. Some of the improvements in agricultural research may be attributed to Roy Newton, recipient of the AIC Gold Medal in 1957.

Roy was born in El Reno, Oklahoma, on May 8, 1896, to Sylvester Warren and Katie (Webb) Newton. After graduating from high school in 1917, he enrolled in

Oklahoma A & M College* where he received his B.S. degree in 1921. He received his doctorate from the University of Chicago in 1924. Thereafter, he joined the research department of Swift & Company where he spent his entire career upgrading Swift's research program. Some of his successes were improvements in lard - using gum guaiac as an antioxidant to reduce its rancidity, margarine, mayonnaise, glue, and gelatin, the result of which he was granted eighty-one foreign and domestic patents.

Dr. Newton is probably best known for his expansion of Swift's research facilities from essentially a one-man laboratory in the early 1920's to a staff of over three hundred researchers in forty-four divisions in 1932. He retired as vice president in charge of research in 1961.

Founder and president of the Institute of Food Technologists, he also served the American Chemical Society as chairman of the Chicago section and as a national councilor and was responsible to a large extent for starting the National Chemical Exposition. He served on the board of trustees for the Industrial Research Institute, George Washington Carver Foundation, Nutrition Foundation, American Meat Institute, and National Research Council. In addition to being an AIC fellow, he was a member of the American Oil Society, American Association for the Advancement of Science, Sigma Xi, and Phi Lambda Upsilon.

Dr. Newton's other awards include the honor scroll of the Chicago Chapter of AIC, the Nicholas Appert Award and the Industrial Research Institute Medal. In 1947, he was designated one of the ten ablest chemists by the

*Now Oklahoma State University.

Chemical Bulletin and was given an honorary D.Sc. degree by Purdue in 1952.

Some of Roy's interests "outside the Laboratory" were serving as a second lieutenant in World War I, for which he was awarded the French Croix de Guerre with Star; airplane pilot using his own plane to commute from Three Rivers, Michigan, to Chicago; and advising young scientists in their careers.

Roy married Ruth Ellen Watkins in 1930. Their children are Wanda Lee (Reed), Roy Maukel and Charles R. Newton.

(Photograph courtesy of The MIT Museum.)

JAMES FLACK NORRIS

The American Institute of Chemists twice honored the distinguished educator and chemist James Norris: in 1937 he was presented the Gold Medal; in 1949 he was made an honorary fellow. Dr. Norris was the recipient of many others honors, including honorary memberships in the Royal Institute of London and the Chemical Society of Rumania.

Norris exerted a great influence on the development of chemistry and chemical education through his researches, teaching, and involvement with national and international scientific organizations. As early as 1904, he served as chairman of the Northeastern Section of the American Chemical Society and later as assistant editor of the Society's journal. In 1925 and 1926, he was the Society's president. He was a member of the executive board of the National Research Council; lecturer on organic chemistry at Harvard, Clark University and Bowdoin College; secretary of the Society of Arts in Boston; president of the Chemistry Teachers' Association of New England and of the Technology Club; vice president of the International Union of Pure and Applied Chemistry; member of the National Academy of Sciences; and fellow of the American Academy of Arts and Sciences.

Recognized as an international authority on organic chemistry, Dr. Norris performed research in several areas of organic chemistry, including condensation reactions and the Friedel-Crafts reaction. He published many papers and books, including twenty papers on "Reactivity of Atoms and Groups in Organic Compounds." In these investigations, Norris and his students measured the reaction rate of substituted benzoyl and benzydryl chlorides with various alcohols, the acidities of substituted benzoic acids, and the reactivities of these with thionyl chloride. He also conducted researches on pyrolysis temperatures, the thermal decomposition of triphenylmethyl alkyl ethers, the production of alcohols from butenes and pentenes through interaction with sulfuric acid, the polymerization of amylenes, the rearrangement of isopropylethylene to trimethylethylene, and pyrogenic decomposition of 2-pentene and trimethylethylene.

James was born in Baltimore, Maryland, on January 20, 1871. At Johns Hopkins, where he received the A.B. (1892) and Ph.D. (1895) degrees, he was impressed by Ira Remsen's courses in organic chemistry and in the history of chemistry. He was a member of the hiking club and debating society. Norris joined the Chemistry

Department at Massachusetts Institute of Technology as an instructor and remained at MIT until 1904, when he became the first professor of chemistry at Simmons College, a new college for women. There he had general supervision of the science courses, developed the chemistry curriculum and organized the laboratories. In 1910-11, he studied physical chemistry in Fritz Haber's laboratory in Karlsruhe. He left Simmons in 1915 for Vanderbilt University, and then returned to MIT in 1916 as professor of organic chemistry. The following year he left MIT to use his talents as a scientist and administrator in the service of this country during the first world war. Prior to 1918, he supervised research at the U. S. Bureau of Mines on war gases; he then entered the army as Lieutenant Colonel in the Chemical Warfare Service and supervised the Service in England. The following year he led the investigation of the manufacture of war gas in Germany. At war's end, he returned to MIT. When the Research Laboratory of Organic Chemistry was formed in 1926, he was appointed its director.

As a young man, James spent summer vacations at his home in North Bridgton, Maine, writing a textbook entitled *Principles of Organic Chemistry* and a laboratory manual that became widely used. In his later years, he spent his summers in walking trips through scenic regions of Europe. His plan to retire on his seventieth birthday was circumvented by his death in Cambridge on August 4, 1940.

ALEXANDER GORDON OBLAD

The Greek word *catalyst*, meaning dissolution or ruin, was taken into English as a political term in the seventeenth century and applied to chemistry by Berzelius in the nineteenth century. It is now used in common speech as a metaphor from science. The mechanisms of homogeneous catalysis, such as the use of sulfuric acid to convert ethanol to ethyl ether, are based on the formation of intermediates. Heterogeneous catalysis, such as platinum, used in the Davy safety lamp, caused combustion of methane (fire damp) without explosive violence. Since Davy's time, there have occurred many important breakthroughs, such as the Haber fixation of nitrogen and the platinum and palladium catalyst converters, which convert hydrocarbons and carbon monoxide to carbon dioxide and water in the exhaust systems of combustion engines. Less well known to the general public are commercial catalytic reactions in petroleum refining, such as cracking and reforming. Many of these catalytic reactions and the explanations for their mechanisms were developed by Alexander Oblad and associates.

While employed by Standard Oil in Whiting, Indiana, in 1937, Oblad calculated the chemical thermodynamic properties of a long series of hydrocarbons and their derivatives. The following year he investigated the addition of carbon monoxide and hydrogen to ethylene, the use of platinum in gamma alumina as a reforming catalyst and the production of aviation gasoline and toluene. In 1942, he accepted a position with Magnolia Petroleum Company in Dallas, Texas, where he investigated the polymerization of 1-olefins and converted propylene to isoprene to produce synthetic rubber; however, Magnolia Petroleum did not recognize the importance of the former research and it was discontinued.

Oblad became Director of Chemical Research of Houdry Process Company in 1947 and spent the next decade developing new processes, such as the production of butadiene from butane, and developing new theories relating to the acidic contents of cracking catalysts to their activities. He and co-workers conceived the idea of dual functionality of reforming catalysts and proposed a concept of separate dehydrogenation sites and the transfer of adsorbed molecules between these sites. He also produced diazabicyclooctane (DABCO), a compound with a diamino cage structure used as a catalyst in the production of polyurethane foams.

Dr. Oblad joined M. W. Kellogg Company in 1957, where, as Vice President of Research and Development, he developed the production of hydrogen from naphthas and planned for the construction of ammonia plants using this source of hydrogen.   He also developed commercial processes for the production of ethylene, propylene, butadiene, benzene, toluene and xylenes from heavy feed stocks and a process for the conversion of chlorine to hydrochloric acid.

In 1970, Alex became Professor of Metallurgical and Fuel Engineering at the University of Utah.

Oblad was born in Salt Lake City, Utah, on November 26, 1909.   He received his B.A. and M.A. degrees from the University of Utah in 1933 and 1934. Four years later, he was awarded his doctorate from Purdue; his dissertation was on the heat capacity of supercooled liquid glycerol under the direction of Professor R. F. Newton.

Named AIC's Chemical Pioneer in 1976, Dr. Oblad was also recipient of the Purdue Chemist Award (1950), Distinguished Alumnus Award from the University of Utah (1962), ACS E. V. Murphree Award (1969) and has been awarded honorary D.Sc. degrees by Purdue (1959) and the University of Utah (1980).   Oblad is a member of the National Academy of Engineering, American Chemical Society, American Institute of Chemical Engineers, American Association for the Advancement of Science, California Catalytic Society, Rocky Mountain Fuel Society, Sigma Xi, Phi Lambda Upsilon, Phi Kappa Phi, Sigma Pi Sigma, and Tau Beta Kappa.   He was co-founder of the Philadelphia Catalyst Society and the International Congress of Catalysis and served as first president of this Congress.   Author of approximately seventy-five scientific reports, he has been granted fifty-five U. S. patents.

Alex married Bessie Elizabeth Baker in 1933.   Their six children are: Dr. Alex Edward Oblad, a metallurgical engineer; Elizabeth Ann Oblad Sonne, a champion marathoner and technical writer at the University of Utah; Virginia Lou Oblad Christensen, a Salt Lake County attorney; John Riley Baker Oblad, a pharmacist in Las Vegas; Haywood Brewster Oblad, a research engineer for Consolidated Coal Company, Library, Pennsylvania; and Jean Rio Baker Calder, a graduate nurse. Alex and Bessie have seventeen grandchildren.

DONALD FREDERICK OTHMER

*The award to the educator lies in his pride in his students' accomplishments. The richness of that reward is the satisfaction in knowing that the frontiers of knowledge have been extended.**

According to Charles Kettering, the ideal inventor must have the faith of a Goodyear, the creative ability of the Wrights, and the production knowledge of a Ford. If Kettering were alive today, he might add "and the versatility of an Othmer."

*From Othmer's biography in *Who's Who in America*.

The versatile Othmer was born to Frederick George and Fredericka Darling (Snyder) on May 11, 1904, in Omaha, Nebraska. After completing high school in 1921, he studied for two years at Illinois Institute of Technology and then transferred to the University of Nebraska, where he received the B.S. degree in 1924. He worked as a chemist at Cudahy Packing Company before undertaking graduate study at the University of Michigan (M.S., 1925; Ph.D., 1927). He then accepted a position as development engineer for Eastman Kodak and Tennessee Eastman Corporation. In 1931, he joined the faculty of the Polytechnic Institute in Brooklyn, was made head of the Department of Chemical Engineering in 1937, and a Distinguished Professor in 1961.

Professor Othmer is probably best known as the founder and co-editor of the Kirk-Othmer Encyclopedia of Chemical Technology, now in its third edition, which is the world's most referenced work in chemistry and related fields. Othmer developed scientific apparatus and methods to determine physicochemical data required in the designing of systems for the separation and purification of materials, which systems generated data necessary for the exact design of industrial operations and plants for the distillation, evaporation, and extraction of both liquids and solids. He also originated processes used by industry in the production of synthetic fibers, photographic film, petrochemicals, synthetic fuels, paints, resins, plastics, and fresh water (desalination) of sea water (and in processes involving solar heating, sewage treatment, sugar and salt refining, and wood pulping). New theoretical developments in physical chemistry and thermodynamics led to the development of his reference-substance method for correlating and predicting chemical and engineering data. This procedure utilizes the fact that the variance of the physical properties of one substance is caused by a physical mechanism identical to that which causes the variance of the physical properties of another, well-studied material under the same conditions. It also simplifies computations by making almost exact predictions, thus supplying, comparatively readily and dependably, otherwise unavailable data essential for the design of equipment and processes. Othmer's theoretical equations for over fifty properties require one or two coefficients to give an accuracy usually within one to three percent, as compared to the empirical equations which require up to 20-24 terms.

Long conscious of the importance of energy to modern industry and lifestyle, Othmer worked for years with processes and equipment to devise novel systems of energy production. One of his developments was the utilization of solar energy absorbed in the surface water of tropical seas to produce not only electric power but also desalinated water and seafood. He recognized that cheap energy alone could not amortize the huge capital costs of such projects, which might be paid for by the added products of fresh water and choice seafood. Othmer's other substantial contributions to the energy picture include the upgrading of seemingly worthless solid fuels, such as peats and lignites, and their conversion into liquid fuels for use in combustion turbines for power production or in motor cars and similar engines. These fuels also hold the promise to produce electric power and automobile fuel less expensively than other proposed systems.

A champion of the use of methanol as a fuel for combusion engines, Othmer states that many more gallons of methanol as opposed to gasoline can be produced from one ton of coal and that methanol can propel a car at one-half the cost of the gasoline from coal.

In addition to receiving the AIC Honor Scroll and Chemical Pioneer Award (1977), Othmer is recipient of the

Perkin Gold Medal, Murphree Award, Award of Merit from the Association of Consulting Chemists and Chemical Engineers, and Tyler Award from the American Institute of Chemical Engineers. He has received honorary degrees from the University of Nebraska, Brooklyn Polytech and New Jersey Institute of Technology. Editor of *Fluidization* (1956), and co-author with Zenz of *Fluidization of Fluid Particle Systems*, he has also published approximately 350 technical reports and been awarded 125 U. S. patents. He is a member of the editorial boards of *Desalination, Chemical Engineer's Handbooks,* and *Pipe, Piping Design and Piping Construction.*

A fellow of the American Institute of Chemists and of the American Association for the Advancement of Science, he also is a member of the New York Academy of Science, American Institute of Chemical Engineers, American Society for Mechanical Engineers, Institute of Chemical Engineers (England), Deutsche Gesellschaft für Chemisches Apparatewesen, Sigma Xi, Tau Beta Pi, Phi Lambda Upsilon, Iota Alpha, Alpha Chi Sigma, and Lambda Chi Alpha.

Othmer married Mildred Jane Topp in 1950. One of his hobbies is siliculture; he has planted thousands of tree seedlings. He also collects old maps and books.

(Reproduced from THE CHEMIST, with permission.)

WILBUR GEORGE PARKS

The Gibson Island Conferences, organized and presided over in 1931 by Professor Neil Gordon, an eminent educator in the field of chemistry, became affilated with the American Association for the Advancement of Science in 1938. Following Gordon's untimely death, the conferences were renamed in his honor. Wilbur Parks at that time became director of the Gordon Conferences.

Wilbur George was born in Rockwood, Pennsylvania, on December 20, 1904, to George and Ruby Parks. After receiving the A.B. degree from the University of Pennsylvania in 1926, he attended Columbia where he received his M.A. and Ph.D. degrees in 1931. He then became an instructor in chemistry at the University of Rhode Island, where he was head of the department from 1950. In addition to investigating textile science, Professor Parks specialized in scientific criminal investigation. In 1965, he became Director of the Laboratories for Scientific Criminal Investigation and held this position until his retirement.

Dr. Parks, a lifetime fellow of the American Institute of Chemists, was named awardee of its prestigious Gold Medal in 1962. He is a member of the New York Academy of Science, American Institute of Chemical Engineers, Phi Lambda Upsilon, Phi Kappa Phi, Sigma Xi, Chemists Club, and American Association of Textile Chemists and Colorists. He also served as director of the American Section of the Société de Chimie Industrielle.

George's hobbies of golf and fishing blended well with his directorship of the Gordon Conferences. He traveled to all of the conferences while spending each summer at Lake Pleasant in New London, New Hampshire.

His 1928 marriage to Margaret Mather Merriman produced Ann Mather and George Merriman. Margaret, who held a doctorate, served as professor of chemistry at Rhode Island State University.

JOHN THOMAS PATTON, JR.

Soya beans, which had been cultivated in the Orient for several centuries, were not introduced into this country until 1804. Still, there was little interest in this important agricultural crop until 1935 when Henry Ford admixed the deoiled dry meal from soya beans, which contain forty-eight percent protein, with phenolic resins to produce a moldable plastic. Ford hired Robert A. Boyer, a nonscientist, to perfect this plastic and John Thomas Patton, Jr., to work with Boyer at the Greenfield Village Research Laboratory. In spite of much newspaper publicity showing Ford striking a soya bean-phenolic impregnated paper plastic trunk with a sledgehammer, this project was not successful. Patton, however, was able to spin fibers from soya bean protein and to isolate lecithin and steroids from soya bean residue. He also investigated the production of vinyl plastics and synthetic rubber while employed by Ford.

The son of John Thomas and Clara Edna (Bohier) Patton, John was born in Jonesboro, Arkansas, on January 30, 1917. After receiving his B.S. degree from Arkansas State University in 1938, he attended Detroit's Henry Ford Trade School as a Ford Scholar; illness saw his return to Jonesboro after four months. After teaching high school chemistry for part of a year, he accepted employment with Ford Motor Company where he worked first in the Rouge soya bean extraction plant and then at Greenfield Village.

While working in the research laboratories of Penick and Ford in Cedar Rapids, Iowa, in 1942, Patton made chemically modified starch used for the production of boxboard for overseas shipments. Unlike Ford, Patton recognized the need for higher education and the next year enrolled in graduate school at Purdue. His first research advisor was Ed Degering; he received his doctorate under Profesor Kornblum in 1947. Thereafter he accepted a position with Wyandotte Chemical Corporation where he investigated block copolymers of ethylene oxide and propylene oxide. These block copolymers, called Pluronics, were used as surfactants.

Dr. Patton spent thirty-five years with Wyandotte before retiring as Deputy Director of the Central Research Laboratories in 1982. Much of his efforts were devoted to the development of polyether polyols used as reactants with diisocyanates for the production of polyurethanes. During his tenure at Wyandotte, the annual use of polyurethanes in this country grew from a few kilograms annually to over 825,000 tons. In spite of Ford's unsuccessful attempt to make car bodies out of soya bean plastics, today the bodies of the popular Pontiac Fiero and automobile bumpers are made from polyurethane by a reaction injection molding process (RIM), that is, the polyol and diisocyanate react in the mold cavity to produce polyurethane plastics in the RIM process.

Patton was described as "Mr. Polyol" by Dr. Hans Schenek, Vice President for Research of BASF AG, which acquired Wyandotte Corporation. The Technical Service Laboratory in Wyandotte was named the John T. Patton, Jr. Laboratory in his honor.

Dr. Patton was selected Chemical Pioneer in 1978. A member of the American Institute of Chemists, American Chemical Society, Society of Plastic Engineers, Phi Lambda Upsilon, Industrial Research Institute, and Sigma Xi, he is the author of ten scientific publications and has been awarded seventy-six U. S. patents and numerous foreign patents.

John married Dorothy Maye Bankle in 1939. They have two sons: John Thomas Patton III and G. Richard Patton. Richard is a professor at the University of Pittsburgh Graduate School of Business.

LINUS CARL PAULING

"Science is the search for truth - it is not a game in which one tries to beat his opponent, to do harm to others. We need the spirit of science in international affairs to make the conduct of international affairs the effort to find the solution."[*]

The letter nominating Linus Pauling for the Priestley Medal in 1984 stated that no one had made a greater contribution to modern chemistry than he and few had participated so actively and effectively in the progress and affairs of the American Chemical Society.

[*]From *No More War,* by Linus Pauling, 1958.

Linus Carl was born on February 28, 1901, in Portland, Oregon to Herman Henry Pauling, a pharmacist, and Lucy Isabelle (Darling) Pauling. He attended Portland's Washington High School but did not take those courses required to graduate. As a result, he is undoubtedly the first scientist to graduate from high school *after* receiving the Nobel Prize. As a matter of fact, Dr. Pauling received his high school diploma the year before he was awarded his *second* Nobel Prize in 1964.

In spite of the fact that he did not have a high school diploma, Linus enrolled in Oregon Agricultural State College* in 1917, which studies were interrupted after his sophomore year by lack of finances. Consequently, he briefly taught quantitative analysis and received his B.S. in 1922. While working as a paving inspector on the Pacific Coast Highway the following summer, he read Bragg's *X-Ray and Crystal Structure.* This led him to the California Institute of Technology where, at the suggestion of A. A. Noyes, he conducted graduate research under the direction or R. G. Dikinson on the determination of crystal structures by using x-ray diffraction techniques. He received his doctorate from Cal Tech in 1925.

Dr. Pauling's first scientific paper was published in 1923; he has published more than three hundred since then. Results of his study on the structure of lithium hydride were not published because similar results were published previously by investigators in Holland; however, data on other crystal structures and his interpretations of molecular structure were published in 1923 and 1924.

As a Guggenheim fellow, he traveled to Europe in 1926 where he worked with Arnold Sommerfeld in Munich, Erwin Schroedinger in Zurich and Niels Bohr in

*Now Oregon State University.

Copenhagen. Thereafter, he returned to Cal Tech to develop the concept of resonance to explain the structure of molecules, such as benzene, to which no single structure could be assigned. Using quantum mechanics, he was able to describe these molecules as hybrids of more than one valence bond structure. He considers his most important contribution to chemistry his description of the tetrahedral bonds in organic compounds in terms of 2s and 2p hybridized orbitals.*

Dr. Pauling met Herman F. Mark, who had invented a technique for the determination of the structure of gas molecules by use of electron diffraction, while in Germany in 1930. Pauling used Mark's technique to compliment his x-ray studies at Cal Tech.

In cooperation with Dr. Robert B. Corey, Pauling published a number of papers on polymers of amino acids which showed that the peptide linkages in proteins were essentially coplanar and that the structure of several proteins was a left handed screw with a number of amino acid residues per turn of the alpha helix. Later, in conjuction with Dr. Harvey A. Itano, he demonstrated that sickle cell anemia was a "molecular disease" caused by a single incorrect amino acid in the hemoglobin polymeric chain.

During the past forty years, Dr. Pauling has championed the use of large doses of Vitamin C to prevent common colds and cancer. As president of the American Chemical Society in 1949, he called on the society to take an active position to prevent a future war. Six years later, he joined with fifteen other Nobel Laureates in a proclamation calling for an end of war as a means of settling conflicts. This led to a contempt of Congress

J. Am. Chem. Soc., 1931.

citation for his refusal to provide a Senate Committee with the names of scientists who had signed the petition to ban nuclear testing.

Dr. Pauling's tokens of esteem are extraordinarly impressive. In addition to receiving the Nobel Prize in Chemistry and the Nobel Peace Prize, he has also been awarded the Presidential Medal for Merit for "exceptional meritorious conduct in the performance of outstanding services in the United States from October 1940 to June 1946," ACS Award in Pure Chemistry, Nichol Medal, Gibbs Medal, Richards Medal, Gilbert Lewis Medal, Sabatier Medal, Davy Medal, Linus Pauling Medal of the Oregon Section of ACS, Roebling Medal of the Mineralogical Society of America, US National Medal of Science, Lomonosov Gold Medal, Chemical Science Award of the National Academy of Science, Thomas Addis Medal, Phillips Medal, Gold Medal of the American College of Physicians, Gold Medal of the Medical Society of New York, Gold Medal of the French Academy of Medicine, Vermeil Medal of the City of Paris, Modern Medicine Award for Distinguished Achievement, Eliaberg and Goldel Medallions in Anesthesiology, Rachel Carson Memorial Award, Martin Luther King Medical Achievement Award, International Lenin Peace Prize, Ghandi Peace Prize, Grotius Medal of Contributions to International Law, Janice Pauling Peace Award (jointly with Eva Helen Pauling), Woman's Strike for Peace Annual Award, Gold Medal of the National Institute of Social Sciences, Volum Award, Award of Merit of the Decalogue Society of Lawyers., and Medal of the Senate of the Republic of Chile. Moreover, he is grand officer of the Order of Merit of the Italian Republic.

Honorary degrees have been conferred upon him by Oregon State and Cal Tech, and from the following institutions or universities: Adelphi, Berlin, Cracow,

Delphi, Liege, London, Marquette, Montpellier, Melbourne, Cambridge, Chicago, Oxford, Paris, Princeton, Reia, Tampa and Toulouse.

The author of *No More War, Science and World Peace, Vitamin C and the Common Cold, The Nature of the Chemical Bond, General Chemistry, College Chemistry* and *Orthomolecular Psychiatry*; he is the co-author of *Treatment of Schizophrenia, The Study of Line Spectra, Introduction to Quantum Mechanics, The Architecture of Molecules,* and *Cancer and Vitamin C and Chemistry* (with son Peter).

Dr. Pauling was promoted to Chairman of the Division of Chemistry and Chemical Engineering at Cal Tech in 1937. In 1963, he accepted a position as research professor of physical and biological sciences at the Center of the Study of Democratic Institutions at Santa Barbara. After spending two years as professor of chemistry at the University of California at San Diego, he accepted a professorship at Stanford (1969) where he is still professor emeritus. Since 1973, he has been a research professor at the Linus Pauling Institute of Science and Medicine in Palo Alto.

Linus' marriage to Ava Helen Miller in 1923 gave them four children: Lewis Paul, Peter Jeffress, Linda Helen and Edward Celin. Ava Helen passed away in 1981. Dr. Pauling has fifteen grandchildren.

(Photograph courtesy of American Institute of Chemists.)

GEORGE R. PETTIT

Dr. George Pettit's acceptance address at the time he received the 1988 AIC Chemical Pioneer award was appropriately titled "Discovery of Naturally Occurring Anticancer Drugs;" for George is Professor of Chemistry, Dalton Professor of Cancer Research and Medicinal Chemistry, and Director of the Arizona State University Cancer Research Institute.

This distinguished gentleman's outstanding researches have been published in more than 320 papers. He is particularly renowned for his pioneering contributions to the chemistry of natural products and cancer chemotherapy, which encompass the isolation, structural elucidation and synthesis of promising anticancer agents from marine organisms and terrestrial plants.

During his career, Dr. Pettit has held important positions in both academia and industry. He was research chemist at E. I. du Pont de Nemours and Company during the summer of 1953, and senior research chemist at Morton-Norwich Company in 1956-57. He was a teaching assistant or professor at Washington State University (1950-52), Wayne State University (1952-56), University of Maine (1957-65), and Arizona State University (1965 to present). In addition, he was Visiting Professor of Chemistry, Stanford University (1965).

Born on June 8, 1929, in Long Branch, New Jersey, George received his B.S. in chemistry from Washington State University in 1952, and (with Professor Carl Djerassi at Wayne State University) his M.S. (Synthetic and Heterocyclic Chemistry) in 1954, and Ph.D. (Structure and Steroid Chemistry) in 1956.

BENJAMIN PHILIPS

Epoxy resins produced by the condensation of bis phenol A and epichlorohydrin were patented by P. Castan in 1943 and improved by S. O. Greenlee in the 1950's. Epoxy (oxirane) compounds were also produced by the condensation of peracids, such as peracetic acid with olefins. The peracetic acid was produced commercially in 1956 by Dr. Benjamin Philips by the autoxidation of acetaldehyde. He also produced epoxydized vegetable oils, used as plasticizers and stabilizers for PVC, and epsilon-caprolactam, used for the production of polyurethane.

Benjamin was born in Galveston, Texas, on April 17, 1917. After completing high school in 1933, he enrolled at the University of the South at Sewanee, Tennessee (B.A.,

1937). He received his doctorate from Johns Hopkins University in 1941. Thereafter he accepted a positon as research chemist with Union Carbide where he served as Assistant Director of Research, Manager of Chemical Research and as an executive in the New York Office.

Dr. Philips was named American Institute of Chemists Chemical Pioneer in 1967. He is a lifetime fellow of AIC and a member of the American Chemical Society and the New York Academy of Science. He has 120 U. S. and foreign patents to his credit.

Benjamin married Marian in 1941. They have four children: Rebekah, Marian, Edith, and Deborah.

(Photograph courtesy of American Institute of Chemists.)

GEORGE CLAUDE PIMENTEL

When he learned he was to receive the American Institute of Chemists's highest honor, Professor George Pimental said: "I am thrilled to be selected as the 1988 recipient of the AIC's Gold Medal. I have devoted my professional life to the joys of research and teaching in chemistry, without thought about such recognition. This adds to the personal pleasure to be so honored - it permits me to speculate inwardly that perhaps I did a few things right." His acceptance speech was entitled "Federal Support for Research: The Feds Pay the Piper; Who Should Call the Tune?"

An enthusiastic teacher, Dr. Pimentel is Director of the Laboratory of Chemical Biodynamics at the Lawrence Berkeley Laboratory, University of California. There he lectures in freshman chemistry as he had done for six years before accepting a Presidential appointment as Deputy Director of the National Science Foundation. He also chaired the committee appointed by the National Research Council, National Academy of Sciences, to identify prime areas for research in the chemical sciences. His report, *Opportunites in Chemistry*, was released by the Academy in 1985. He is author or co-author of many research papers, eight books (four of which are textbooks and three of which concern areas of his research).

Dr. Pimentel's research has been in the fields of infrared spectroscopy, chemical lasers, molecular structure, free radicals, and hydrogen bonding. His interests have centered on the application of spectroscopic methods to the study of unusual chemical bonding. A major contribution was the development and exploitation of the matrix isolation method for the spectroscopic detection of highly unstable molecules. This involves stabilization of such molecules in a matrix of frozen inert gas, such as argon, at very low temperature to permit leisurely spectroscopic study. Application of this matrix isolation method led to the discovery of unusual and highly reactive molecules that could not otherwise have been detected.

His pioneering development of rapid scan techniques for infrared spectroscopy extended to the gas phase these spectroscopic studies of normally transient species. This work led to the design of a unique infrared spectrometer for the 1969 Mariner interplanetary spacecraft to determine the composition of the atmosphere of Mars.

During studies of photochemical reactions, Dr. Pimentel and his students discovered the first chemically pumped laser. Flash photolysis methods on the microsecond time scale permitted the measurement through laser emissions, of nascent population inversions produced in the normal course of a chemical reaction. Quite a variety of chemically pumped vibrational and rotational lasers have been discovered in his laboratory, providing valuable state-to-state kinetic information.

George has received many honors and awards. In 1987, he was named an honorary fellow of the Royal Society of Chemistry and received the AIC Members and Fellows Lecture Award. Other major honors include the ACS Priestley Medal (1989), Robert A. Welch Award in Chemistry (1986), Benjamin Franklin Medal of the Franklin Institute (1985), Sigma Xi William Proctor Prize (1985), ACS Peter Debye Award in Physical Chemistry (1983), and National Medal of Science (1983). He is a member of the National Academy of Sciences, American Chemical Society, American Institute of Chemists, American Physical Society, and American Academy of Arts and Sciences.

Dr. Pimental, was born on May 2, 1922, in Rolinda, California. He has long been associated with the University of California: He studied for his B.A. degree on the Los Angeles campus; his doctorate was granted by Berkeley. Following his involvement with the Manhattan Project and the Office of Naval Research during World War II, he returned to the Berkeley campus in 1949.

HERMAN PINES

Herman Pines was co-discoverer with Vladimir Ipatieff in 1932 of the catalytic process for the alkylation of isoparaffins with olefins, which discovery was essential for the production of aviation gasoline during the second world war. Fifty years following this most important discovery, Dr. Pines was named American Institute of Chemists Chemical Pioneer.

Prior to the discovery of the alkylation of isobutane, most organic chemists maintained that paraffins (which were named after "parum affins") had little affinity for chemical reaction.

Herman was born in Lodz, Poland, on January 17,

1902, to Isaac and Eugenia (Grynfeld) Pines. He received his B.S. in chemical Engineering from Ecole Superiéure de Chimie Industrielle at Lyons, France in 1927; his Ph.D. from the University of Chicago in 1935.

For two years following his immigration to this country in 1928, Herman worked at several routine jobs. He then accepted a position as routine analyst for UOP in Chicago. His questioning of the validity of the routine tests for olefins was considered audacious by his superior and met with admonishment. Herman was not to be denied, however, and persisted. After making a patentable discovery, he was transferred to the research department. From 1941 until his retirement in 1970, he served as a member of the chemistry faculty at Northwestern University; from 1945 through 1951 in the dual function of UOP's coordinator of Exploratory Research.

Dr. Pines received the American Institute of Chemists Chemical Pioneer Award in 1982 and the following honors: ACS Fritzche Award (1956), ACS Petroleum Chemistry Award (1981), Houdry Award of the Catalyst Society (1981), ACS Murphree Award (1983) ACS Midwest Section Award (1983), and honorary doctoral degree from Claude Bernard University, Lyons, France (1983). A lifetime fellow of AIC, Herman is a member of the American Chemical Society, Sigma Xi, and Phi Lambda Upsilon. He is the author of *The Chemistry of Catalytic Hydrocarbon Conversions*, the co-author (with W. M. Stalick) of *Base-Catalyzed Reactions in the Chemistry of Hydrocarbons;* and since 1961 has also served as co-editor of *Advances in Catalysis.*

Herman married Dorothy Mlolek in 1927. Their daughter Judith is the mother of three children.

(Photograph courtesy of Lawrence Berkeley Laboratory,
University of California.)

KENNETH SANBORN PITZER

Kenneth Sanborn Pitzer, recipient of AIC's Gold Medal in 1976, was named one of America's ten outstanding young men by the Junior Chamber of Commerce in 1950.

Kenneth was born to Russell Kelly and Flora Anna (Sanborn) Pitzer in Pomona, California, on January 6, 1914. His mother, who was a mathematics teacher, died when he was thirteen years old. After completing high school, Kenneth entered the California Institute of Technology where he received his B.S. in 1935. He then enrolled as a graduate student and teaching assistant at the University of

California at Berkeley (Ph.D., 1937) and later was granted a Shell fellowship. Upon completion of his doctorate, he joined Berkeley's faculty but took a leave of absence during the second world war (1943-44) to serve as Technical Director of the Maryland Research Laboratories. Upon his return to Berkeley, he was promoted to Professor of Chemistry in 1945. A second leave (1949-51) placed him in the position of Director of the Division of Research of the Atomic Energy Commission. He was made Dean of Berkeley's College of Chemistry in 1951. He also served on the General Advisory Committee of the Atomic Energy Commission (1958-65) and was a member of the President's Science Advisory Committee (1964-67).

In 1961, Pitzer became President and Professor of Chemistry at Rice University. Seven years later he accepted a comparable position at Stanford University. In 1971, he returned to teaching and research as Professor of Chemistry at the University of California. He shares with Norman Hackerman* and James Bryant Conant the distinction of being university presidents chosen for AIC's Gold Medal.

Professor Pitzer pioneered in the development of approximations which made possible the chemical thermodynamic properties of a host of chemical compounds, which approximations provided a means of using statistical rate theory in order to interpret reaction rates. He developed statistical methods for measuring the restrictive force which prevents free rotation about single carbon-carbon bonds. This value of 12.55 kilojoules (3 Kcal) was applicable to many hydrocarbons. He obtained a good approximation for the properties of normal fluids by including a parameter called the acentric factor, which

*Norman Hackerman was president of Rice University from 1970 to 1985.

was related to vapor pressure and temperature, and applied these theoretical methods to estimate the properties of aqueous electrolytes including sea water.

Ken is the author or co-author of *Selected Values of Properties of Hydrocarbons, Quantum Chemistry,* and *Thermodynamics,* the latter being a revision of the classic textbook by Lewis and Randall. He has also published more than two hundred scientific articles.

Named a Guggenheim Fellow in 1950, Dr. Pitzer also received that year the Precision Scientific Company Award in Petroleum Chemistry. Other honors include the Clayton Prize from the Institute of Mechanical Engineering (London), Priestley Memorial Award, Priestley Medal, National Medal for Science, ACS Pure Chemistry Award, G. S. Lewis Medal, and Willard Gibbs Medal.

He is a fellow of AIC and a member of the American Chemical Society, American Physical Society, American Association for the Advancement of Science, National Academy of Science, Chemical Society of London, American Council on Education, Philosophical Society, Nuclear Society, Faraday Society, American Academy of Arts and Sciences, Chemists Club, Bohemian Club, Cosmos Club, Pi Kappa Dalta, Tau Beta Pi, and Sigma Xi.

Ken married Jean Mosher in 1935. Their children are Ann, Russell and John. Russell, who holds a doctorate in physics, is a faculty member at Cal Tech. Russell is the father of three children. Besides education and research, Kenneth is interested in traveling, boat design, boat building and sailing the boats he has designed and built.

CHARLES JOSEPH PLANK

One of the major breakthroughs in industrial catalysis occurred in the late 1920's when Eugene J. Houdrey used pelletized San Diego clay as a catalyst for cracking petroleum. After a successful pilot plant run at the Paulsboro Laboratories of Vacuum Oil Company in 1934,* Houdrey formed the Houdrey Process Company to exploit this catalytic system. Five years later, Socony had several Houdrey units in operation which were able to produce high octane gasoline for military aircraft. Later, the Houdrey fixed bed catalyst was replaced by a moving bed catalyst process (TCC) and fluid catalytic cracking (FCC). As FCC required a more rugged catalyst than acid-

*In 1931, Vacuum Oil joined with Standard Oil to form Socony-Vacuum Oil Co.

treated clay, Socony hired several scientists to develop a new catalytic cracking system. Charles Plank was one of these men.

Born in Calcutta, India, on November 8, 1915, to missionary parents, Charles attended high school in Lafayette, Indiana - his father's hometown. Purdue University, which is in West Lafayette, conferred upon him the B.S. (1936), M.S. (1939), and Ph.D. (1942) degrees. In 1941, he became a research chemist with Socony-Mobile.*

Dr. Plank soon learned the shortcoming of Nobel Laureate Ostwald's definition of a catalyst, i.e., "a material which changes the rate of chemical reaction without itself appearing in the product." Since U. S. oil refineries must replenish more than 2,000 tons of catalysts daily, Plank defined "industrial catalysis" as "the science of dirty surfaces."

In his attempt to develop a superior catalytic system with a long life, Charles used the CAT-a-test developed by Alexander Shimp of Houdrey for testing his experimental catalysts. His first efforts were devoted to improving the synthetic silica-alumina gels, which were more stable and more active than Houdrey's acid-treated clay. He soon discovered, however, that the system he sought could not be measured by the CAT-a-test. It was in 1956 that he and Edward J. Rosinski began to obtain a catalyst with active sites located in pores whose sizes were in the same order as the molecules to be cracked. These investigations led to the development of the early Zeolite Cracking Catalysts (REAY), which were patented in 1964. By use of fluid-bed pilot tests, Plank and Rosinski developed improved zeolite catalysts (REHY) which increased the yield from 51 to 54 percent. This crystalline

*Now Mobil Oil Company.

zeolite catalyst composite consists of a finely divided crystalline alumino-silicate having uniform pore openings of 0.6 to 1.5 nm, dispersed in an inorganic oxide matrix, with a low sodium content.

It has been estimated that the use of zeolite catalysts has saved this country's petroleum industry 200 million barrels of imported oil annually.   It is also recognized that 90 percent of all cracking catalysts used by the American Petroleum Industry are molecular sieve catalysts - the largest use of catalysts by industry - related to Plank's invention.   These molecular sieve catalysts are zeolitic or crystalline alumino-silicates in which the shape and size of the pores and the internal shape permits only certain molecules to enter into the cavity. The catalyst itself is believed to be dependent upon the ions associated with each particular zeolite.

Charles was named AIC Chemical Pioneer in 1974. He and Rosinski were inducted into the Inventors Hall of Fame in 1979, which signal honor they share with Thomas Edison, Nobel Laureate John Bardeen, Charles M. Hall, Leo Baekeland, Carl Djerassi and Roy Plunkett.   Other honors include the Award of the Catalysts Club of Philadelphia (1969), Outstanding Patent Award by the New Jersey Council for Research and Development (1970), Eugene J. Houdrey Award in Applied Catalysis (1973), and honorary doctorate by Purdue (1977).

Charles is an ardent golfer and enjoys bird photography, bridge and traveling. His marriage to Helen Bechtol Eichel produced two children: C. Laurence and Lois Plank Abby. Laurence is an attorney and district manger of a title insurance firm in Vero Beach, Florida. Lois, who is the mother of two, is a teacher of remedial reading in Longmont, Colorado.

ROY J. PLUNKETT

*A few years ago at a social affair I was
introduced by a doctor friend of mine to a
man who had been suffering from a heart
defect. "See that fellow dancing over there?"
asked my friend. "He's alive today because
he is wearing a 'Teflon' aorta which I
installed." That sort of makes the occasional
discouragements of research a lot easier -- I
believe I've been more than just helpful; I've
made a real contribution.**

*From Roy Plunkett's acceptance speech at the time he was
presented AIC's Chemical Pioneer Award.   (Taken from *THE
CHEMIST*, July 1969.)

Fluorine is one of the most reactive of all elements. It is derived from the mineral fluorspar, named for the Latin word *fluo* (meaning *flow*), which was used, prior to 1500, as a flux in metallurgy. It was Henri Moissan who, in 1886, obtained fluorine by the electrolysis of a solution of potassium acid fluoride in anhydrous hydrofluoric acid. Then in the 1920's, Thomas Midgley and Albert Henne used the Swarts reaction to develop the Freons, the first of the industrially important organic fluorides. One of the most important developments in the fluorochemical industry was the polymerization of tetrafluoroethylene by Roy Plunkett in 1938. This new polymer (Teflon) was used as a liner for vessels containing fluorine for the conversion of isotopes of uranium hexafluoride and more recently for frictionless surfaces, including cookware.

Born in New Carlisle, Ohio, on June 26, 1910, Roy attended Manchester College (B.A., 1932) and Ohio State University (M.S., 1933; Ph.D., 1936) with Paul Flory. Both men then accepted employment with Du Pont. Roy was promoted to Chief Chemist in 1939, the year following his discovery of Teflon; to Director of Research in 1960; and Director of Operations of the Freon Production Division in 1970. He retired from Du Pont in 1975.

Roy's discovery of polytetrafluoroethylene (PTFE) has been accredited to both a flash of genius and serendipity.* Of course, as in all major discoveries, luck also played a role. The need to develop a new product to compete with Freon was also an incentive for Roy, essentially the "new kid on the block," who prepared

---

*Serendipity is the faculty of making fortunate discoveries by accident. The word was coined by Horace Walpole based on the old fairy tale "The Three Princes of Serendip."

about 50 kg of TFE and stored it in cylinders cooled by dry ice. When he and his associate Jack Rebok opened the valve, instead of gas in the cylinder, they found a solid. Instead of discarding the solid, they took it to polymer chemists in the Central Research Department for characterization. Roy wrote in his laboratory notebook (dated April 6, 1938), "A white solid material was obtained which was supposed to be a polymerized product of C_2F_4." The U. S. Patent office issued Roy a patent on PTFE in 1949, the same year the trademark "Teflon" was coined. Roy subsequently received approximately thirty patents for this discovery.

The first use of PTFE was for gaskets and packing in plants in Oak Ridge, Tennessee, producing uranium hexafluoride and for nose cones covering the proximity fuses on artillery shells. Its application to cookware was delayed until the 1960's.

Dr. Plunkett received the American Institute of Chemists Pioneer Award in 1969. He was installed into the Plastics Hall of Fame in 1973 and the National Inventors Hall of Fame in 1985. His other honors include the John Scott Medal from the city of Philadelphia (1978), a citation from the Society of the Plastics Industry on the occasion of the silver anniversary of the discovery of Teflon (1963), Modern Pioneer Award of the National Association of Manufacturers (1960), Centennial Achievement Award from Ohio State University (1970), and honorary doctoral degrees from Manchester (1952) and Ohio State (1977). An AIC fellow, Roy is a member of the American Chemical Society, American Institute of Chemical Engineers, American Association for the Advancement of Science, Gamma Alpha and Sigma Xi. Moreover, Roy has been extremely active in the Boy Scouts of America, United Fund, Selective Service System, and Salem County (New Jersey) Community College.

Roy's 1935 marriage to Dorothy E. Detrick gave them two sons: Michael R. and Patrick L. Michael is a mechanical engineer for Du Pont in Charlotte, North Carolina; Patrick is a computer scientist in Washington, D.C. Two grandchildren are students at Appalachian College. Roy married Lois M. Koch in 1965. They moved to Padre Island, Texas, when he retired in 1975. Since 1979, he has served as president of the Padre Island Property Owners Association. Roy and Lois, ardent "fisherpeople" who enjoy traveling and golf, are members of the Padre Island Country Club.

CHARLES COALE PRICE

In Job XXVIII, Verse 18, one may find the verse, "The price of wisdom is above rubies." Charles Coale Price, recipient of the 1966 Chemical Pioneer Award, is definitely a "price of wisdom."

At the age of thirty-nine, Charles was a Democratic nominee for Congress, a faculty squash champion at the Universities of Illinois and Notre Dame, and a winner of sailboat races (from 1953 through 1967) on the Great Lakes and Chesapeake Bay. In 1970 he sailed his Proton II across the Atlantic Ocean to Ireland, returning to Annapolis, Maryland, in 1971 by way of the Canary Islands and Antigua. Since 1982, he has organized Academic Leaders for Alternatives to War, which resulted in fifty college and university presidents and board chairs signing petitions leading to useful meetings with Schultz, Weinberger, Clark, Adelman, etc.

Charles was born in Passaic, New Jersey, on July 13, 1913, to Thornton W. and Helen Farley Price. After graduating from high school in 1930, he enrolled in Swarthmore College (B.A., 1934). Graduate studies were undertaken at Harvard (M.A., 1935; Ph.D., 1936) where his research advisor was Louis F. Fieser. He then became research assistant to Roger Adams at the University of Illinois, was promoted to assistant professor in 1941 and associate professor in 1942. During World War II, he directed research projects for the National Defense Research Committee, the Chemical Warfare Service, and the Committee on Medical Research. The summer of 1945 was spent as a visiting lecturer at the Polytechnic Institute of Brooklyn; in 1946 he became Professor and Head of Chemistry at Notre Dame. Eight years later, he was named Blanchard Professor and chairman of the chemistry department at the University of Pennsylvania. He served as a Fulbright Lecturer at Kyoto and Osaka in 1963. Resigning the chair at the University of Pennsylvania in 1965, he was appointed Benjamin Franklin Professor of Chemistry the following year. The fall semester of 1970 saw him on academic leave at the Max Planck Institute in Munich.

Dr. Price's research has been concerned principally with the mechanism of organic reactions; he is probably best known for the synthesis of polypropylene glycol polyurethane elastomers which he produced at Notre Dame in 1941. This polymerization, which contained ether rather than ester repeat units, is now produced on a large scale around the world.

Charles served as a member of the Atomic Energy Committee National Fellowship Selection Committee

(1946-48), National Institute of Health (1958-63), Chemical Education Material Study Steering Committee (1962-74); as chairman of the National Science Foundation Divisional Committee for Mathematical, Physical and Engineering Science (1953-58), ACS Advisory Committee to the Chemical Corps (1955-58), and National Science Foundation's Advisory Council on College Chemistry (1962-66). He was President of ACS in 1965 and Vice President and Chairman of the Chemistry Section of the American Association for the Advancement of Science. Moreover, he was on the editorial boards of "Organic Synthesis," *Chemical Reviews*, the *Journal of Polymer Science*, the *Journal of Organic Chemistry*, "Chemico-biological Interactions," "Organic Reactions," "Macromolecular Synthesis," *International Science and Technology*, and "Concepts of Chemistry" series; and was chairman of the Chemistry-Biology Interface Series and on the Award Jury of Phi Beta Kappa science books. What is more, he served as chair of the St. Joseph County Chapter (1948-50) and the Indiana State Branch (1950-52) of the United World Federalists, as well as vice president of the Philadelphia Area Council and Pennsylvania State Branch (1955). He was a member of the National Executive Council (1950-53, 1956-65), First Vice-President (1958-59) and President (1958-61); is Honorary Vice-President of World Federalists USA and was president of the World Federalists Educational Fund (1972-74); was chairman of the Statutes Committee of the World Movement for World Federal Government (1953-57) and chairman of the Board of the Council for a Livable World (1973-77); was chair of the Board of Managers of Swarthmore College (1977-81), on the Board of Directors of the Wistar Institute (1960-72), Franklin Institute (1973-79), World Affairs Council of Philadelphia (1976-78), American Association for the United Nations (1958-62), American Friends Service Committee (1968-72), Commission to Study the Organization of Peace, and Friends Committee on National

Legislation (1955-65); and chaired the organizing committee of the Global Interdependence Center of Philadelphia (1976-78).

Dr. Price is the author of "A Brief Course in Organic Chemistry" (1941), "Reactions of the Carbon Carbon Double Bond" (1946), *Sulfur Bonding* (1961), *Geometry of Molecules* (1971), *The Synthesis of Life* (1974), *Energy and Order: Some Reflections on Evolution* (1983), *Coordination Polymerization* (1985), and of approximately three hundred scientific publications.

In addition to the AIC Chemical Pioneer Award, Dr. Price has received the AIC Honor Scroll from the Chicago (1955) and Philadelphia (1960) Chapters, ACS Award in Pure Chemistry (1946), Army-Navy Certificate of Appreciation Award (1948), Indiana Junior Chamber of Commerce Distinguished Service Award (1948), Army Commendation for Meritorious Civilian Service Award (1958), Philadelphia Section ACS Award (1963), ACS Charles L. Parsons Award for Distinguished Public Service (1973), and the ACS Award for Creative Invention (1974). He has been awarded honorary doctoral degrees from Swarthmore College (1950), Wilkes College (1964), Case Institute of Technology (1965), Haverford College (1966), LaSalle College (1975), Rensselaer Polytechnic Institute (1977), Philadlephia College of Pharmacy and Science (1979), and University of Pennsylvania (1983).

This esteemed international chemist, educator and politician continues to sail, play squash and golf. His 1936 marriage to Mary Elma White made him the father of four daughters and one son. After Mary's death in 1982, Charles married Anne Parker Gill.

ROY LAVELLE PRUETT

Roy Lavelle Pruett, who was recipient of the American Institute of Chemists Pioneer Award in 1982, has been credited with the discovery of many organometallic reactions, to wit: Mannich, cyclopentadienyl rhenium tricarbonyl, substituted arene chromium tricarbonyl, the use of the Chatt-Dewar model for olefin metal bonding, the Wacker process for the production of acetaldehyde via the nuceophilic attack of water on the ethylene-palladium (II) chloride complex, and the production of butyraldehyde via the addition of hydrogen and carbon monoxide to propylene (hydroformylation).

Born in Union City, Tennessee, on November 26, 1924, he graduated from Union City high school to enroll in Murray State Teachers College (B.S. 1944). During the second world war, he served as a Lieutenant J. G. in the United States Navy. He joined Union Carbide in 1948, the year he received his M.S. degree. His doctorate was awarded him by the University of Tennessee in 1951. He became chief scientist of Exxon Chemical Company's Baton Rouge, Louisiana, branch in the late 1950's.

Dr. Pruett is a lifetime fellow of the American Institute of Chemists and a member of the American Chemical Society. He has been granted forty patents by the U. S. Patent Office.

He was married in 1945.

IRA EDWIN PUDDINGTON

Twenty Canadian Citizens are members of the American Institute of Chemists. Of these, Ira Puddington is the only one to receive the AIC Chemical Pioneer Award. He is also one of the few colloid and surface chemists to receive this prestigious award.

Dr. Puddington's investigations involved spherical agglomeration and its applications in the mining industry for upgrading low quality coals and in the continuous separation of bitumen from tar sands. He also applied the spherical agglomerate technology to several other industrial problems, such as catalyst supports, selective mineral processing and ball bearing production. In 1952, Dr. D. I. Stock observed that, when shaken in benzene, finely divided barium sulfate formed quite uniform dense microspheres.　Dr. Puddington discovered that there was a fairly critical amount of water required for the formation of these dense spheres which was related to the interfacial tension between the two liquid phases.　He used this preferential wetting technique for many practical applications.　Dr. Puddington demonstrates his discovery, which is based on colloid and surface science, by showing that two pieces of plate glass can be cohered by selectively wetting the two surfaces by adding a drop of water and squeezing.

To eliminate lead poisoning of ducks (while game birds die from lead poisoning from eating spent lead shot, the effect of lead is nullified in the presence of iron), Dr. Puddington has made spherical agglomerates by selective wetting of iron and lead powder and gluing these particles together either with a water-soluble glue or by sintering.

Dr. Puddington also developed an alternative approach for the recovery of the bitumen content in oil sands in Alberta, Canada - presently recovered by the Clark Hot Water Process - by using his spherical agglomeration technology.　This has proven to be especially useful in recovering bitumens from lower grade or high fines oil sands.

In addition, he has used his knowledge of colloidal science for the collection and beneficiation of coal fines; the latter representing as much as twenty percent of the output of bituminous coal mines.　For example, in the Sidney Mines there is a 500,000 ton waste pile consisting of 80 percent carbon and twenty percent ash.　Useful coal is now being recovered from this waste pile by preferential wetting, yielding an energy source which produces little sulfur dioxide and hence does not contribute to acid rain.

Ira was born in Clifton, New Brunswick, on January

8, 1911, to Charles E. and Elizabeth Currie Puddington. After graduating from the Provincial Normal School in Fredericton in 1929, he obtained a Grammar School teacher's license and from 1929 until 1932 taught school in the Province of New Brunswick. He then enrolled in Mount Allison University in Sackville, New Brunswick, where he was a chemistry instructor, and received his B.S. with honors in chemistry in 1933. Thereafter, he attended McGill University where he was a lecturer in chemistry and received his M.S. (1936) in agricultural chemistry and Ph.D. (1938). During 1937-38, he was also a lecturer in chemistry at Sir George Williams University.* Upon receipt of his doctorate, he joined the National Research Council as a Research Officer; he remained with NRC until his retirement as Director of the Chemistry Division in 1974. While employed at NRC, he taught courses in colloid science at the University of Ottawa (1952-56) and at Carlton University (1962-72). He has been an honorary adjunct professor at Carlton since 1972. Since retiring from NRC, he has served as their special consultant.

In addition to being named Chemical Pioneer of 1984, he has been awarded honorary degrees from Mount Allison, Carleton, Memorial and McGill Universities, received the Montreal Medal of the Chemical Institute of Canada and the R. S. Jane Award for Creative Contributions to Applied Science. Author of over one hundred scientific reports, he has been awarded over forty U. S. patents, an equal number by the Patent Office in Canada, and an additional forty plus in foreign patents. In addition to being a lifetime fellow of AIC, Ira is a fellow of the Chemical Institute of Canada, Royal Society of Canada and a member of the International Union of Pure and Applied Chemistry (IUPAC). He was president of the Chemical Institute of Canada, secretary of the Applied Chemistry

*Now Concordia.

Division of IUPAC, and secretary of the Research Committee of the Technical Section of the Canadian Pulp and Paper Association.

Ira married Hazel Jean Duncan in 1936. They have one son, James.

WILSON ALVIN REEVES

Cotton, which occurs in the bolls of the perennial *Gossypium hirsumtium* plant, is the world's most important vegetable fiber. Woven for more than seven thousand years, cotton was "king" prior to World War II. Since then, however, polyester, nylon and acrylic fibers have decreased cotton's share of the U. S. fiber market to less than twenty-five percent. Fortunately for the cotton planters, research at the United States Department of Agriculture Southern Regional Research Laboratory has modified this fiber so that it can now be used in many applications which were unsuitable for the unmodified cotton fiber. Many of these modifications were developed under the supervision of Dr. Wilson A. Reeves. These developments include flame resistant cotton fabrics treated with tetrakis (hydroxymethyl) phosphonium chloride (THPC) in combination with THPC-methylolmelamine-urea tris (1-aziridinyl) phosphine oxide (APO) and ammonia. The use of the THPC and APO processes has led to an expansion in the use of cotton fabric and the commercial production of these new phosphorus compounds.

Another of Dr. Reeves' developments is a "poly-set" process which uses a buffered Lewis acid with N-methylol agents to obtain durable press cotton. Another development is the use of THPOH-NH$_3$ (Firestop) flame retardant treatment which meets Federal standards for children's sleepwear. Dr. Reeves and coworkers also developed a cross-linking process for water-swollen cotton which resulted in "durable press" work-wear cotton fabrics. Over three thousand million meters of cotton and polyester-cotton fabrics are treated annually in this country using this process. He also developed a commercial durable press cotton fabric based on the use of aluminium dichlorohydroxide and a cross-linking agent and developed the slack mercerizing process which is used by over twenty companies to produce all-cotton stretch yarns and fabrics. Other Reeves' development are: a rot and mildew resistant cotton fabric based on treatment with a formic acid colloid of methylolmelamine, a steam process for removal of formaldehyde from treated cotton and a liquid ammonia mercerizing process.

Wilson Alvin was born in Mittie, Louisiana, on July 14, 1919, to Darcy W. and Cora Simmons Reeves. After graduating from Fairview High School, he enrolled in the University of Southwestern Louisiana where he received his B.S. degree in 1941. He was granted his M.S. degree from Tulane University in 1950 and doctorate from Clemson University in 1969.

In 1942 he was with the USDA Southern Regional

Laboratory in New Orleans. The next three years were spent as an officer in the U. S. Naval Air Corps. From 1959 to 1975, he was head of USDA's Textile Finishing Laboratory. Since 1976, he has been a Professor of Textiles at Louisiana State University at Baton Rouge where he continued to investigate textile finishing until his recent retirement.

Dr. Reeves was awarded AIC's Honor Scroll and named Chemical Pioneer in 1976. He has also received the John Scott Award, Olney Medal of AATCC, Anselme Payen Award of the ACS, Certificate of Merit from the Mayor of New Orleans, Southern Chemists Award, Distinguished Service Award from the New Orleans Federal Business Association, and several superior service and distinguished service and certificate of merit awards from the USDA. A life fellow of AIC, he is a member of the American Association for Textile Chemists and Colorists (AATCC), American Chemical Society, Sigma Xi, Fiber Society, and Delta Sigma Gamma. He was president of the New Orleans Branch of the Research Society of America and chairman of the Cellulose, Wood and Fiber Division of ACS. Author of 270 technical reports, two books and nine book chapters, he has presented lectures on cotton textile finishing in England, Japan, Hong King, India, the Netherlands, the Philippines, Switzerland, Taiwan, Thailand, and the United States, and has been awarded more than seventy U. S. patents.

Wilson married Emily L. Weilbacher in 1942. They have four children - Kay, Paul, Jean and Lynn - and two grandchildren.

(Photograph courtesy of E. F. Smith Memorial Collection, Center for History of Chemistry, University of Pennsylvania.)

EBENEZER EMMET REID

Ebenezer Emmet Reid received the 1972 Chemical Pioneer award approximately one month before he celebrated his 100th birthday. The citation read: "Dean of American organic chemists, whose contributions to the knowledge of organic sulfur compounds occupy a classical position in the world's literature. Mentor to countless students and other chemists of many lands."

Dr. Reid's contributions to the organic chemistry of sulfur have been outstanding, both experimentally and as the author of the six-volume treatise *Organic Chemistry of Bivalent Sulfur.* His principal areas of research were organic sulfur compounds, identification of acids, phthalic esters and their plasticizing properties, physical properties and molecular structure, chloroacetophenone, and lachrymators.

Few can match the lengevity record* set by Emmet Reid. In 1972, he published "an interim report" (his words) entitled *My First One Hundred Years*. This 290-page book covers not only his life story but also the history of American chemistry. Reid conducted graduate studies under the great Ira Remsen and was active in 1907 when *Chemical Abstracts* were started. He lived through the era in which the chemical industry sprang from its infancy to its present giant dimensions.

Reid was also the author of *Introduction to Organic Research* (1924); *College Organic Chemistry* (1929); *Organic Chemistry of Bivalent Sulfur* (six volumes, 1958); *Invitation to Chemical Research* (1961); *Catalysis Then and Now* (1965); and *Chemistry Through the Language Barrier* (1970). Only two of his seven books were published prior to 1937 when - at the age of sixty-five - Dr. Reid was made emeritus professor at Johns Hopkins University. Of the 138 research articles published by Dr. Reid, sixty-six were published after his so-called retirement. His failing vision and eventual blindness during the last two decades of his life failed to discourage him from achievement.

In addition to the Chemical Pioneer award, Dr. Reid's contributions to science have been recognized as follows: Phi Beta Kappa, Herty Medal, Maryland Chemist Award, Leon P. Smith Medal, honorary membership in the American Institute of Chemists, and honorary degrees

*Dr. Joel Hildebrand, University of California, Berkeley, lived to be 101 years of age.

from Richmond and Johns Hopkins Universities. Moreover, he is listed in *World's Who's Who in Science* as one of the greatest scientists in all the world in all history.

Emmet received his M.A. from Richmond College in 1892 and his doctorate from Johns Hopkins in 1898. In 1892 he was a professor of science and mathematics at Mt. Lebanon College. He taught at Baylor University and was a Carnegie assistant at Johns Hopkins in 1908-9 and a Johnson Scholar from 1909-11. After serving as a research chemist at Colgate & Company from 1911 to 1914, he joined the faculty of Johns Hopkins as Associate Professor. He was made a full professor in 1917, which post he held for twenty years; in 1937, he was named emeritus professor. Reid was a consultant to the U. S. Bureau of Mines, the U. S. War Department, Du Pont, Edgewood Arsenal, Thiokol Corporation, Hercules Powder Company, Socony Vacuum Company, and numerous colleges and universities.

Dr. Reid was a member of the American Institute of Chemists, American Chemical Society, American Association for the Advancement of Science, German and French Chemical Societies, Sigma Xi, and Johns Hopkins Club.

He was born in Fincastle, Virginia, on June 27, 1872, to Thomas Alfred and Virginia (Ammen) Reid. He married Margaret Kendall on December 28, 1915; their children are Emmet Kendall, Alfred Gray, and Martha Reid Hudson. Dr. Reid's hobby was music.

Dr. Reid died in Baltimore at the age of 102.

EUGENE GEORGE ROCHOW

The name Kipping is a favorite with polymer chemists because in 1900 he investigated organic silicon chemistry which, in 1927, led him to the recognition that polysiloxanes were macromolecules. He mistakenly called these polymers silicones because he believed them to be ketones instead of siloxanes. A second error on Kipping's part occurred in 1937 when he concluded that "the prospects of any immediate and important advance in organosilicon chemistry did not seem to be very hopeful." This error in judgment was corrected by Russia's Andrianov, Hyde and Sullivan at Corning Glass Company, McGregor at the Mellon Institute, and Rochow, Patnode and Marshall at General Electric. It is Dr. Eugene George Rochow who is credited with the basic patents on silicone polymers. He is also credited with the basic patent on the direct synthesis of organosilicon halides by the reaction of silicon with gaseous methyl chloride in the presence of copper.

Eugene was born in Newark, New Jersey, on October 4, 1909. After completing high school, he enrolled at Cornell (B.C., 1931; Ph.D., 1935) where he conducted graduate research under Dr. L. M. Dennis on the preparation of oxyacids of fluorine, and on germanium, gallium and indium, as well as organic compounds of indium and thallium. As a Hecksher Research Fellow, he also worked with Dr. Alfred Stock. His plan to undertake post-doctoral studies with Dr. Honigschmidt in Berlin did not materialize because of the unsettled conditions in Europe at that time. As a result, he accepted a position with General Electric's Research Laboratories in Schenectady, New York, where he conducted his meritorious research on organosilicon chemistry. In 1948, Dr. Rochow joined the faculty at Harvard (where he was given an honorary A.M. degree) and remained there until he retired twenty-two years later. He directed research on siloxanes, silazanes and stannanes.

For excellence in teaching, Dr. Rochow was awarded the Chemistry Manufacturers Association Catalyst Award in 1970 and the James Flack Norris Award from the Northeastern Section of the American Chemical Society in 1973. He received the Baekeland Medal (1949), Mayer Award from the American Ceramics Society (1951), Mattiello Award from the Federation of Paint and Varnish Producers (1958), AIC's Honor Scroll from the New England Chapter (1964), ACS Perkin Medal and Frederick Stanley Kipping Award (1965), Chemical Pioneer award (1968), Inventors Award from General Electric (1971), and the Alfred Stock Gedächtnis Preis from the Gesellschaft Deutscher Chemiker (1983). He is also the recipient of an honorary doctoral degree from Braunschweig University and has served as a visiting lecturer at a number of universities.

Dr. Rochow has authored or co-authored eleven books, two of which are co-authored with his scientist brother Theodore, who, formerly with American Cyanamid Company, is now a professor at North Carolina State University. Awardee of eight U. S. patents and twenty foreign patents, Dr. Rochow has published more than 170 scientific articles.

In addition to being a fellow of AIC, Rochow is a member of the American Chemical Society, American Academy of Arts and Sciences, Société de Chimie Industrielle and the International Academy of Law and Science. He has served on the editorial board of the *Journal of Organic Metallic Chemistry* since its inception in 1963. A special issue of the journal was dedicated to him on the occasion of his seventieth birthday.

Eugene's 1935 marriage to Priscilla Ferguson gave him Stephen, Jennifer and Eugene, Jr. Priscilla passed away in 1950. Eugene married Helen Louise Smith in 1951. Eugene and Helen have a son Eugene, Jr. They now live in Captiva, Florida - a tiny island far removed from the hustle and bustle of New York and Massachusetts.

BARNETT ROSENBERG

Most recently, organometallic compounds based on noble metals have been used for the treatment of human cancer. One of the leading investigators in this important field is Barnett Rosenberg, a member of the faculty of Michigan State University. Dr. Rosenberg developed platinum derivatives as chemotherapeutic agents.

Unlike many of the other Pioneers, who were born in small midwestern towns, Barnett was born in New York City on November 11, 1926. After attending public schools in New York, he enrolled in Brooklyn College where he received his B.S. degree in physics in 1948. He spent the following year at Hochschule, Zürich, Switzerland, and then returned to New York University to receive the M.S. (1950) and Ph.D. (1955) degrees.

Thereafter he accepted a post-doctoral scholarship at New York University's Institute of Mathematical Science.

Following a brief career as Senior Research Physicist with Westinghouse Electric Company, in 1958 he returned to his alma mater as a research scientist. Three years later he joined the faculty of Biophysics at Michigan State University, where he remained as professor and cofounder of the department before being named professor of chemistry in 1983. That same year he was elected President of Barros Research Institute. Two years later the Barnett Rosenberg Chair was endowed in his honor at Michigan State.

Most of Dr. Rosenberg's fifty early publications were related to the visual receptor process and photoconductivity. His eighty or more subsequent publications have been related to platinum complexes in cancer chemotherapy, kinetics and thermodynamics of aging, and death and methods for controlling brain analgesia.

Recipient of the American Institute of Chemists Pioneer award of 1979, he has also received the Gold Plaque at International Symposium on Platinum Cancer Research (1976), Gold Medal for Chemotherapy Foundation (1978), A Michiganian of the Year Award - *Detroit News* (1980), H. J. Albert Medal - International Precious Metals Institute (1981), Cain Memorial Award - American Association of Cancer Research (1983), Bristol Myers Cancer Chemotherapy Award at 13th International Congress of Chemotherapy (1983), and Harvey Prize from the Technion, Israel (1985).

Dr. Rosenberg is a fellow of AIC and a member of the American Chemical Society.

JAMES FRANK ROTH

James was born in Rahway, New Jersey, on December 7, 1925, to Louis and Eleanor Roth. After graduating from the first class of the Bronx High School of Science, he entered the University of West Virginia where he received his B.A. degree in 1947. His doctorate was awarded him by the University of Maryland in 1951. Thereafter, he accepted employment as a senior research chemist with the Franklin Institute. Three years later he became chief chemist for Lehigh Paints and Chemicals. From 1956 to 1959, he was a research chemist for GAF. He then returned for one year to the Franklin Institute as manager of the chemistry laboratory before joining Monsanto where he spent twenty years as Director of Process Sciences.

The American Institute of Chemists bestowed the Chemical Pioneer award upon Dr. Roth in recognition of his invention of the novel homogeneous rhodium catalytic low pressure carbonylation of methanol for the production of acetic acid and the heterogeneous platinum-based catalytic dehydrogenation of paraffins for the production of linear olefins. Although Borden's Louisiana plant has operated a catalytic type acetic acid production unit using a cobalt iodide catalyst at high pressures, the rhodium complex-phosphine process developed for Monsanto by Dr. Roth is more selective and functions at low pressure. Roth also produced linear olefins which are used to make biodegradable linear alkylbenzene sulfonates.

Dr. Roth was selected Chemical Pioneer in 1986. He is also the recipient of the St. Louis Section Award of the American Chemical Society, ACS Murphree Award, Richard J. Kokes Award of Johns Hopkins University and the Philadelphia Award of the Catalysis Club. He has been a Cecil L. Brown Lecturer at Seton Hall University and a Charles D. Hurd Lecturer at Northwestern University.

James is a fellow of the American Institute of Chemists and a member of the National Academy of Engineers, American Chemical Society, Catalysis Society, and Catalysis Club of Philadelphia. He is a member of the editorial board of the *Journal of Catalysis and Catalysis Reviews* and is regional editor for the Americas of *Applied Catalysis*. He was a member of the advisory board of the Center for Catalytic Science and Technology, University of Delaware, and is serving in a second term on the Visiting Committee of the Chemistry Department, Lehigh University. Author of over thirty scientific reports, he has been awarded twenty-four patents by the U. S. Patent Office.

Dr. Roth is the father of three children by a prior marriage: Lawrence, Edward and Sandra. He married Sharon Mattes in 1969.

ALLEN STEPHENSON RUSSELL

After many unsuccessful commercial adventures, Charles Martin Hall and Alfred Hunt formed the Pittsburgh Reduction Company. With the completion of its New Kensington, Pennsylvania, plant, the company name was changed to Aluminum Company of America (Alcoa). Allen Russell joined Alcoa in 1940. Thirty-eight years later,

*In 1888, Charles Martin Hall, a graduate of Oberlin College and the first chemist inducted into the Inventors Hall of Fame, produced aluminum by an electrolytic process which caused the price of the metal to drop below the longstanding price of eight dollars per pound.

he was named Vice President-Science and Technology. His principal contribution was to assist the development of the Alcoa Smelting Process, the first breakthrough in aluminum production since the development of the Hall process.* The Alcoa Smelting Process produces aluminum using thirty percent less electricity and provides a safer environment than the Hall process. Dr. Russell and his associates have also made important strides in aluminum recycling, which saves energy and basic materials. These developments have made it possible for the aluminum industry in this country to recycle 600,000 tons of aluminum cans annually.

Dr. Russell was named Chemical Pioneer in 1983. He received the Karl Joseph Bayer Medal at the International Light Metals Congress in Vienna in 1981, the first American to be so honored, which medal was named for the developer of the process for extracting pure alumina from bauxite. He is also recipient of the Pennsylvania State Alumni Fellow (1980) and the Gold Medal of the American Society of Metals (AMS) (1982). He is a fellow of both AIC and AMS and a member of the American Chemical Society, American Institute of Mining, Metallurgical and Petroleum Engineers, American Society for Metals, Directors of Industrial Research, National Academy of Engineering, Research Society of America, Phi Lambda Upsilon, Sigma Pi Sigma, and Sigma Xi. He was the Extractive Metallurgy Lecturer for the Metallurgical Society of AIME in 1981. In 1979, he was the fourteenth to be named Scientist of the Year by *Industrial Research/Development.**

*Some of the other recipients of this honor were John Bardeen, co-developer of the transistor and winner of two Nobel Prizes; AIC Gold Medalist W. O. Baker; William P. Lear, inventor of the Lear Jet; and Wernher von Braun and William H. Pickering, aerospace scientists.

Author or co-author of thirty-seven scientific articles, Dr. Russell has been granted ten U. S. patents. Two of his early publications were co-authored by his faculty advisor, J. H. Simons; another publication was entitled "A New Process to Produce High Purity Aluminum."

Allen, whose birthday is May 27, 1915, was one of six children born to Ruth Stephenson and Arthur Stanton Russell of Bedford, Pennsylvania. His father ran a wholesale grocery business which had been founded by Allen's grandfather. Two of Arthur's sons later joined the wholesale grocery business. Following Allen's graduation from Bedford High School in 1932, he entered Pennsylvania State University where he received his B.S. (1936), M.S. (1938) and Ph.D. (1941) degrees.

In 1941, Allen married Judith Sexauer, whom he met at a Thanksgiving party at a local church. He has travelled extensively and enjoys bridge, music, golf and swimming. Since retirement, he has served as an adjunct professor at the Universities of Pittsburgh, Florida, and Trondheim, Norway.

Dr. Russell's research philosophy is summarized in part by the following statement: "Successful research depends a great deal on making the right decisions on which way to go. Investigating a blind alley is costly in time and money, but an alley is sometimes so poorly marked that you don't know it's blind until you have reached the end."

(Photograph courtesy of Clark University Archives.)

ROBERT PRICE RUSSELL

Robert Russell, a talented scientist, competent executive, and president of the Standard Oil Development Company, received the AIC Gold Medal in 1946. Three distinguished men - Gustav Egloff, Warren K. Lewis, and Major General A. H. Wait - commemorated him at that ceremony. Lewis did not attempt a comprehensive survey of the accomplishments of Russell's organization, but attention was called to three achievements of outstanding importance. The first was development of the techniques of polymerization of isobutylene and the utilization of the products. The second was the development of methods of manufacture and purification of butadiene from petroleum raw materials, for over ninety percent of the butadiene produced from petroleum in this country for use in the rubber program employed in its manufacture one or more of the processes developed by Russell's men. The third, perhaps of even greater importance than either of the other two, was the development of the so-called fluid catalyst process for the cracking of oil, which process was used in connection with the manufacture of more than half the aviation gasoline produced in this country during the second world war.

Robert was born on July 16, 1898, in Worcester, Massachusetts; his father was a bank clerk. He helped pay for his education at Clark University with an assortment of jobs that included house-to-house selling of brushes. Clark presented him his A.B. degree in 1917 and an honorary D.Sc. degree in 1946. Before enrolling at the Massachusetts Institute of Technology (M.S., 1922), he studied at the University of Michigan and Worcester Polytechnic Institute. He held important positions at MIT until 1927, when he became director of research and development of the Standard Oil Company of Louisiana at Baton Rouge.

A pleasing personality and the knack of delegating responsibility made Bob Russell a top-flight executive as well as a scientist. In gathering men around him in petroleum research, he demanded two things: first, they must have a sound and thorough technical background; second, and perhaps even more important, they must be able to get along with other people. Bob advanced rapidly to positions of importance in Standard Oil before becoming president in 1944. Under his leadership, the Standard Oil Development Company grew into one of the world's leading organizations devoted to research on petroleum and its products. In addition to new and improved uses for crude oil, the laboratory worked on the production of liquid hydrocarbons from coal and natural gas, on better synthetic rubbers, and in the field of plastics. In 1947, Russell became vice president of the International Basic Economy Corporation, Caracas, Venezuela.

In addition to those already mentioned, Russell's many honors included the Chevalier, Legion d'honneur; Cadman Medal, British Institute of Petroleum; civilian with the Office of Scientific Research and Development; member of the National Defense Research Committee; and honorary fellow of AIC. He was a member of the American Chemical Society, American Institute of Chemical Engineers, American Petroleum Institute, American Society of Automotive Engineers, and American Institute of Chemists.

Robert was married in 1923 and fathered two children.

ALFRED SAFFER

Though all recipients of the American Institute of Chemists Pioneer award have made major contributions to the advancement of chemistry, few have had the opportunity to start new corporations for the production and sale of the end results of their research. One of these few fortunate individuals is Alfred Saffer, who founded and served as chief executive officer of Oxirane International and Halcon Catalyst Industries and was the co-inventor of the bromine-assisted oxidation process for the production of terephthalic acid from p-xylene. Oxirane International produces propylene oxide, styrene, tertiary butyl alcohol, isobutylene, tertiary butyl hydroperoxide, and methyl methacrylate; Halcon Catalyst Industries produces catalysts and terephthalic acid.

Born in New York City on December 3, 1918, Alfred received his B.S. (1939), M.S. (1941) and Ph.D. (1943) degrees from New York University. He then joined the Manhattan Project at Princeton where he was a senior research associate and group leader in atomic energy research. He left this position in 1945 to become senior research chemist for Firestone Tire & Rubber Company. Three years later he joined Halcon as a research chemist and in 1957 founded Halcon Catalyst Industries. He became affiliated with Oxirane when it was created in 1966 as a joint venture of Halcon and Atlantic Richfield Company, and became president in 1976; but two years later he returned to Halcon as vice chairman.

Dr. Saffer was named Chemical Pioneer in 1982. He is a member of the National Academy of Engineering, American Institute of Chemists, American Institute of Chemical Engineers, and Society of Chemistry Industry. Awardee of thirty-two U. S. patents, he has authored or co-authored three papers describing his technology in *Chemical Week, Chemical Engineering Progress* and *Chemical Technology.*

(Photograph courtesy of Merck & Co.)

LEWIS HASTINGS SARETT

A few Nobel prizes have been awarded as a result of the isolation and synthesis of cortisone, namely, to Philip S. Hench, Edward C. Kendall and Tadeus Reichstein in 1950 for the discovery of cortical hormones or corticoids; and to Robert B. Woodward in 1965 for the synthesis of cortisone which took place in 1951. Prior to that time, in 1944, Lewis Sarett used cattle bile in a step-by-step synthesis of cortisone, which was followed by the total synthesis of cortisone. The efficacy of this hormone against rheumatoid arthritis was demonstrated by Dr. Hench at the Mayo Clinic in 1948. Five years later, Dr. Sarett's achievements in this regard were cited as the most outstanding in the *Annual Review of Chemistry*.

Sarett subsequently participated in the synthesis of dexamethasone, which is thirty-five percent more potent than cortisone. He also headed the Merck research team which discovered amprolium for the treatment of coccidiosis in poultry; thiabendazole, which controls gastrointestinal parasites in livestock; and indomethacin, an anti-inflammatory agent used for certain arthritic disorders.

Lewis Hastings Sarett was born in Champaigne, Illinois on December 22, 1917, and grew up in the small lumbering town of Laona, Wisconsin. His father was a professor of speech. Lewis' choice of a career in chemistry was catalyzed by the gift of a chemistry set. After completing high school, Lewis enrolled in Northwestern University (B.S., 1939). Graduate work was conducted at Princeton (Ph.D., 1944). He then joined the Merck Research Laboratory, a pharmaceutical firm, and spent forty years with them before retiring as Senior Vice President for Science and Technology in 1982.

The American Institute of Chemists awarded Sarett its Gold Medal in 1971 and named him Chemical Pioneer in 1972. He was inducted in the National Inventors Hall of Fame in 1981. His other awards include the Northwestern Alumni Association Award of Merit (1951), Merck Board of Directors Scientific Award (1951), Leo Hendrick Baekeland Award for the North Jersey Section of ACS (1951), Eastern Union County (New Jersey) Chamber of Commerce Award (1952), Julius W. Sturmar Memorial Lecture Award (1959), ACS Award for Creative Work in Synthetic Organic Chemistry (1964), William Scheele Lecture Award of the Pharmaceutical Institute of Sweden (1974), Synthetic Organic Chemical Manufacturers Association Medal for Creative Research in Synthetic Organic Chemistry (1964), New Jersey Patent Award from the New Jersey Council for

Research and Development (1966), National Cystic Fibrosis Foundation Award (1969), National Medal of Science (1975), Perkin Medal of the Society of Chemical Industry (1976), Industrial Research Institute Medal (1980), Commonwealth Award of Distinguished Service of the Commonwealth Fund of Wilmington (Delaware) (1980), and Procter Medal of the Philadelphia Drug Exchange (1982). He also received honorary doctoral degrees from Northwestern (1972) and Bucknell (1977) Universities.

Dr. Sarett is a member of AIC, the National Academy of Sciences, American Chemical Society, Society of Chemical Industry, Phi Beta Kappa, Phi Eta Sigma, Phi Lambda Upsilon, New York Academy of Science, and Sigma Xi. He has been a member of many boards and committees, including a membership in the advisory committee of the University of Alexandria (Egypt) Research Center, Industrial Advisory Committee of the University of California at San Diego, Advisory Council for the Department of Chemistry at Princeton, Board of Trustees at Cold Spring Harbor Laboratory for Quantitative Biology, and the Editorial Advisory Board of *Chemical and Engineering News*. The author of approximately eighty scientific reports, he has been awarded over 180 U. S. patents.

Lewis was married to Mary Adams in 1944 and has two children.

(Photograph courtesy of Lawrence Berkeley Laboratory, University of California.)

GLENN THEODORE SEABORG

While Aristotle believed that the world was made of four elements - heat, cold, wetness and dryness - the phlogistionists and their successors discovered the chemical elements hydrogen (Cavendish, 1776), oxygen (Priestley, 1770), chlorine (Scheele, 1777), to name but a few. Some discoverers of elements, such as Lord Rayleigh and Sir William Ramsay were knighted for the discovery of argon, neon, krypton and xenon; others, such as Marie Curie, were made Nobel Laureates. In other words, the eminence of many pre-twentieth century chemists was the result of their discovery of one or more element.

One scientist of this century - Glenn Theodore Seaborg - discovered or co-discovered more elements than any of his predecessors: plutonium (1940), americium (1945), curium (1944), berkelium (1949), californium (1950), einsteinium (1952), fermium (1953), mendelevium (1955), nobelium (1958), and element 106 (1974). He and his colleagues have also discovered more than one hundred isotopes of elements, including uranium-233. He is also the originator of the actinide concept for placing the heavy elements in the periodic table.

Glenn was born in Ishpeming, Michigan, on April 19, 1912, to H. Theodore Seaborg, a machinist, and Selma Erickson Seaborg. As a result of taking a course in chemistry from an inspiring high school teacher, Dwight Logan Reid, at Jordan High School in Los Angeles, Glenn decided to major in chemistry. After receiving his A.B. from the University of California at Los Angeles in 1934, he commenced graduate research at the University of California in Berkeley where his research advisor was Dr. Ernest Gibson. Upon receipt of his doctorate in 1937, he served as a research assistant to G. N. Lewis and then joined Berkeley's faculty, where he is presently a University Professor, Associate Director of Lawrence Berkeley Laboratory, and Chairman of the Lawrence Hall of Science. Moreover, he served as Berkeley's Chancellor from 1958 to 1961.

His service at the University of California was twice broken. During World War II, he went to the University of Chicago's Metallurgical Laboratory to work on the chemical extraction process used in the production of plutonium for the Manhattan Project. In 1961, President Kennedy appointed him Chairman of the Atomic Energy Commission, in which capacity he served for ten years. Prior to that time, he had served as a member of the

General Advisory Committee to the AEC (1946-50) and as a member of the President's Science Advisory Committee (1959-61). While Chairman of the AEC, Dr. Seaborg visited sixty foreign countries. In 1963, he headed the United States delegation which signed the "Memorandum on Cooperation in the Field of Utilization of Atomic Energy for Peaceful Purposes" and he was also part of the U.S. delegation for the signing of the Limited Nuclear Test Ban Treaty. In 1971, he served as president of the Fourth U.N. Conference on the Peaceful Uses of Atomic Energy held at Geneva, Switzerland. Two years later, he visited the People's Republic of China as a member of the first delegation of the Committee for Scholarly Communication with the People's Republic and again in 1978 as chairman of a delegation of chemists and chemical engineers under this committee's auspices.

Glenn Seaborg was recipient of the Nobel Prize in chemistry with E. M. McMillan in 1951. The American Institute of Chemists named him Gold Medalist in 1968. The citation of his Chemical Pioneer award (1973) credited him with inspiring and creative leadership and organizational skill in scientific, educational and governmental affairs. Glenn's other honors include the ACS Award in Pure Chemistry (1947), Nichols Medal from the New York Section of ACS (1948), John Scott Medal from the city of Philadelphia (1953), Perkin Medal (1957), Enrico Fermi Award (1959), Joseph Priestley Memorial Award from Dickinson College (1960), Science and Engineering Award from Drexel Institute (1962), Leif Erickson Foundation Award (1962), Swedish American of the Year (1962), Franklin Medal (1963), Spirit of St. Louis Award (1964), Charles L. Parsons Award from ACS (1964), Willard Gibbs Medal from the Chicago Section of ACS (1964), Washington Award (1965), Arches of Science Award (1968), International Platform Association Award (1969), Prometheus Award (1969), Nuclear Pioneer Award

(1971), Oliver Townsend Award (1971), Distinguished Honor Award from U. S. Department of State (1971), The Golden Plate Award (1972), Madison Marshall Award from the North Alabama Section of ACS (1972), Priestley Medal (1979), John R. Kuebler Alpha Chi Sigma Award (1978), Founders Medal from Hebrew University (Jerusalem) (1980), Henry DeWolf-Smyth Award (1982), Great Swedish Heritage Award (1984), and the first annual Glenn T. Seaborg Actinide Award (1984). He is the recipient of forty-nine honorary doctoral degrees.

A fellow of AIC, Glenn is a member of the American Chemical Society, American Physical Society, American Nuclear Society, American Philosophical Society, Royal Swedish Academy of Engineering Sciences; the national academies of science of Argentina, Bavaria, Poland, Scotland, Spain, Sweden, and USSR; the Deutsche Akademie der Naturforscher Lepoldina (East Germany), Society of Nuclear Medicine, World Association of Federalists, Federation of American Scientists, National Academy of Public Administration, International Platform Association, Phi Beta Kappa, Sigma Xi, Pi Mu Epsilon, Alpha Chi Sigma, Phi Lambda Upsilon, American Hiking Society, Bohemian Club, Chemists Club, Cosmos Club, University Club, and the University of California Faculty Club, to name but a few. He is the Chairman of the Board at Kevex Corporation and serves on the boards of several other private and community service organizations. He was president of the American Association for the Advancement of Science (1972), ACS (1976), and continues to serve as president of Science Service (1966-) and the International Organization for Chemical Sciences in Development (1981-). He was also a member of the National Commission on Excellence in Education (1981-84) and chaired the Chemical Education Materials Study (1959-74).

His many book$ include *Chemistry of the Actinide Elements, The Transuranium Elements, Kennedy, Khrushchev and the Test Ban,* and close to four hundred scientific papers. He has been awarded forty patents by the U. S. Patent Office, including those on the elements americium and curium.

Glenn is a sports enthusiast. He hikes regularly and is an avid football fan. He served as the Faculty Athletic Representative of the Berkeley campus to the Pacific Coast Intercollegiate Athletic Conference from 1953 to 1958. An ardent conservationist, he aided in the development of a twenty-year master plan for the East Bay Regional Park District in the San Francisco area and serves as chairman of Citizens for Urban Wilderness Areas.

He married Helen L. Griggs, who had been secretary to Dr. Ernest O. Lawrence. The Seaborgs' six children are Peter, Lynne (Cobb), David, Stephen, John Eric and Dianne.

RAYMOND BENEDICT SEYMOUR

While many chemists attribute their choice of vocation to inspiration from a chemistry teacher or role model, Ray's choice of profession was related to the things he did not want to do or was not capable of doing. For, prior to his university experience, he had spent many hours after school and on summer vacations pulling weeds, picking vegetables, making hay, in a bakery, as a bottle washer in a dairy, in a cotton mill, as a dishwasher and soda jerk in a tea room, as a paperboy, as a book salesman, and as a laborer building roads for the New Hampshire Highway Department. This wide experience was attributable in part to the lack of job opportunities during the depression and the need to find new jobs periodically during summer vacations.

Ray was born in Brookline, Massachusetts, on July 26, 1912, to Walter A. Seymour, a salesman, and Marie E. (Doherty) Seymour. Following high school graduation, he accepted a four-year partial scholarship to Massachusetts Institute of Technology. However, since MIT increased its tuition prior to his enrollment, he decided to commute to the University of New Hampshire, which was approximately six miles from home. There he competed on the cross country and track teams and served as a teaching assistant during his junior and senior years. After receiving his B.S. degree and the Opdyke Prize for proficiency in physical chemistry (1933), a graduate teaching assistantship allowed him to remain with the University of New Hampshire to obtain his M.S. degree (1935). On the advice of his research advisor, Professor Harold A. Iddles, Ray then applied for a teaching assistantship and in 1937 received his doctorate from the University of Iowa.

Dr. Seymour began his professional career in accelerator research with Goodyear in Akron, Ohio. Because of the lack of challenge in this field, Ray moved into the field of synthetic rubber research and was able to show that the so-called modifier, dodecyl mercaptan used in the emulsion copolymerization of butadiene and styrene, was actually a chain transfer agent. This additive reacted with a growing polymer chain and hence the molecular weight, as measured by the Mooney viscosity, was inversely proportional to the concentration of dodecyl mercaptan. Because of the growing popularity of research on synthetic rubber, Ray then directed his research to plastics based on copolymers of vinyl chloride. As a result, he developed and patented Goodyear's first commercial vinyl chloride-vinylidene chloride copolyer (Plioflex).

Ray left Goodyear in 1939 to accept a position as

chief chemist for Atlas Mineral Products Company in Mertztown, Pennsylvania. There he developed the first commercial vinyl chloride copolymer coatings (Zerok), the first natural rubber latex tank lining (Rewbon), the first plastic concrete (Alkor) and the first interpenetrating network system (Alkor 25). The latter, based on the *in situ* polymerization of solutions of polybutyl methacrylate in furfuryl alcohol, was patented.

In 1941, Dr. Seymour became Research Group Leader at Monsanto's Central Research Laboratories in Dayton, Ohio. There he directed development of and patented textile coatings (Stymer), high impact polystyrene (Styron), high performance Polymer (Cadon), low density crosslinked styrene-maleic anhydride copolymer, silica-filled polymethyl methacrylate dentures and oil soluble polymers and contributed to the styrene production and polyacrylonitrile fiber (Acrilan) programs.

Four years later, Ray accepted a position as Director of Research at the University of Chattanooga.* In this capacity, he directed the development of a spectrographic procedure for monitoring engine wear of diesel engines on the Southern Railroad; a continuous method for the mercerization of cotton, plastic composites reinforced by nylon, cotton and orlon fibers; bonded fabrics (Sterilon); plastic impregnated Coca Cola cases; controlled release biocides; ionomers; abrasion resistant clear plastics; and a commercial process for making glycine. He also introduced the nation's first undergraduate course in polymer science.

Ray joined Johnson and Johnson in New Brunswick, New Jersey, in 1948, where he directed the development of x-ray opaque surgical sponges, reinforced plastic casts

*Now the University of Tennessee at Chattanooga.

nd plastic adhesive bandages. Six months later he became President and Technical Director of Atlas Mineral Products Company where he directed the development a new line of products, which included simulated marble (Vitroplast), four epoxy resin concrete and coatings (Alfane), rigid polyvinyl chloride pipe and structures (PEE VEE CEE, Amcoflex), reinforced plastic pipe and structures, root resistant joints for sewer pipe and polyurethane foam and coatings.

From 1955 to 1959, Dr. Seymour was President and Technical Director of Loven Chemical of California. The next years he was Professor, Chairman of the Department of Chemistry and Dean of the Science Division of Sul Ross State University in Alpine, Texas. In 1964, he accepted a position as Professor and Associate Chairman of the Department of Chemistry and Associate Director of Research at the University of Houston where he remained until his retirement. He became Distinguished Professor at the University of Southern Mississippi in 1976.

Ray was Edison Scholar (1929) and recipient of AIC's Honor Scroll from the Louisiana Section (1982) and Chemical Pioneer award (1985). His other honors include Western Plastics Award (1960), Southeast Texas ACS Award (1972), Plastics Pioneer Award (1973), University of Houston Excellence in Teaching Award (1975), Outstanding Educator of America Award (1976), Chemical Manufacturers' Catalyst Excellence in Teaching Award (1976), Western Plastics Pioneer Award (1977), Tam Kang University Chair in Chemistry (1978), Western Plastics Hall of Fame (1981), Southern Chemist Award (1981), SPE International Excellence in Teaching Award (1982), ACS Herty Award (1985), and ACS Outstanding Chemist in Mississippi (1986).

Professor Seymour has been an ACS tour speaker

on eight different occasions. He has also been a tour speaker for Sigma Xi, The Society for Coatings Technology and NACE. He has served as a visiting scientist for AAAS in the southwest; U. S. Department of Commerce in Bangladesh; National Academy of Sciences in Yugoslavia; Coatings, Rubber and Plastics Societies in Australia; and National Science Council of Taiwan. He was a symposium chairman at the North American Chemical Conference in Mexico City, delegate to the International Union of Pure and Applied Chemistry Conference in the USSR, plenary speaker at an international reinforced plastics and composites conference in Czechoslovakia, and speaker and session chairman at the IUPAC meeting in Jerusalem. In addition to presenting seminars at over one hundred universities in this country, he has presented seminars at the University of the West Indies in Trinidad, Simon Fraser University, University of British Columbia, University of Belgrade, University of Zagreb, University of Ljubljana, National University of Taiwan, Tam Kang University, and the Universities of Tainan and Taichung.

A fellow of AIC and of the American Association for the Advancement of Science, Ray is a fifty-year member and former national councilor and section chairman of ACS. He is also a member of the American Institute of Chemical Engineers, National Association of Corrosion Engineers, Society of Plastics Engineers, Society of the Plastics Industry, Society of Coatings Technologists, American Association of Textile Chemists and Colorists (AATCC), Technical Association of Pulp and Paper Industry, Mississippi Academy of Science, Alpha Chi Sigma, Phi Lambda Upsilon, Phi Kappa Phi, Gamma Sigma Epsilon and Sigma Xi. Moreover, he served as vice president of the Tennessee and Texas Academy of Sciences, National Director and chairman of the Southern California Section of the Society of Plastics Industry, chairman of the Education Committee of the Polymer

Division and Chairman of the Polymer Group of ACS, and chairman of the South Central Section of AATCC. He was also the director of the Allentown Kiwanis Club and of the Rotary Clubs of Chattanooga and Alpine. Awardee of forty-five U.S. patents and over one hundred foreign patents, he has published thirty-five books, two audio courses, 150 chapters in books and encyclopedias, and more than 1500 articles in scientific journals around the world. He served as Technical Editor of *Modern Plastics* encyclopedia and on the editorial advisory committees of *Southern Chemist, Western Plastics, Popular Plastics, Plastics, Polymer News, Polimeri* and the *ACS Advances in Chemistry* series. His dedication to teaching has been recognized by the establishment of annual best student awards in his honor at the Universities of New Hampshire, Sul Ross, Houston, and Southern Mississippi.

While a student at the University of Iowa in 1936, Ray married Frances B. Horan. Four children were born of this union. Dr. David Ray Seymour is an economist at the University of Nevada at Reno. Peter Jerome is the proprietor of an interior and exterior decorating company in Houston. Susan Jayne Seymour Smith is an interior decorator for her brother's company. Phillip Allen is a music composer and artist in San Francisco. Ray and Frances have ten grandchildren.

(Photograph courtesy of American Institute of Chemists.)

KARL BARRY SHARPLESS

Karl Sharpless, who was named AIC's Chemical Pioneer in 1988, is well known for his pioneering work on novel organic synthesis methodology in general and asymmetric synthesis methods in particular. His outstanding work has brought together metal chemistry and organic chemistry in a truly synergistic manner. His current research interests include developing new homogeneous catalysts for the oxidation of organic compounds, using inorganic reagents to effect new transformations in organic chemistry, and asymmetric catalysis involving both early and late transition metal-mediated processes.

Born on April 28, 1941, in Philadelphia, Dr. Sharpless received his B.A. from Dartmouth College (1963), where he was introduced to organic chemistry and research. His doctorate was granted by Stanford (1968) under the direction of E. V. van Tamelen. Following postdoctoral years with James P. Collman at Stanford and with Konrad Bloch at Harvard, Karl became professor of chemistry at the Massachusetts Institute of Technology in 1970. From 1977 through 1980 he was on Stanford's chemistry faculty.

A former A. P. Sloan Fellow, Camille and Henry Dreyfus Teacher-Scholar and Sherman Fairchild Distinguished Scholar at the California Institute of Technology, Dr. Sharpless serves on the board of editors of *Organic Syntheses.* He is a fellow of the American Academy of Arts and Sciences and the American Association for the Advancement of Science, and a member of the National Academy of Sciences.

Recipient of the American Chemical Society's Award for Creative Work in Organic Synthesis, he has also been awarded the Arthur C. Cope Scholars Award, Allan R. Day Award of the Philadelphia Organic Chemists Club, Dr. Paul Janssen Prize for Creativity in Organic Synthesis (Belgium) and the Harrison Howe Award of the Rochester Section of the American Chemical Society. During the 1987-1988 academic year, he was a Guggenheim Fellow.

Karl was married in 1965.

(Photograph courtesy of the National Academy of Sciences.)

HENRY CLAPP SHERMAN

Henry Clapp Sherman was born on October 16, 1875, in Ash Grove, Virginia. His early education was in a rural one-room school and at home. In 1893 he received his B.S. from the Maryland Agricultural College.* He then obtained a fellowship at Columbia University, where he received the M.S. (1896) and Ph.D. (1897) degrees. His doctoral thesis was concerned with the insoluble carbohydrates of wheat. Thereafter, he worked with Wilbur Atwater on energy metabolism and nutrition. Early in his career, he was an assistant in the laboratory of the State Chemist of Maryland. The paper resulting from this

*Now the University of Maryland.

work was entitled "Determination of Nitrogen in Fertilizers Containing Nitrates." In 1899, he joined Columbia as a lecturer and supervisor of the quantitative organic analysis course. Two years later, he became an instructor; in 1905, adjunct professor. He also published his first book that year - *Methods of Organic Analysis*. In 1907 he became professor of chemistry.

During World War I, he served as a member of the American Red Cross mission to Russia. At war's end, he returned to Columbia as executive officer of the Chemistry Department and remained in this position until 1939. In 1924, he was elected Mitchell Professor of Chemistry. During the second world war he once again left Columbia to serve his country as chief of the Bureau of Human Nutrition in the Department of Agriculture. He became chairman of the Commission of Dietary Allowances of the National Research Council in 1948.

Dr. Sherman's research included the requirements of humans for calcium, phosphorus, iron and protein, which led him to the conclusion that the optimal intake of "fuel food" is close to the actual need, and that for protein and certain mineral elements a margin of about fifty percent may be desirable. He showed enzymes to be protein-like, a conclusion contrary to the view then held by many chemists. He developed biological assay methods for vitamin A, thiamine, ascorbic acid and riboflavin. His studies of the effect of diet on the life span led him to the conclusion that old age could be postponed by following a diet rich in the "protective foods" of fruits, vegetables and milk.

In 1922, Sherman (with S. L. Smith) published the ACS Monograph "The Vitamins," the second edition of which was published in 1931. At the tercentenary of the American Chemical Society in 1935, he presented a paper entitled "Food Supply and Human Progress." His book *The Science of Nutrition* was published in 1943.

Sherman received many honors because of his creative and important researches on foods, vitamins and nutrition. Named Gold Medalist by the American Institute of Chemists and elected to the National Academy of Sciences in 1933, the following year he was presented the Nichols Medal from the New York Section of the American Chemical Society with the citation, "So large a quantity of the literature on vitamins is valueless and there was needed a critically minded investigator who had the patience and capacity to review all that was published on the subject and eliminate what was worthless." The Associated Grocery Manufacturers of America presented him an award in 1937. In 1947, he received the Franklin Medal of the Franklin Institute of Philadelphia. Columbia University and the University of Maryland awarded him honorary doctoral degrees.

Henry married Cora Aldrich Bowen in 1903 and became the father of two boys and a girl. One of his sons became a physician. His daughter, Caroline Sherman Lanford, assisted her father in writing the book *Essentials of Nutrition*. Sherman continued to publish until he was seventy-five. He died just short of his eightieth birthday on October 7, 1955, in Rensselaer, New York.

JOSEPH H. SIMONS

Fluorine is three times as abundant in nature as carbon. In spite of this knowledge, those chemists who listened to Joseph Simons' talk at the Chattanooga, Tennesee, ACS meeting in 1946 were startled by his prediction that "because of their stability, fluorocarbons and their derivatives would outnumber all isolatable organic compounds in the future." It was Simons whose electrochemical fluorination techniques in hydrogen fluoride made possible the production of many old and new organic fluoride compounds.

The son of David and Esther Simons, Joseph was born in Chicago on May 10, 1897. After completing high school, he enrolled at the University of Illinois where he received his B.S. (1919) and M.S. (1922) degrees in chemistry. He then accepted a fellowship at the University of California where he was awarded his doctorate (1923) for his investigations in the use of trifluoromethyl radicals. Thereafter, he joined Atmospheric Nitrogen Corporation as a research chemist but left industry two years later to begin his long career as a professor. He was with the Universities of Puerto Rico, Northwestern, Pennsylvania State and Florida, becoming professor emeritus at the University of Florida at the time of his retirement in 1967.

Dr. Simons was recipient of the AIC Pioneer award in 1971. As executor of the will of Gertrude Monroe of Chicago and his own donations made possible a Simons-Monroe endowment of $100,000 to Sigma Xi to support research in the more speculative and innovative aspects of science. He was editor of five volumes of *Fluorine Chemistry* published by Academic Press and author of several scientific publications. In addition to being a fellow of AIC, Professor Simons was a member of the American Chemical Society, American Institute for the Advancement of Science, American Association of University Professors, Alpha Chi Sigma, Sigma Xi, Phi Lambda Upsilon and Sigma Phi Sigma.

Joseph married Eleanor Mae Whittaker. Their children are Dorothy E. and Robert W. Simons.

Professor Simons passed away in 1984, but his name lives on in the Simons fluorination process, the Simons-Monroe Sigma Xi Endowment, and in the five volumes he edited on fluorine chemistry.

JOHN HENRY SINFELT

The word *catalysis,* used as a political term in England in the seventeenth century, was adopted as a chemical term in 1836 by Berzelius. His colleague Sir Humphry Davy made use of the heterogeneous catalyst, platinum, to produce the miners' safety lamp which causes "fire damp" (methane) to combine with oxygen to produce a glow instead of an explosion. Catalysis has come a long way since Davy invented the safety lamp, however. Many of the major contributions to the development of catalysis can be attributed to John Henry Sinfelt.

John's investigations have emphasized bifunctional, bimetallic catalysts, primarily from periodic Group VIII and Group IB. His work on elucidating reaction mechanisms in heterogeneous catalysis formed the basis for a kinetic model of the complex reforming process which has been used worldwide in the design of reforming units. In his investigation of the kinetics of ethane hydrogenolysis, he showed that the hydrogenolysis activity of Group VIII metals is decreased in the presence of a Group IB metal but that the dehydrogenation activity is virtually unaffected. As a result, the selectivity of Group VIII metals for the aromatiziation of alkanes and cycloalkanes was greatly enhanced. Dr. Sinfelt developed a concept that the atoms of both metallic elements are in a highly dispersed state, which he named "bimetallic clusters." Metallic clusters of ruthenium-copper and osmium-copper, which are less than 10 nm in size, provide excellent examples of these systems. Bimetallic catalysts are widely used in the reforming process in the conversion of saturated hydrocarbons to aromatic hydrocarbons to produce unleaded gasoline with a high octane number. Sinfelt's bimetallic clusters of platinum and iridium are 1 nm in size and the accumulation of carbonaceous residues is several fold lower than on a platinum catalyst. In addition to his catalyst system which produces high octane number, low lead, antipolluting gasoline, Dr. Sinfelt developed a commercial process for the production of para-xylene. When oxidized, it produces terephthalic acid which is a reactant used in the production of polyester fibers and plastics.

John, the oldest of three children, was born on February 18, 1931, in the central Pennsylvania town of Munson. His father, Henry Gustave Sinfelt, who was a foreman in the Pennsylvania coal mines, was probably familiar with Davy's safety lamp. John's mother was June Lillian (McDonald) Sinfelt. After graduating from Philipsburg high school as class valedictorian, John majored in chemical engineering at Penn State (B.S., 1951). Graduate studies were undertaken on molecular diffusion through a liquid-liquid interface at the University of Illinois (Ph.D., 1954) under the direction of Professor Harry G. Drickamer. John then accepted a position with Exxon Research and Engineering Company, where he has been Senior Scientific Advisor since 1979; his entire industrial career at Exxon has been in the field of catalysis.

In addition to receiving the Chemical Pioneer award in 1981, Dr. Sinfelt has been honored with the Alpha Chi Sigma Award in Chemical Engineering Research (1971), Professional Progress Award for Outstanding Progress in Chemical Engineering from AIChE (1975), Paul H. Emmett Award in Fundamental Catalysis (1973), ACS Award in Petroleum Chemistry (1976), Dickson Prize in Science and Engineering from Carnegie-Mellon University (1977), American Physical Society International Prize for New Materials (1978), President's National Medal of Science (1979), Perkin Medal of the Society of Chemical Industry (1984), and honorary D.Sc. degree from the University of Illinois in 1981.

Dr. Sinfelt was a visiting professor at the University of Minnesota, and has served as name lecturer as follows: William N. Lacey Lecturer, Cal Tech (1973); Peter C. Reilly Lecturer, University of Notre Dame (1974); Frontiers in Chemistry Lecturer, Case Western Reserve University (1978); Matthew Van Winkle Lecturer, University of Texas (1979); Francois Gault Lecturer in Catalysis for the Council of Europe Research Group in Catalysis with lectures at various universities and institutes in France, Germany, Belgium, Netherlands and Wales (1980); Mobay Lecturer in Chemistry, University of Pittsburgh (1980); Distinguished Visiting Lecturer in Chemistry, University of Texas (1981); Camille and Henry Dreyfus Lecturer in Chemistry, University of California at Los Angeles (1982); Carothers Lecturer for the Delaware Section of the ACS (1982); Distinguished Visiting Lecturer at the University of Alberta

(1983); and the Edward Clark Lee Memorial Lecturer in Chemistry at the University of Chicago (1983). Moreover, he was chairman of the Gordon Conference on Catalysis; a member of the Board of Directors of the Catalysis Society and a member of the Board of Fellowships and Associateships for the National Research Council Committee on Human Resources; and on the Advisory Board of the University of Illinois Materials Research Laboratory. His book *Bimetallic Catalysts: Discoveries, Concepts and Applications* was published by John Wiley and Sons in 1983. Exxon's most honored scientist, he has been awarded forty-five U. S. patents and has published more than one hundred scientific articles.

A fellow of AIC and of the American Academy of Arts and Sciences, John is a member of the American Chemical Society, American Institute of Chemical Engineers, Catalysis Society, National Academy of Sciences, National Academy of Engineering, Phi Lambda Upsilon and Tau Beta Pi.

John married Muriel Jean Vadersen in 1956. They have one son: Klaus Herbert Sinfelt.

FOSTER DEE SNELL

"One of the nation's most distinguished consulting chemists, he has applied the principles of his life work with empathy, sage counsel, illuminating vision, and persuasive leadership, to the challenge of transmuting the organization of alumni of the Graduate Faculties into an active and vital entity in the life of the University. . . ."

*Citation of the Alumni Federation of Columbia University in honoring Dr. Snell.

Dr. Snell, a remarkably successful scientist and consultant, was first honored by the American Institute of Chemists when he was elected president for the period of 1946-48. He was made an honorary member of AIC in 1959 and received the Chemical Pioneer award in 1970. While president of the AIC, Dr. Snell thought it would be well for the AIC to take over the professional activities of the American Chemical Society. Because of his vigor, intelligence and persuasiveness, he almost achieved this goal.

In the early part of his career, Foster taught industrial chemistry at the Pratt Institute. Even after establishing his consulting and business firm in 1928, he retained his interest in chemical education. The books he wrote reflect this: *Chemicals of Commerce*, first published in 1939 and revised in 1952; *Chemistry Made Easy*, the second edition of which was published in Spanish; *Colorimetric Methods of Analysis*, published in 1921, revised in 1936, enlarged to four volumes in 1948, 1949, 1953 and 1954. His favorite co-author, herself a renowned chemist, was his wife, Dr. Cornelia T. Snell.

Although he held a doctorate in chemistry, Dr. Snell chose business as a career. His firm blossomed into what was to become one of the largest private chemical and engineering consulting groups in the country. After World War II, the firm moved into a ten-story building in Manhattan and the company gained an international reputation. At its peak, the Snell organization had a staff of more than one hundred fifty chemists and engineers with offices in several international locations and satellite laboratories in Baltimore, Maryland, and Bainbridge, New York. The firm's list of clients, amassed over more than fifty years, represented a who's who in business.

Dr. Snell gave extensive and devoted service to his

fellow chemists and the advancement of the profession. He spearheaded a movement to encourage the legislature of the state of New York to license chemists as professionals. The conviction and the effort behind his endeavor was not political in the usual connotation but rather a manifestation of these attributes which made Foster a professional chemist.

For more than thirty years, he served both the local section of the American Chemical Society and the society at large as councilor, committeeman and in other capacities. He was an officer of the American Oil Chemists Society, chairman of several committees, and continued to serve this organization as representative to the National Research Council. As a member of this latter body, he was chairman of the Fats and Oils Committee. His work for the Society of Chemical Industry during his long tenure in various offices, from secretary through chairman of the American Section and vice president of the International Society, was well known. He was active in many other organizations as well. During World War II he served on the Referee Board of the Office of Production, Research and Development. He was a member of the New York City Community College Advisory Board; the Advisory Committee to the State University of New York; Institute of Applied Arts & Sciences; and the Detergents Advisory Committee of the National Security Industrial Association. He was also active in the affairs of the American Institute of Management and he served on the President's Council of Advisors. In 1962, Governor Nelson A. Rockefeller appointed Snell a member of the Advisory Council for Industrial Research and Development of New York State.

Dr. Snell's many honors were well deserved. When he received the Gold Medal of the Society of the Chemical Industry in London, he was known as "Mr. Synthetic Detergents" or "Syn Dets" because of his prodigious work in the field of surface chemistry and detergency. He had more than fifty patents to his credit and was well known for his work on pressurized shaving cream and for his litigation in successfully defending the patent structure of his composition, which resulted in a landmark decision by the United States Supreme Court. Colgate awarded him an honorary doctor of science in 1963; the Alumni Federation of Columbia awarded him an Alumni Medal in 1964.

QUENTIN FRANCIS SOPER

Quentin Francis Soper, who is known for the biosynthesis of new penicillins, received the American Institute of Chemists Pioneer Award in 1981.

Quentin was born in Buhl, Minnesota, on December 3, 1919. He received the B.S. degree in chemistry from the University of Minnesota in 1940 and the Ph.D. degree from the University of Illinois in 1943.

When Eli Lilly and Company began research in agriculture in the late 1950's, it decided to look at the many thousands of compounds which had been made for pharmaceutical testing to determine whether any of these compounds had biological activity in the agricultural areas. The company picked the right biologists and the programs were started. During his career at Lilly Research Laboratories, in addition to the biosynthesis of new penicillins, Dr. Soper was also credited with the discovery of dinitroaniline herbicides which, by making it possible to grow weedfree crops, results in an annual savings of over one billion dollars annually to American farmers. The major dinitroaniline herbicide, trifluralin, is mainly used to control the grassy weeds in cotton and soybeans, although it has a major use in other crops, such as rapeseed in France and Canada. The main weeds controlled are foxtail and crabgrass with no injury to the crops. The weed in the rape crop is the poppy. Trifluralin also possesses the ability to control certain broadleaf weeds. Those scientists working with Dr. Soper also discovered the use of 4-nitropiazthiole as a non-selective postemergent herbicide, which is effective against a number of broadleaf and grassy weeds.

Quentin married in 1946 and is the father of four children: John, Julia, Dan and Jean.

WILLIAM JOSEPH SPARKS

It was William Sparks' fate to play an important role in one of the miracles of the twentieth century: namely, the development in less than four decades of a vast and versatile synthetic rubber industry. This industry, which was critically important during the second world war, still contributes in a major way to our economy and well-being.

In 1937 - only one year after receiving his doctorate under the direction of Dr. Carl S. Marvel from the University of Illinois - Bill decided to start inventing. His first big invention was with colleague Robert M. Thomas. Bob and Bill copolymerized a monoene (isobutylene) with small proportions of a diene (usually less than two percent isoprene) to obtain a novel and highly useful product - butyl rubber. Unlike the diene rubbers, butyl rubber is substantially free of olefinic linkages after vulcanization and hence resistant to oxidation and weathering. Butyl, one of the major synthetic rubbers, is manufactured on a large scale in at least six countries. Butyl rubber was and is enormously successful both technologically and in the business sense.

Bill Sparks' research was scarcely limited to synthetic rubber. His publications and some 145 patents (many with co-inventors) were concerned with a variety of subjects, including a leavening process, refining hydrocarbons, plastics, manufacture of alkyl nitrates, lubricants, additives, corrosion-proof liners, diesel fuel, alcohol-gasoline compositions, plasticizers, stabilized polymers, paving compositions, seed treatment, rocket propellant, and encapsulated oxidants. Many of Sparks inventions and co-inventions were also commercially successful. For example, styrene-isobutylene copolymers as coatings for paper and paper milk bottles; styrene-isoprene copolymers as artificial leather; colored asphalt paving materials; oxo alcohols; and oxo ester plasticizers. During his brief period of employment as a research supervisor at USDA's Northern Regional Research Center in Peoria, Illinois, Dr. Sparks initiated work on dimer acids and polymers made from vegetable oils; continuation of this work by NRRC scientists led to the development of the elastomer called Norepol.

Bill did not feel society should support him and his personal preferences in research. Instead, he believed research should benefit society and pay for itself. His belief was manifested when he helped establish AIC's Chemical Pioneer Award program. His talks and publications also emphasized the value of useful inventions.

Dr. Sparks' achievements as a scientist and inventor

and his dedicated services to his profession were rewarded by many important honors. These included AIC's Gold Medal and honorary membership (1954); Distinguished Alumni Award from Indiana University (1956); Charles Goodyear Medal (1963); Perkin Medal, Society of Chemical Industry (1964); ACS Priestley Medal (1965); honorary D.Sc. degrees from Indiana University and Michigan Technological Institute (1966); elected to National Academy of Engineering (1967); and Chemical Pioneer Award (1970). The Library of Congress requested an autographed photograph and list of publications to be placed in its Collection of Photographs of Famous Scientists. In 1987, Exxon Chemical Company sponsored the annual Sparks-Thomas Scientific Award through the Rubber Division of ACS.

Bill's services to science and technology included active participation in the American Chemical Society (President, 1966), American Institute of Chemists (Board of Directors, 1960-63), American Institute of Chemical Engineers, Society of the Chemical Industry, American Association for the Advancement of Science, Association of Research Directors, National Academy of Engineering, Armed Forces Chemical Association, American Academy of Achievement, Cosmos Club (Washington), Chemists Club (New York), Sigma Xi, Alpha Chi Sigma, and Phi Lambda Upsilon.

As a diplomat, he headed the U. S. Delegation to the Stockholm meeting of the International Union of Pure and Applied Chemistry in 1953 and delegate 1955 and 1957. He was a member of the Governing Board, National Academy of Sciences, 1953-55; Policy Committee Member, National Academy of Engineering; Advisory Committee Member, International Technological Assistance; Committee Chairman, Chemical and Biological Warfare, Armed Forces Chemical Association; and Vice President, Chemists Club

(New York). Moreover, he was an advisor to the U. S. State Department, Department of Agriculture and Army; Rutgers University and Rensselaer Polytechnic Institute; and national chairman of the Division of Chemistry and Chemical Technology of the National Research Council, the Scientific Research Society of America, and the Society of Sigma Xi.

William Joseph was born in Wilkinson, Indiana, on February 26, 1904; his parents were Charles Edward and Daisy (McDaniel) Sparks. Young Sparks lived on the family farm until he started his college education at Indiana University. Before entering graduate school, he worked as an industrial chemist. The fact that Bill minored in economics at the University of Illinois may have been indicative of his interest in the economic importance of research. The fact is, Bill made many wise decisions. At the age of eighteen, he decided upon a college education over the gift of a new Model T Ford. While a sophomore, he accepted the advice of Professor Frank Mathers to change his major from history to chemistry. In 1930, he asked classmate Meredith Pleasant to become his wife.

Of Dr. Sparks' 145 patents, two were issued prior to the time he received his doctorate, twelve were issued to protect his post-retirement inventions, and his last was issued two years after his death. Bill spent most of his career with Esso.* He was Director of the Chemical Division from 1946 to 1958 and held the prestigious position of Scientific Advisor from 1958 to 1970. Prior to his career with Esso, he undertook research at Sherwin-Williams (1926-29), Du Pont (1929-34), and USDA's Northern Regional Research Center (1939-40). Following his retirement from Exxon in 1970, Bill continued to invent and serve the chemical profession. During two years of

*Now Exxon.

this co-called retirement, he was national chairman of the Scientific Research Society of America.

Sparks' heavy involvement in research and other professional activities left little time for hobbies. Still, he occasionally enjoyed poker and golf. He was a member of the Echo Lake Country Club in Westfield, New Jersey, and the Riviera Country Club in Coral Gables, Florida. He passed away on October 23, 1976, in Coral Gables.

Meredith and Bill have four children.

Meredith also received her doctorate from the University of Illinois, conducting her thesis work under the direction of the late Dr. Roger Adams. She received a law degree in 1958 and is conducting a successful business as an attorney specializing in patents and technical matters. Herself the recipient of many honors, she served as President of the National Association of Women Lawyers in 1981-82. She was named to *Who's Who in the World* (1987/88).

JEROME S. SPEVACK

Deuterium, or heavy water, can be separated from ordinary water by continued electrolysis, continued distillation or the hydrogen sulfide-water exchange. The latter system, called the "GS" process and which costs about two cents per gallon of water, was developed by Jerome S. Spevack. Two 400-ton per year "GS" heavy water plants are in operation in Savannah River, South Carolina, and Dana, Indiana. The "GS" process is also used to produce over three thousand tons annually of heavy water in Canada. Canada's success with heavy water moderated nuclear reactors, coupled with its low cost heavy water production by the "GS" process, is enabling it to conserve its fossil fuels, to extend the value of its uranium mineral resources, and to sell its nuclear power technology to worldwide markets. The availability of low cost heavy water by Spevack's "GS" process also has helped Canada to achieve pre-eminence among the nuclear electric power producing nations of the world.

The growing international acceptance of the heavy water moderated nuclear power reactor and the emergence of controlled thermonuclear fusion power may soon challenge physical and financial capabilities to construct needed heavy water production facilities. Spevack and Deuterium Corporation, the company he organized over fifteen years ago to commercialize heavy water production by the "GS" process, have been able to make further improvements and to economize the "GS" process.

Dr. Spevack was named Chemical Pioneer in 1976 by the American Institute of Chemists.

LEO HENRYK STERNBACH

The ancients used mushrooms for physiological effects, and the early Egyptians used opium for the relief of pain. Tranquilizers, for the relief of stress and anxiety, were not introduced until recently. Librium® and Valium®, the first tranquilizers of the 1,4-benzodiazepine type, introduced in 1960 and 1963, respectively, were synthesized by Leo Henryk Sternbach.

In addition to Valium®, which for many years was the most commonly prescribed drug in this country, and Librium®, Dr. Sternbach and co-workers synthesized the tranquilizers Nobrium® and Lexotanil®, the anticonvulsant Clonopin®, the hypnotics MogadonR, Dalmane® and Rohypnol®, the anticholinergic Quarzan®, which is the anticholinergic component of Librax®, and the ganglionic blocker Arfonad®, which is used in bloodless surgery. He was also responsible for the technical synthesis of biotin.

This prolific creater of new drugs was born to Michael Abraham and Piroska Cohn Sternback in Abbazia, Austria, on May 7, 1908. Naturalized in this country in 1946, he received the Outstanding Naturalized Citizen Award by the Newark chapter of UNICO National in 1977. Dr. Sternbach also received the ACS Medicinal Chemistry Award (1978), Chemical Pioneer Award (1979), ACS Creative Invention Award (1979), and the John Scott Medal from the Board of Directors of City Trusts of Philadelphia (1982).

Leo attended secondary schools in Austria and Poland and then entered the University of Cracow in 1929, where he received the Master of Pharmacy (1929) and Ph.D. (1931). Until 1937, he served as a research assistant with Professor K. Dziewonski at Cracow. He then accepted a position as a research fellow with Nobel Laureate L. Ruzicka in Zürich. He joined Hoffman-La Roche as a research chemist in Basel in 1940; one year later he was transferred to Nutley, New Jersey. Promoted from Group Chief to Senior Group, Section Chief and Director of Medicinal Chemistry, he retired from Hoffmann-La Roche in 1973 but has served as a consultant since that time.

Dr. Sternbach is a member of the American Chemical Society, Swiss Chemical Society, International Society of Heterocyclic Chemistry, Chemical Society of London, and Sigma Xi. Author or co-author of over one hundred twenty scientific articles and five monographs, he has been awarded over 230 patents by the U. S. Patent Office.

Leo married a Swiss miss by the name of Herta Kreuzer in 1941. He and Herta have two sons. Michael is a sales representative for Hoffmann-La Roche. Daniel is Assistant Professor of Organic Chemistry at Duke University. Leo's hobbies are skiing, hiking and bridge.

One of Dr. Sternbach colleagues made the statement: "Leo's sustained and outstanding creativity in the field of medicinal chemistry has contributed significantly to the material prosperity and happiness of people all over the world." Dr. Sternbach ascribes his success to "my love for chemical research and particularly to my deep interest in organic chemical laboratory bench work."

RAYMOND STEVENS

In 1956, the AIC Gold Medal was awarded to Raymond Stevens, president of A. D. Little, Inc., Cambridge, Massachusetts, in recognition of his "Contributions to the wider understanding of essential procedures for the management and operation of industrial research." That same year, he was made an honorary fellow of AIC. Dr. Lawrence W. Bass, who spoke for Stevens at the Gold Medal banquet, praised the recipient for his drive, enthusiasm, communicating skill and ability to get very busy people to work with him.

Raymond was born to David and Nettie (Knowles) Stevens in Nashua, New Hampshire, on April 15, 1894. In 1917 he received his B.S. from the Massachusetts Institute of Technology. From 1919 to 1920, he was assistant superintendent of the Isko Company. He then began a long and unusually successful career with A. D. Little, Inc.: From 1920 to 1930, he was assistant to Arthur Dehon Little; from 1930 to 1956, vice president; from 1956 to 1960 and from 1961 to 1962, president; from 1960 to 1961, chairman of the executive committee; from 1962 to 1963, chairman of the board. Stevens was also president of the Massachusetts Small Business Investment Corporation from 1962 to 1964, and chairman of the board from 1964 to 1968.

In 1918, Stevens served as Second Lieutenant, Chemical Warfare Service, U. S. Army, and received the Department of Army's Civilian Service Award. He was chairman of the Northeastern Section of the American Chemical Society, 1932 and 1933, and Councilor, 1933 to 1947; honorary chairman of the American Section of the Society of the Chemical Industry, 1955 and 1956; president of the Alumni Association of M.I.T., 1944 and 1945; and president of the Cambridge Industrial Association, 1935 and 1936. Moreover, he was editor of Volume II of the important document, "Research - A National Resource," published by the National Research Council.

Some of the subjects investigated at A. D. Little under Stevens' direction were marketing research, low temperature research, operations research, computation, automation, flavor and odor research, and the development of latent patents. Despite his devotion to A. D. Little's expanding activities over the years, Stevens always found time for public and professional service. During World War II, he was chairman of the Committee on War Use of Research Facilities. Other positions included: chairman of the advisory board on Quartermaster Research and Development, 1955 to 1958; director, Brockton Edison Company; trustee of the Eastern Utilities Association; corporate president, Woods

Hole Oceanographic Institution, 1955 to 1961.

A Republican and Unitarian, he was a member of the American Academy of Arts and Sciences, American Association for the Advancement of Science, Institute of Food Technologists, American Chemical Society, Society of the Chemical Industry, Kappa Sigma, Chemists Club (New York) and the Brookline Country Club.

Raymond married Katherine Andrews in 1920 and became the father of three children. He passed away in 1983.

CHARLES ALLEN THOMAS

Charles was born in Scott County, Kentucky, on February 15, 1900, to Charles Allen and Francis (Carrick) Thomas.

In 1920 he received his A.B. degree from Transylvania University and in 1924 his M.S. degree from the Massachusetts Institute of Technology. He began his career in 1923 with General Motors in Dayton, Ohio, working on the problem of anti-knock gasoline with Thomas Midgley, Jr. and C. A. Hochwalt, with whom he was so closely allied career-wise throughout his life. In those days it was recognized that tetraethyl lead was satisfactory from the standpoint of preventing the knock, but something had to be done to get rid of the lead. A bromine compound was found to do it, but at that time bromine was a relatively scarce material and controlled by the Germans. As a result, Thomas took to the sea and sampled sea water at various locations. The result was the "good ship Ethyl," by which he was able to develop the extraction of bromine from sea water by means of chlorine, and for a considerable period of time this was the big factor in establishing the supply of bromine for this country.

To continue their researches, Thomas and Hochwalt worked out an arrangement with the University of Dayton for the use of its laboratory in the evenings. There they developed the fundamentals of what turned out to be a very interesting discovery in fire extinguishers. This led to their first publication on the effect of alkali metal compounds on combustion, in which they showed that the elements of the first group of the Periodic Table have a definite negative catalytic effect on the combustion of hydrocarbons, and that even potassium chlorate in water solution will instantly extinguish gasoline flames.

About this time General Motors decided to move their laboratory from Dayton. Hochwalt was a native of Dayton and Thomas had found another interest outside of chemistry. Deciding to strike out for themselves, the Thomas and Hochwalt Laboratories were founded as a consulting research firm, with the first laboratories in the attic of a downtown Dayton building. With General Motors as their first client, they were assigned the problem of working on synthetic rubber. They later joined Monsanto, and the Thomas and Hochwalt Laboratories became Monsanto's Central Research Laboratory. The positions Thomas held at Monsanto were vice president and technical director (1945-46); executive vice president (1947-51); president (1951-60); chairman of the board (1960-65); and chairman of the finance committee (1965-70). Moreover, he served as chairman of the Scientific Manpower Advisory Committee of the National Security Resources Board; project director of the Clinton Laboratories at Oak Ridge, Tennessee; and member of the scientific panel of the United Nations Atomic Energy Commission. He was one of the five co-authors of "A Report on the International Control of Atomic Energy," prepared in 1946 for the Secretary of State's Committee on Atomic Energy; and author of the monograph, "Anhydrous Aluminum Chloride in Organic Chemistry."

Charles was awarded the U. S. Medal for Merit (1946); Industrial Research Institute Medal (1947); an honorary D.Sc. from Washington University (1947); AIC Gold Medal (1948) and honorary fellowship (1949); Missouri Honor Award for Distinguished Service in Engineering (1952); Perkin Medal of the Society of the Chemical Industry (1953); Priestley Medal of the American Chemical Society (1955); decorated Knight of Order of Leopold; and Palladium Medal of the American Section, Société de Chimie Industrielle (1963). President of the American Chemical Society in 1948 and chairman of the Board of Directors in 1950 and 1951, he received honorary degrees from many universities.

Thomas was a member of the National Academy of Sciences, Society of Chemical Industries, Electrochemical Society, American Chemical Society, American Institute of Chemists, American Association for the Advancement of Science, National Academy of Arts and Sciences, American Philosophical Society, American Institute of Chemical Engineers, National Academy of Engineering, Chemical Society (London), Phi Lambda, Phi Beta Kappa, Sigma Xi, Alpha Sigma and Chi Sigma.

Charles and Margaret Stoddard Talbert, whom he married in 1926, had four children. He died in 1982.

(Photograph courtesy of The Firestone Tire
and Rubber Company.)

JOHN WEBSTER THOMAS

John Thomas, a chemist who rose to distinction as
president and chairman of The Firestone Tire & Rubber
Company, became an outstanding performer early in life.
He was born on November 18, 1880, on a farm outside the
beautiful New England style village of Tallmadge, which is
five miles east of Akron, Ohio. His father was a Welsh coal
miner. He and his wife had eight children - six sons and
two daughters. It was on this farm that John learned the
first lesson essential to success: namely, the virtue of
honest work and the value of money in terms of the hard
work necessary to procure it. In 1897, at the age of
seventeen, he had the highest marks in Summit County

and won a scholarship to the academy of Buchtel College.* His outstanding academic record at the academy was rewarded with a scholarship to Buchtel.

John obtained a great deal of exercise while attending Buchtel because he walked between home and school - a distance of ten miles. In addition, he worked on the family farm. Moreover, he went out for football in his junior year and was elected captain. He was also class president and delivered a highly praised address when he received the Ph.B. degree in chemistry in 1904.

Following his graduation from college, Thomas spent four years as a chemist in an early rubber compounding laboratory at Akron, and his work won the attention of Harvey S. Firestone. The two met one evening in the Firestone home in 1908; the astute industrialist and the eager young chemist immediately recognized in each other the qualities that were to become the foundations of one of the world's great industrial organizations. It was then that John agreed to work for Firestone at $100 per month.

As the rubber industry progressed, Thomas hired more and more scientists. It was his interest in science, in fact, that was the cornerstone for the striking growth of Firestone's research program. After the laboratory had been well established, Firestone made John supervisor of the wash lines, mills and calendars of the night shift. Working twelve hours per night six nights per week, he managed factory operations for more than a year. (This drive remained with him throughout his career. Well into his sixties, he usually arrived at his office at 7:30 in the morning and remained until after six in the evening.) John's performance as both a scientist and manager was so

*Now the University of Akron.

good that his steady advancement at Firestone was assured. After only three years, he was made general superintendent of the Firestone plants. He was appointed a director in 1916, vice president in 1919, president in 1932, and later chairman and chief executive.

One of the first major industrial executives to consider research an important arm of business, he indoctrinated the entire Firestone organization with this philosophy. During his thirty-eight years at Firestone, the research and development staff expanded from one lone chemist to more than one thousand chemists, physicists, engineers, and other technical workers. Thomas stated years later that his upward progress was " . . . simply a matter of hard work and common sense." He retired in 1946, but for several years continued with Firestone as a member of the board of directors.

Under Thomas' leadership, Firestone initiated a major research program in the early 1930's to develop synthetic rubber for tires. This early experience gave Firestone the knowhow needed to construct and operate in Akron the first government-owned synthetic rubber plant in this country and Firestone was the first to provide synthetic rubber tires for airplanes to the United States Army. Thomas' silver-winged, twin-engine aircraft covered hundreds of miles a day in racing him to the half-a-hundred war plants and the thousands of store and dealer units for which he was responsible. Dignified, white-haired, soft-spoken, he was characterized particularly by his readiness to accept the new. Though he was quick to spot a flaw, he was equally quick to praise.

The Akron facility, which went into production in 1942, paved the way for the construction and operation of later plants built as a part of the government's synthetic rubber program during World War II. These plants benefitted from the standards established by Firestone.

John was also active in civic affairs. He served on the board of the University of Akron, during which time enrollment increased from 827 to 5,291. In recognition of his achievements in the industrial world and his service to his alma mater, the university conferred upon him the honorary D.Sc. degree in June 1945. He also received the AIC's Gold Medal that year; in 1949, he was named AIC honorary fellow.

John Thomas passed away eight days after celebrating his seventy-first birthday.

(Photograph courtesy of the American Chemical Society.)

MAX TISHLER

Centuries ago, chemistry or alchemy, medicine and pharmacy were one pseudoscience, controlled to some extent by magic and religion. When chemistry became more of a science it displaced alchemy. It was Frederick II who in 1242 separated medicine from pharmacy. In that each of these sciences became self-sufficient, it is surprising that a scientist of our times was able to make contributions to all three disciplines.

Max Tishler's first contact with pharmacy was as a pharmacist's helper and delivery boy at the age of twelve. At the age of twenty-one, while still an undergraduate student at Tufts University (B.S., 1928), he actually became a registered pharmacist in Massachusetts. Thereafter, he accepted an Austin Teaching Fellowship at Harvard (M.A., 1933; Ph.D., 1934). For the next two years he was a research associate at Harvard; during 1936 and 1937, an instructor. He left Harvard to join Merck & Company as a research chemist, where he remained until 1969 when he retired as Senior Vice President of Research and Development.

While a graduate student at Harvard, Max's resolution of a substituted allene settled an important consequence of the tetrahedral carbon atom. Through use of the Grignard reaction of alpha-haloketones, he contributed to the understanding of nucleophilic reactions of the Grignard reagent and of the reactivity of the enolate anions in alkylation. His first publication with Professor E. P. Kohler in the *Journal of American Chemical Society* was followed by five other reports with Kohler and ten other reports with C. F. Fieser, W. L. Sampson and N. L. Wendler in the *Journal*. The latter reports were on a rational synthesis of Vitamin K and this vitamin's relationships of biological activity to structural variations.

Subsequent investigations at Merck led to the synthesis of other vitamins, such as pantothenic acid, biocytin vitamins, nicotinic acid and riboflavin, as well as aminopyrazine, aminoquinoxoline, sulfaquinoxaline, tryptophan, and threonile. Tishler also collaborated with Selman Waksman and co-workers in the production of actinomycin, penicillin, and streptomycin. Much of this work was reported in over forty articles in the *Journal of American Chemical Society*. Toward the end of his industrial research career and since his retirement in 1975, he has published many provocative reports, such as "The Challenge Ahead," "Reflections on the Future of Research," and "The Debt of Discovery to Learning."

In 1970, Dr. Tishler joined Wesleyan University as Professor of Chemistry, since which time he has continued to direct research and teach chemistry. He later became chairman of the department and was named University Professor of the Sciences, Emeritus. The eighteen research reports he published while a member of the faculty at Wesleyan make a total of 115 publications, which include "Chemistry of Organic Compounds" (with J. B. Conant, 1937), "Streptomycin" (with S. Waksman, 1949), and "Chemistry in the Economy" (1976). He has served as editor of *Organic Syntheses* and is on the editorial boards of *Biotechnology Polymer Digest* and *Separation Science*. Awardee of approximately one hundred U. S. patents, he has received a like number of foreign patents.

Dr. Tishler was recipient of AIC's Honor Scroll (Massachusetts and New Jersey), Freedman Federation Patent and Gold Medal. He has also been awarded the Industrial Research Institute Medal, Medal of the Society of Chemical Industry, Priestley Medal of the American Chemical Society, Eli Whitney Award for Inventions, and was elected into the National Inventors Hall of Fame in 1972. Honorary Doctor of Science degrees have been conferred upon him by Tufts; Bucknell; Philadelphia College of Pharmacy and Science; Stevens Institute of Technology; University of Strathclyde, Glasgow, Scotland; Fairfield University; Upsala College; and Doctor of Engineering degree by Stevens Institute of Technology; and the President's National Medal of Science. In 1986, a special symposium was held at Wesleyan University in Tishler's honor on the occasion of his eightieth birthday.

Max is a trustee or member of the board of visitors or governors at Columbia, Harvard, Massachusetts Institute of Technology, Princeton, State University of New York, Union College of New Jersey, University of Pennsylvania, Rutgers, Tufts and The Weizmann Institute. A member of the American Chemical Society, he served as president in 1972 and as chairman of the Organic Chemistry Division in 1951. He is a fellow of AIC, the New York Academy of Sciences, American Association for the Advancement of Science, and Chemical Society of London. He served as chairman of the American section of the Society of the Chemical Industry, Alfred P. Sloan Foundation, and a conference on raw materials of chemical intermediates for the International Union of Pure and Applied Chemistry. He is president of the Association of Harvard Chemists, an honorary member of the Royal Society of Chemistry and Société Chimie de France, and a member of the Agricultural Chemical Society of Japan, Academy of Independent Scholars, Chemical Society of Japan, American Academy of Arts and Sciences, National Society of Sciences, Swiss Academy of Sciences, Connecticut Academy of Sciences, Sigma Xi, Phi Lambda Phi, Phi Beta Kappa, and Chemists Club.

The son of Samuel and Anna Gray Tishler, Max was born in Boston on October 30, 1906. He had five brothers and sisters. He married Elizabeth M. Verveer in 1934; their children are Peter Verveer and Carl Lewis.

Dr. Tishler maintains that "instead of broadening the scientist," as some suggest, it is more important to train future leaders "to understand science so that they can govern it."

WILLIAM GRIDLEY TOLAND, JR.

According to Massachusetts' Horace Mann (1796-1859), "The scientific or well-being of a community is to be estimated, not so much by its possessing a few men of great knowledge, as its having men of competent knowledge."

William G. Toland meets both criteria. Born in Springfield, Massachusetts, on November 29, 1917, Bill completed the local high school in 1935. He then attended Antioch College* in Yellow Springs, Ohio (B.S., 1940). For two years as an undergraduate, he worked part-time at Eastman Kodak, which caused him to change his major

---

*Horace Mann was president of Antioch from 1853 until his death.

from pre-med to chemistry. Graduate studies were conducted at Purdue, where he received his doctorate in 1944. He then joined California Research Corporation* in Richmond, California.

During his thirty-eight years with Chevron, Toland was responsible for the development of a process for making phenol from cumene and for making terephthalic acid from p-xylene. His main research areas were in the field of liquid and vapor phase catalytic air oxidation of hydrocarbons which included the use of sulfur as an oxidant.

Dr. Toland was recipient of the AIC Chemical Pioneer Award in 1969. A member of AIC, the American Chemical Society and the American Association for the Advancement of Science, he is the author of twenty-four reports in scientific journals and has been awarded eighty patents by the U. S. Patent Office.

Bill was married in 1939 and fathered two children. He retired from Chevron as Vice President of New Ventures in 1982 and is now active as a chemical consultant.

*Now Chevron Research Company.

(Photograph courtesy of the University of Wisconsin.)

BARRY MARTIN TROST

The word *thespian* is derived from Thespis of Attica who, in 536 B.C., traveled from place to place on a cart to give performances.   Perhaps some future lexicographer will coin the word *Trostian* to describe Barry Trost, Thespis' scientific counterpart, who travels from place to place in an airplane to present seminars.

Trost has presented plenary lectures at over seventy national and international meetings.   These include: Timmie Lecturer at Emory University (1965); Humble Lecturer in Science (1972); Sherwin-Williams Lecturer, University of Illinois (1974); American Swiss Foundation Lecturer (1975); Visiting Distinguished Professor,

University of Iowa (1976); Merck Lecturer at Buchnell University (1976); Whitemore Lecturer at Kent State University (1976); Visiting Distinguished Professor, University of Texas, Austin (1977); Denkewalter Lecturer at Loyola University of Chicago (1978); Friedman Lecturer at Rutgers University (1978); Lemieux Lecturer at the University of Ottawa (1978); Arthur D. Little Lecturer at Northeastern University (1979); Frank B. Daines Lecturer, University of Kansas (1979); Ritter Memorial Lecturer at Miami University (1980); Presidential Lecturer at University of Arizona (1980); McNeal-Ortho Lecturer at Philadelphia (1980); Sandia Lecturer, University of New Mexico (1981); Bachman Lecturer, University of Michigan (1981); Frontiers in Chemistry Lecturer, Western Reserve University (1981); Arapahoe Lecturer at the University of Colorado (1982); Ayerst Lecturer at University of Montreal (1983); Georgeselie-Amyot Lecturer at the University of Nevada (1983); Lecturer at the University of Gröningen (1983); Arnold Lecturer at University of Southern Illinois (1983); R. P. Scherer Lecturer at University of South Florida (1983); Lecturer at the University of Connecticut (1983); Frontiers in Chemical Research Lecturer, Texas A & M University (1984); Bachman-Pierce Lecturer at Purdue University (1984).

From 1967 onward, Dr. Trost has also presented plenary lectures at ACS conferences and at the following: Burgenstock Conference, Switzerland (1972); Société Chimie, Marseilles, France (1973); International Conference on Organosulphur Chemistry, Wales (1974); IUPAC Conference on Organic Synthesis at Louvain-Laineuve (1974); International Symposium on Medicinal Chemistry, Paris (1976); International Conference on the Chemistry of Platinum Group Metals, Frisco, England (1976); International Symposium on Present and Potential Uses of Metals in Organic Synthesis, St. Raphael (1976); Yugoslav Symposium on Organic Chemistry (1977); IUPAC

Symposion on National Products, Varna, Bulgaria (1978); Workshop on Stereo-Selective Synthesis of Natural Products, Ulm, Germany (1978); International Symposium on Organic Synthesis, Cambridge, England (1976); International Kioto on New Aspects of Organic Chemistry (1979); Sino-U.S. Symposium on the Chemistry of Natural Products, Shanghai (1978); International Symposium on Chemistry of Cations at Vanguard, Wales (1979); Royal Society of Chemists Symposium at London (1982); Sheffield Symposium at Sheffield (1982); Royal Dutch Chemical Society Symposium at Vwaegenin (1982); IUPAC Symposium on Organic Synthesis at Tokyo (1982); Highlights in Organic Synthesis at Sapporo (1982); International Symposium on Homogeneous Catalysis at Milan (1982); Ospra Symposium, University of Cincinnati (1982); Additional Chemistry Symposium at Cambridge, England (1982); World Society of Chemistry Annual Conference at London (1983); Symposium of Organic Chemistry of Natural Products in Industry Chemistry at Pisa, Italy (1983); Organic Chemistry Conference at Pretoria, South Africa (1983); GECO XXIV Cap d'jde Herault (1983); and Royal Australian Chemical Institute (1984).

Moreover, he was a visiting professor of chemistry at the Universities of Marburg and Copenhagen in 1972 and 1979, respectively.

What does Dr. Trost speak about that is of such interest to so many? His pioneering research which led to major advances in the synthetic reactors and reagents, investigations of model biogenetic systems, and the total synthesis of biologically important molecules.

Barry was born in Philadelphia on June 13, 1941, to Joseph and Esther Trost. A Philadelphia Board of Education Scholar, he received his B.A. from the

University of Pennsylvania in 1961. After attending M.I.T. as a National Science Foundation Fellow (Ph.D. in 1965), he accepted a faculty position at the University of Wisconsin, where he served as chairman of the department from 1980-82 and is now a Vilas Research and Helfaer Professor of Chemistry.

Named Chemical Pioneer in 1985, Barry was presented the ACS Award in Pure Chemistry, ACS Award for Creative Work in Organic Chemistry, and the Baekeland Medal. He is a fellow of AIC and a member of the American Chemical Society, American Academy of Arts and Sciences, Chemist Society, National Academy of Sciences, and Phi Beta Kappa. He has served on the advisory board of editors of *Journal of Organic Chemistry and Organometallics* and as associate editor of the *Journal of American Chemical Society*. He has also served on the editorial board of *Organic Reaction Theories* and *Dictionary of Organic Compounds, Dictionary of Organometallics*; is editor of *Structure and Reactivity, Concepts in Organic Chemistry*; and is the author of "Spectroscopy" (1967) and "Sulfylids-Emerging Synthetic Intermediates" (1975) as well the author or co-author of over 280 scientific reports. Barry has been awarded three U. S. patents.

Barry married Susan Paula Shapiro in 1967. They have two children: Aaron David and Carey Daniel Trost.

HAROLD CLAYTON UREY

In 1931, Harold Urey and assistants discovered heavy hydrogen, or the isotope deuterium. For this discovery, Urey was awarded the Nobel Prize in chemistry in 1934.

Deuterium, which is used as a chemical tracer, has proved to be a source of power for the hydrogen bomb and useful in obtaining power from uranium fission. Dr. Urey prepared deuterium by the fractional distillation of the usual liquid hydrogen. Deuterium and heavy water, deuterium oxide, are now made commercially. Aside from his discovery of this isotope, Urey was productive in many fields of research: entropy of gases; atomic structure; absorption spectra and structure of molecules; properties and separation of isotopes; exchange reactions;

measurement of paleo-temperatures; and chemical problems of the origin of the earth, meteorites, moon, and solar system.

Urey correlated the abundance of oxygen-18 in carbonate shells with the temperature at which they were formed, thereby providing a method of studying past climates. Work on paleotemperatures led him to the study of geochemistry, with emphasis on the abundance of elements and isotopes. His publications include *Atoms, Molecules, and Quanta* (with A. E. Ruark), 1930, revised in 1964; and *The Planets*, 1952.

In addition to the Nobel Prize, Dr. Urey received the Gibbs Medal (1934); Davy Medal (1940); Franklin Medal (1943); Medal for Merit (1946); Cordoza Award (1954); Hamilton Award (1961); Remsen Award (1963); National Medal of Science (1964); American Academy Achievement Award (1966); Gold Medal, Royal Astron Society (1966); Leonard Medal (1969); Linus Pauling Award (1970); Johann Kepler Medal (1971); Gold Medal, American Institute of Chemists (1972); and Priestley Award (1973). The recipient of twenty-three honorary degrees from American and foreign universities, he was elected to the National Academy of Sciences and named as one of the greatest scientists in all history by *World's Who's Who in Science*, 1968.

The son of Samuel C., a schoolteacher and lay minister, and Clara Rebecca (Reinuhl) Urey, Harold was born on April 29, 1893, at Walkerton, Indiana. He received his B.S. in zoology from the University of Montana in 1917, during which time he served as instructor; his Ph.D. in chemistry from the University of California in 1923. The next academic year, he was a fellow at Niels Bohr's Institute of Theoretical Physics in Copenhagen. From 1924 to 1929, he was associate in chemistry at Johns Hopkins. The following sixteen years he served Columbia as professor; during the war years, he was director of Columbia's SAM Laboratories, investigating the separation of uranium, hydrogen and boron isotopes. From 1945 to 1958, he was Distinguished Service Professor at the University of Chicago. Beginning in 1958, he was Professor of Chemistry at Large at the University of California.

Harold married Frieda Daum in 1926. They had four children: Gertrude Elizabeth, Frieda Rebecca, Mary Alice and John Clayton.

Dr. Urey passed away on January 6, 1981, at the age of eighty-seven.

CHRISTIAAN PIETER VAN DIJK

The most recent commercial process for the production of chlorine from hydrochloric acid is the Kel-Chlor process, which was developed by Christiaan Van Dijk. This process differs from the Deacon process* in that it uses nitrogen oxides with other catalysts to oxidize

---

*In 1868, Henry Deacon used copper (II) chloride at a catalyst at 400oC. This industrial reaction was displaced by an electrochemical process at the end of the nineteenth century. However, the Deacon reaction, in which five volumes of reactant produced four volumes of gaseous products, is still used to demonstrate the effect of pressure on equilibrium reactions.

the hydrochloric acid by the use of oxygen at elevated temperatures. The nitrosyl chloride produced in this process is converted to nitrogen oxides by treatment with sulfuric acid. The first commercial use of the Kel-Chlor process was in a 600-ton a day plant built by Du Pont at Corpus Christi, Texas, in 1974. However, smaller Kel-Chlor plants with capacities as low as 150 tons a day can be built and used to produce chlorine on a profitable basis.

Christiaan was born in Amsterdam, Netherlands, on November 10, 1915. He later became a United States citizen. On June 28, 1955, he married Judith F. Rottschaefer to become the father of three children, Rudolf Dirk, Willem Leendert and Margaret Elaine.

He obtained his B.S. (1936) and M.S. (1940) degrees from Amsterdam Municipal University; his Ph.D. in organic chemistry (1946) from Delft University of Technology.

He was with the Royal Dutch Shell Company in The Netherlands from 1948-57; with Dow Chemical from 1957-60; with M. W. Kellogg Co., New Jersey, from 1960-75. Since 1975 he has been with Pullman Kellogg Research & Development Center in Houston.

Dr. Van Dijk was named American Institute of Chemists Chemical Pioneer in 1975. In addition to being a fellow of AIC, he is a member of the American Chemical Society, American Institute of Chemical Engineers, Royal Netherlands Chemical Society, Alpha Chi Sigma, Phi Lambda Upsilon and Sigma Xi.

Christiaan continues to work with M. W. Kellogg Company as a senior scientist in Houston.

BARTHOLOMEUS VAN'T RIET

Methylene blue or basic blue 9 is a thiazene dye that has been used extensively in biological oxidation-reduction experiments and in medicine. Bart van't Reit reasoned that since the ionic dye was chemisorbed on crystals it might be used to treat kidney stones. Consequently, he proposed this treatment to Dr. William H. McKinney, who persuaded W. H. Boyce of North Carolina to make clinical tests. Because of the characteristic blue color of the urine resulting from the ingestion of methylene blue, placebos could not be used. In spite of this, test data showing that the effects of methylene blue on stones consisting mainly of calcium oxalate monohydrate were published in 1967. Later, reproducible growth of calcium oxalate stones was produced by the addition of 0.75 percent ethylene glycol to the drinking water of rats. It was then demonstrated that oral ingestion of 65 mg, three times a day, plus vitamin C would reduce the frequency of occurrence of kidney stones. The results of ten years of testing with this dye were published in 1978.

When van't Riet discovered that methylene blue was not chemisorbed on calcium oxalate, he proposed a different mechanism. He now believes that methylene blue is absorbed by organic material present in the kidney stones. He also proposed that vitamin C reduces the methylene blue so that it is more readily absorbed by the organic matter; and that modifications of methylene blue, such as the removal of one methyl group from the amine, are not effective in the treatment of kidney stones.

Bart was named Chemical Pioneer in 1976. In addition to being a fellow of AIC, he is also a member of the American Chemical Society. He has authored many scientific reports and been granted several patents by the U. S. Patent Office.

Born in Arnhem, Netherlands, on June 25, 1922, he received a B.S. degree in chemistry and physics from the Vrije (Free) University at Amsterdam in 1950, where he was an assistant (1948-1951). The University of Minnesota awarded him his doctorate in 1957. He then joined the faculty of the University of Virginia in Charlottesville. Seven years later he accepted an associate professorship at the Medical College of Virginia in Richmond and was promoted to full professor in 1970.

Bart's 1955 marriage produced three little van't Riets.

HERVEY HARPER VOGE

Hervey Voge and B. S. Greensfelder were asked to investigate the reactions of catalyst cracking when Voge joined Shell Development Company in Emeryville, California, in 1938. His most important investigations were the development of new heterogeneous catalytic systems and the attempt to determine the mechanism involved in catalytic cracking of petroleum. He and his associates noted the similarities between catalytic cracking and low temperature acid-catalyzed reactions and applied the concept of the carbonium ion intermediate as proposed by Dr. Frank Whitmore in 1932.*

Dr. Voge and co-workers developed an iron oxide catalyst (Shell 205) and used this in the presence of steam at 620°C as a catalyst for the dehydrogenation of n-butene for the production of butadiene. The use of Shell catalyst 205, which consists of Fe_2O_3 (87.9%), Cr_2O_3 (2.5%) and K_2O (9.6%) made possible the dehydrogenation of butene on a continuous basis. This catalyst was also effective for the production of styrene by the dehydrogenation of ethylbenzene. Later, Shell catalyst 405 was developed by Voge and associates for the decomposition of hydrazene to gaseous hydrogen and nitrogen. This catalyst is used worldwide to control the orientation of numerous satellites. The production of butadiene and styrene was essential for the production of SBR, the general purpose synthetic elastomer. The production of nitrogen and hydrogen from hydrazine was essential for the thrustors used to orient and control space age satellites.

When Dr. Voge was sent to the Shell Laboratory at Amsterdam in 1956, he used the carbonium ion to explain the reactions of cyclopentanes and cyclohexanes over platinum-alumina-halogen reforming catalysts. He also investigated catalytic oxidation for the production of ethylene oxide, acrolein and acrylonitrile.

Hervey was born on June 29, 1912, in Zürich, Switzerland. His father was an American citizen who was developing a Dewey Decimal System for the classification of chemical compounds in Switzerland. The Voges returned to California when Hervey was eighteen months

---

*Whitmore suggested the presence of carbonium ions to explain the deep color of solutions of the phenol methyl chloride in sulfuric acid.

old. In that his parents were divorced at World War I's end, Hervey worked at odd jobs in order to help his mother support the family, which included two younger brothers and a sister. He attributes his interest in chemistry to the inspiration generated by a high school teacher. Hervey attended San Jose College for three years before transferring to the University of California at Berkeley (B.S., 1931). He then enrolled in the University of Wisconsin (M.S., 1932). He received his doctorate from Berkeley in 1934.

Named Chemical Pioneer by AIC in 1960 , Dr. Voge is a fellow of AIC and a member of the American Chemical Society, Sigma Xi and Phi Beta Kappa. Since his first publication in the *Journal of the American Chemical Society* in 1933, he has authored or co-authored approximately forty other scientific reports and two nontechnical reports, i.e., "A Climber's Guide to the High Sierra" (1963) and "A Forest Liberated" (1980). Dr. Voge has been granted twenty-seven U. S. patents. He chaired the Gordon Conference on catalysis in 1956.

Hervey married Esther Kocher in 1937. Their daughter Suzanne is head nurse in a California hospital; son Gregory is an academic dean at Sierra Nevada College in Lake Tahoe, California; daughter Tamara is a social worker. Hervey and Esther, who were divorced in 1951, have five grandchildren. In 1952, Hervey married Rhea Barrere DeLasaux, a widow with four small children. Hervey and Rhea are parents of Brendan, a computer science major at Berkeley.

Dr. Voge retired from Shell in 1972 when it moved its research facilities to Houston. He then joined the faculty at the Universidad Autónoma de San Luis Potosí in Mexico. In 1974, he accepted a Latin American Teaching Fellowship at Universidad Técnica Federico Santa Maria in

Valparaiso, Chile. In addition to raising fruits and vegetables and working on his forty acres of woodlands, Dr. Voge makes furniture in his home workshop.

OTTO VOGL

Otto Vogl has contributed significantly to a number of fields of polymer chemistry. He discovered the polymerization, especially the sterospecific polymerization of higher aldehydes, poly (alkylene oxide) ionomers, functional oxirane polymers, and the cryotachensic polymerization. He has contributed to the understanding of regular copolyamides and their use as reverse osmosis membranes, polymerizable and polymeric U.V. stabilizers, polymeric drugs and head-to-head polymers. Most recently, he demonstrated the existence of optically active polymers based on molecular asymmetry. Moreover, Professor Vogl played a leading role in the establishment of the Center of the University of Massachusetts-Industry Research on Polymers, which represents a novel concept of cooperation between government, industry and academia.

Otto was born in Traiskirchen, Austria, on November 6, 1927, to Franz and Leopolidene Scholz Vogl. He received his doctorate from the University of Vienna in 1950, where he conducted research on steroids and alkaloids under the direction of Professor Galinovsky. He also served the university as an instructor of chemistry from 1948 to 1953.

Otto then emigrated to the United States where, as a research associate, he spent two years at the University of Michigan and one year at Princeton. The next fourteen years were with the Central Research Department of Du Pont. Otto joined the University of Massachusetts as a Professor of Polymer Science and Engineering in 1970 and was named Professor Emeritus in 1983, when he became the Herman F. Mark Professor of Polymer Science at the Polytechnic Institute of New York.

Dr. Vogl has served as a guest lecturer at the universities Kyoto (1968, 1980); Osaka (1968); Royal Institute of Technology in Sweden (1971); Freiburg (1973); Louis Pasteur at Strasbourg (1976); Berlin (1977); and Dresden (1982). He has been a guest lecturer for the Soviet Academy of Science (1973), Polish Academy of Science (1973) and the Academy of Science of Rumania (1974, 1976). He was a Fulbright Fellow (1976), Senior Scientist Fellow in Japan (1980), and Foreign Member of the GDR Academy of Sciences (1983).

Recipient of AIC's Chemical Pioneer award in 1985, he was named a Pioneer in Polymer Science by *Polymer News* (1982) and received the Humboldt Award (1977). He is a fellow of AIC and a member of the American Chemical Society, American Association for the Advancement of Science, Austrian Chemical Society and

Sigma Xi. He was awarded the Dr. Rer. Nat. degree honoris causa from the University of Jena in 1983. He served as chairman of the ACS Polymer Division (1974), of the Connecticut Valley Section of the ACS (1970), of the Gordon Research Conference on Polymers (1981), of the National Academy of Sciences Committee on Macromolecular Chemistry (1977-79); as General Secretary for the ACS Secretariat for Macromolecules (1976); as a member of the Academy's *Ad Hoc* Panel for National Needs in Polymer Science (1980-81); and on the Advisory Committe of the International Division of the National Science Foundation.

The author of eight books and chapters in several books, he has published over two hundred scientific reports and been awarded thirty U. S. patents. He has also served on the advisory or editorial boards of *Macromolecules, Journal of Polymer Science, Macromolecular Synthesis, Journal of Macromolecular Science & Chemistry, Macromolecular Science, Polymer, Die Makromolekulare Chemie, Monatshefte für Chemie, Polymer News, Acta Polymerica, Dalchemist* and the *Delaware Chemical Bulletin.*

Otto married Katherine Jane Cunningham of Sag Harbor, New York, in 1955. They have two children, Eric and Yvonne. Wife Jane is in charge of the business office of the ACS Division of Polymer Science at Polytechnic Institute of New York. Son Eric is a petroleum geologist working in New Orleans, Louisiana. In his younger days Otto, who became a naturalized U. S. citizen in 1959, was an avid soccer player and referee. His outside interests center on history, languages, music - especially opera, and travel. Photography and stamp collecting are his favorite hobbies.

ERNEST HENRY VOLWILER

*"Dr. Volwiler epitomizes the highest quality
of leader in the pharmaceutical industry. His
brilliant perception, his depth of understanding, not
only of his chosen field of science, but also of the
people he worked with at Abbott and the many
other organizations he devoted his time to, make
him truly a giant. He has added a unique luster to
AFPE, and we have incurred a debt to him we can
never repay."**

*Dr. C. R. Walgreen, chairman of the American Foundation
for Pharmaceutical Education, in his tribute to Volwiler.

Ernest Volwiler, who was educated as a chemist, is an honorary member of the American Foundation for Pharmaceutical Education. Not only did Dr. Volwiler aid in the development of pharmaceutical science, but he was also one of the major supporters of the American Chemical Society. He joined ACS in 1916 and served as councilor from 1931 to 1934, chairman from 1944 to 1956, and president in 1950, the Diamond Jubilee year. He was also a strong supporter of and served as chairman of the Division of Medicinal Chemistry.

Ernest was born on a farm near Hamilton, Ohio, on August 22, 1893, to Jacob and Dorothea Targe (Mann) Volwiler. After receiving his A.B. from Miami University in 1914, he accepted a fellowship to undertake graduate work in chemistry at the University of Illinois (A.M., 1916; Ph.D., 1918). Before entering Miami, he earned money for his college education by teaching all eight grades in a country school. He began his career as a research chemist working for Dr. Wallace C. Abbott, the founder of Abbott Laboratories. He was named chief chemist in 1933, executive vice president in 1944, president in 1950, and chairman of the board in 1958. Ernest served as a major in Chemical Warfare Research and was the head of Chemical Warfare Services and medical teams in Germany in 1945. While at Abbott, he and his associates made history by synthesizing many new barbiturates, including Nembutal and Pentothal. Dr. Volwiler, who also contributed to the development of antihistamines, sulfa drugs, and drugs for the treatment of epilepsy, initiated the investigations that led to the marketing of Sucaryl - the trade name for salts of cyclohexylsulfamic acid.

Recipient of AIC's Honor Scroll (1947) and Gold Medal (1960), Dr. Volwiler has been awarded the Modern Pioneer Award from National Manufacturers Association (1939), Centennial Award from Northwestern University

(1951), Medal of the Society of Chemical Industry (1954), Sesquicentennial Medal from Miami University (1959), Priestley Medal (1959), Perkin Medal (1965), and Industrial Research Institute Medal (1968). He has received honorary doctoral degrees from Miami University (1946), Northwestern (1949), Coe College (1953), Knox College (1954), Philadelphia College of Pharmacy and Science (1954), Southwestern University at Memphis (1958), St. Louis College of Pharmacy and Allied Sciences (1958), Illinois (1954), and Lake Forest (1980).

In addition to those affiliations already mentioned, Ernest has been a member of the American Institute of Chemists, American Association for the Advancement of Science, American Institute of Chemical Engineers, Society of Chemistry (London), American Drug Manufacturing Association, Phi Beta Kappa, Sigma Xi, Phi Lambda Upsilon, Alpha Chi Sigma, Beta Gamma Sigma, Phi Kappa Tau, and Gamma Alpha Phi. He served as President of the Chicago Chemistry Club, was a member of the Board of Regents of the National Library of Medicine, as chairman of the Division of Chemicals and Chemical Technology of NRC, and on the board of directors of NSF and McCormick Theology Seminary.

Ernest's 1920 marriage to Lillien F. Huggler gave him three children: Doris Volwiler (Semler), Marjorie Volwiler (Grinnell), and Wallace Volwiler. Ernest and Lillien have nine grandchildren. Ernest's hobbies include travel, photography, golf and higher education. Since his retirement in 1959, he has served as Trustee of Lake Forest College and as chairman of its board. He and Lillien endowed the first chair at Lake Forest, specifically designated for the natural sciences and mathematics.

JOHN CHRISTIAN WARNER

John Christian Warner, who is known to his friends as "Jake," was born in Goshen, Indiana, on May 28, 1897. His grandfather, who was a farmer and a potter, had migrated to Indiana from Saxony in the 1850's. John's father Elias was a farmer and logger-lumberman; his mother Addie Plank taught in a country school before her marriage.

After attending a one-room rural school, John graduated from Goshen High School in 1915. He then enrolled in Indiana University. Following his junior year, he accepted a position as a chemist with the Barrett Company in Philadelphia, but returned to Indiana University to complete his education (A.B., 1919; M.A., 1920; Ph.D., 1923). The year following the receipt of his

Masters, he spent working as a chemist for Cosden Oil Company of Tulsa, Oklahoma. He served as an instructor in chemistry during the last two years of his graduate studies and the year following the receipt of his doctorate. Thereafter, he joined Wayne Chemical Corporation in Fort Wayne, Indiana, as a research chemist. Two years later, he joined the faculty of Carnegie Institute of Technology, where he served as professor and head of the department of chemistry, dean of graduate studies, and president. During the years 1943 to 1945, John was granted a leave of absence to supervise research on the chemistry and metallurgy of plutonium for the Manhattan Project at the Central Research Laboratories of Monsanto in Dayton, Ohio. In 1965, he became professor and president emeritus of Carnegie Institute of Technology.

Dr. Warner's most important contributions to science were concerned with the kinetics of reactions in solutions and the properties of solutions. He even went back to the Wohler reaction (1828) and showed that the experimental results of the conversion of the inorganic compound ammonium cyanate to the organic compound, urea, were in agreement with theory. He showed that the reason for great disagreement between experimental and calculated results for rate constants for bimolecular reactions in solution were due to the use of incorrect energies of activation. These were obtained from collisions of gases in which there is no appreciable change in environment of reacting molecules with temperature. He and his associates derived mathematical expressions which were in accord with experimental data for reactions between ions of like and unlike signs and for a variety of reactions between ions and uncharged molecules. Warner also did important work on the relation between reaction rates and the true acid-base strengths of halohydrins and various solvents in epoxide formation.

John Warner's honors include: AIC Gold Medal (1953), Pittsburgh Junior Chamber of Commerce Man of the Year Award (1958), Pittsburgh Graphic Arts Council Award (1963), Horatio Alger Award (1964), Western Pennsylvania Board of Industrial Realtors Award (1965), Pennsylvania Award for Excellence in Education (1966), and Distinguished Alumnus Award from Indiana University (1968); honorary doctoral degrees from Northwestern University (1953), University of Pittsburgh (1953), Indiana University (1954), University of Maryland (1955), Bucknell University (1955), Worchester Polytechnic Institute (1956), Youngstown University (1959), University of Toledo (1960), Duquesne University (1963), Grove City College (1964), Geneva College (1965), Rose Polytechnic Institute (1965), Carnegie Institute of Technology (1965), and Washington and Jefferson College (1965).

In addition to his educational responsibilities, Dr. Warner has taken an active interest in civic, business and professional society affairs. He served as a director of: Jones and Laughlin Steel Corporation (1951-70), Dravo Corporation (1961-65), the Pittsburgh Branch of the Federal Reserve Bank of Cleveland (1954-60); and chairman (1957-60), Magnetics, Inc. (1964-70), Spang Company (1970-73), P P G Industries, Inc. (1965-69), Eriez Manufacturing Company (1965-69), and Cyrus W. Rice Company (1967-70). He was chairman of the board of Nuclear Science and Engineering Corporation (1964-66), a member of the Governor's Council on Science and Technology (1963-65), a trustee of Shadyside Academy (1964-66), and a member of the Advisory Board and Research Council of the Center for Strategic and International Studies, Georgetown University (1967-77).

He has been a member of the Advisory Committee of the Oakland Branch of the Mellon National Bank since 1950, a member of the Pennsylvania State Planning Board, and director of the Regional Industrial Development Corporation, the Vocational Rehabilitation Center, and St. Barnabus Inc. A trustee of Carnegie-Mellon University, the Carnegie Institute, the Pittsburgh Playhouse (1953-67 - chairman, 1958 and 1967), and Argonne Universities Association, Inc. (1965-69 - president 1965-6); he was a member of the Research Advisory Board of Cities Service Corporation (1968-71) and chairman of the NAS-NAE Committee on Science and Technology in Support of the Puerto Rican Economy (1966-67), NAS Committee for Science Cooperation with the Philippines (1965-66), NRC Panel on Shipbuilding Research and Development (1973) and NRC Committee on the Treatment and Disposal of High Energy Materials (1973).

John was also a member of the Honorary Board of Judges of the Fisher Body Craftsman's Guild (1957-66), served on the Commission on Higher Institutions of the Middle States Association of Colleges and Universities (1950-56), and was president of the Pennsylvania Association of Colleges and Universities (1954-55). A member of the Policy Advisory Board of the Argonne National Laboratory and of the Board of Visitors, Air University (1964-67 - chairman, 1967), he attended the Second U. N. International Conference on Peaceful Uses of Atomic Energy held in Geneva, Switzerland, in 1958, as a technical consultant to the U. S. delegation.

In addition to being an honorary fellow of AIC and a member of the American Chemical Society, Professor Warner was a fellow of the New York Academy of Sciences and American Association for the Advancement of Science, and is or has been a member of the Pittsburgh Chemist Club, National Academy of Sciences, American Institute of Mining and Metallurgical Engineers, American Society for Engineering Education, Electrochemical Society, Delta Upsilon, Phi Beta Kappa, Sigma Xi, Alpha

Chi Sigma, University Club (Pittsburgh), Duquesne Club (Pittsburgh), Pike Run Country Club (Jones Mills, Pennsylvania), and Cosmos Club (Washington, D.C.). He served the American Chemical Society as a national councilor and chairman of the Pittsburgh Section and as director and president. He was also president of the Electrochemical Society and the Pittsburgh Chemists Club.

Dr. Warner is the author or co-author of *General Chemistry* (1931), *Chemistry of Engineering Materials* (1942), *Chemistry, Metallurgy and Purification of Plutonium* (1945), *Metallurgy of Uranium and Its Alloys* (1953), and *Uranium Technology* (1951) as well the author of approximately forty scientific reports.

(Photograph courtesy of Mobil Research &
Development Corp.)

PAUL BURG WEISZ

Paul Weisz investigated the catalytic cracking of petroleum and devoted considerable time to elucidate diffusion transport phenomena and their influence on the course of chemical transformations in heterogeneous catalytically active systems. He also devised methods for measuring diffusivity of catalysts and evolved simple criteria for the existence of diffusional effects. These criteria, which rely only on observable quantities, now provide systematic guidance in catalyst research, design and development.

Dr. Weisz' work with Dr. V. J. Frilette led to the discovery of intracrystalline catalysis in zeolites, and the development of molecular shape-selective catalysts. The first commercial shape-selective catalytic process, called Selectoforming, was designed to increase the octane number in gasoline. These successful results and the discovery of new zeolite structures have led to other catalytic processes, such as the hydrodewaxing of petroleum distillates, a selective conversion of methanol to gasoline (MTG), and the isomerization of xylenes. The world's first commercial MTG plant has gone on stream in New Zealand where it will supply one-third of the country's automotive fuel from domestic natural gas.

Paul was born in Pilsen, Czechoslovakia, on July 2, 1919, to Alexander and Amalia Sulc Weisz. From 1937 through 1939, he studied physics at the Technical University in Berlin and received the B.S. degree from Auburn University in 1940.

That same year, he accepted a position with the Bartol Research Foundation in Swarthmore, Pennsylvania, where he investigated cosmic rays, radiation detection, loran and radar related electronics. Weisz joined Socony-Vaccum Oil Company* at Paulsboro, New Jersey, and was named a senior scientist in 1962. Seven years later, he became manager of Mobil's Central Research Laboratory at Princeton, New Jersey; he served Mobil as a science advisor from 1982 to 1984. Weisz became Distinguished Professor of Chemical and Bio-Engineering Science at the University of Pennsylvania and a consultant in R&D strategy in 1984.

Dr. Weisz was named Chemical Pioneer in 1974. Other honors include Scientific Award, South Jersey

*Now Mobil Oil Corporation.

Section of ACS (1963); E. V. Murphree ACS Award (1972); Philadelphia Catalysis Club Award (1973); Leo Friend ACS Award (1976); R. H. Wilhelm Award of AIChE (1978); Lavoisier Medal of Société Chimique de France (1983); ACS Chemistry of Contemporary Technological Problems Award (1986); and Society of Chemical Industry's Perkin Medal (1985). He was elected to the National Academy of Engineering in 1977 and was awarded an honorary doctoral degree by the Swiss Federal Institute of Technology in 1965.

In addition to being a member of AIC, the American Chemical Society and the New York Academy of Sciences, Paul is a fellow of the American Physical Society and of the American Institute of Chemical Engineers. He has published approximately one hundred fifty scientific papers and been granted seventy-one U. S. patents. He writes a column, "The Science of the Possible," for *ChemTech*.

Paul married Rhoda A. M. Burg in 1943. They have two children, Ingrid B. and P. Randall. Paul became a United States citizen in 1946. His vacation time is often devoted to visitations to the world of marine biology with fins, mask, scuba and underwater camera.

(Photograph courtesy of American Institute of Chemists.)

ROBERT CULBERTSON WEST

Distinguished and versatile Robert West, who was born March 18, 1928, in Glen Ridge, New Jersey, began receiving honors in school and continues to receive them. At Cornell University, where he received his B.A. degree in 1950, he was a member of Phi Beta Kappa, Phi Kappa Phi, and Sigma Xi. During graduate work at Harvard (M.A. 1952, Ph.D. 1954), he was a National Science Foundation Predoctoral Fellow and National Defense Education Act Fellow for Japanese Language Study (summer 1952). His doctoral thesis, conducted under the direction of Professor Eugene Rochow, was entitled "Cyclic Organosilicon Compounds."

Interestingly, twenty-two years after Dr. Rochow received the Chemical Pioneer Award, Dr. West was selected for the same high honor. Robert was cited for his pioneering discovery of organosilicon species with silicon-silicon double bonds, the synthesis of organosilicon polymers used as precursors in the manufacture of silicon carbide, and the development of "revolutionary chemistry," an academic course that has been a model for chemistry courses for non-scientists.

Dr. West, who in 1985 was named Outstanding Science Innovator by *Science Digest*, was recipient of the American Chemical Society Kipping Award in organosilicon chemistry (1970), Amoco Distinguished Teaching Award (1974) and Eugene G. Rochow Professorship (1980).

Robert has served as lecturer or visiting professor at many universities, including Kyoto and Osaka Universities (1964-65), University of Wurzburg (1968-69), Haile Sellassie I University, Ethiopia (1972), Tohoku University, Japan (1976), University of California, Santa Cruz (1977), Hebrew University, Jerusalem (1979), University of Utah (1981), Institute of Chemical Physics, Chinese Academy of Science, Lanzhou, Gansu, Peoples Republic (1984), Justus Liebig University, Giessen, West Germany (1984), Southern Oregon State College (1984), Gunma University, Japan (1987); Abbott Lecturer, University of North Dakota (1964), Seydel-Wooley Lecturer, Georgia Institute of Technology (1970), Sun Oil Lecturer, Ohio University (1971), Edgar C. Britton Lecturer, Midland, Michigan (1971), Jean Day Memorial Lecturer, Rutgers University (1973), Cecil and Ida Green Honors Professor, Texas Christian University (1983), Karcher Lecturer, University of Oklahoma (1986), Broberg Lecturer, North Dakota State University (1986), and Xerox Lecturer, University of British Columbia (1986).

Dr. West's interests are broad. His more than 360 scientific papers deal with such topics as: Organosilicon chemistry - synthesis and study of chemical bonding in multiple-bonded silicon compounds, including disilenes, $R_2Si=SiR_2$; silenes, $R_2Si=CR_2$; and silanones, $R2Si=O$. Synthesis and electronic properties of cyclic polysilanes. Polysilane high polymers - synthesis, characterization and photochemistry. Similar studies on germanium compounds. Nuclear magnetic resonance, electron spin resonance, electrochemistry, and x-ray crystallography of silicon and germanium compounds. Highly conjugated organic molecules including oxocarbons, quinocycloalkanes and polyquinones. He is also the author of papers on mountain exploration and glaciology in British Columbia and Alaska, and Japanese language study and modern Japanese culture.

That Dr. West has developed and is using novel methods of teaching is aptly demonstrated, for he has developed a new approach to the teaching of general chemistry which emphasizes the application of chemistry to social and environmental problems; a seminar in chemical education for graduate teaching assistants in organometallic chemistry and spectroscopy; and student-centered seminars and courses on energy, population, the biological revolution, and liberation of men, women and children.

A member of the American Chemical Society, Chemical Society (London), Japan Chemical Society, American Institute of Chemists and the American Association for the Advancement of Science, Robert has served as a member of many important committees and advisory and editorial boards. He has also served in various non-chemical positions, which include president, Madison Community School (free high school) (1971-81);

coordinator, Congress on Optimum Population/ Environment (1970); founder and member of board of directors, Women's Medical Fund of Wisconsin; national board of directors, Zero Population Growth (1980-86); board of directors and vice president, Protect Abortion Rights, Inc. (1980 to present); and lay minister, Prairie Unitarian Universalist Society (1982).

Dr. West's avocations include exploration and mountaineering, skiing, flying aircraft, and nature study.

He was married in 1950 and is the father of two children.

DAVID WILSON YOUNG

Many of America's great chemists have been accomplished musicians and David Wilson Young is no exception. He has served for over ten years as a tour speaker for the American Chemical Society, his topic entitled "Antonio Stradivari, the Artist and the Chemist." This accomplished violinist "possesses" his own Stradivarius violin and intrigues his audience by mixing music and chemistry in his talks. In 1971, the American Institute of Chemists named Dr. Young an honorary member for his defense of the rights of chemists, the development of standards for professional employment, and *the sweetness of his violin.*

David was born in Oblong, Illinois, on August 16, 1909, the only child of William Lee and Bertha Fay (Wilson)

Young. He graduated from Lexington Senior High School, Lexington, Kentucky, in 1927, and attended the University of Kentucky where he majored in chemistry (B.S., 1931; M.S., 1935). He was awarded the Sc.D. degree from Transylvania University (1936) and Queens College, England (1968). He financed his college education by playing his violin as background music in local movie theaters for silent films before the advent of "talkies."

From 1931 to 1935, he worked as a chemist for the Kentucky Agricultural Experiment Station and then accepted a position in the Laurel Hill Research Laboratories of General Chemical Company. In 1940, he joined Esso Research Engineering in Linden, New Jersey, as a senior research chemist. Fifteen years later, he accepted a position with Sinclair Research, Inc. in Harvey, Illinois. In 1969, he became research associate at Atlantic-Richfield Company. Thereafter he was Vice President of Compino Labs in Forest Park, Illinois; R & D director for Heritage Environmental Research Institute at Anaheim, California, and a partner of R. B. MacMullin Associates, Niagara Falls, New York. He then founded David W. Young & Associates, Inc. (now Young & Kather Associates, Inc.) where he is still active as president emeritus.

While employed at General Chemical, David worked with titanium; while with Esso, he developed and patented many new products. Some of his developments are low temperature polymerization of olefins, acyl-p-aminophenol antioxidants for nylon, isooctanyl esters as plasticizers and high impact polystyrene. While at Sinclair, he developed polyester titanium lubricants, titanium compounds to improve the lubricity of kerosene used for rocket boosters and activated metal halide polymerization catalyst, 2,4-dichloro-phenoxyacetate (2-4D), low molecular weight butadiene polymers and new uses for styrene-maleic anhydride copolymers (SMA).

Dr. Young has been awarded AIC's Honor Scroll from the Chicago Section and Chemical Pioneer Award, as well as the Kentucky Colonel Award (1959), Merit Award from the Chicago Technical Society Council (1961), Honor Award from the Commissioner of Patents (1964-65), and the President's Honor Award from Stanislaus College (1969).

In addition to serving as president of AIC (1971-73), chairman of the Kentucky Section (1935), and director of the Chicago Section of ACS, David is a member of the American Association for the Advancement of Science, Sigma Xi, Phi Kappa Alpha, Phi Mu Alpha, Alpha Chi Sigma, and the American Legion. Awardee of 264 patents by the U. S. Patent Office and more than 235 by foreign patent offices, he has published fifty scientific reports.

David married Eloise Conner in 1935. Eloise, who received her M.A. from the University of Kentucky in 1931, is active in her local church and various charitable organizations. Their daughter, Susan Wilson Young Caron, received her M.S. degree in education from Purdue University and is presently assisting in a variety of areas at Conners Prairie Pioneer Settlement, a restored village near Indianapolis, Indiana. Susan has two sons: Jay P. Caron and David Young Caron.

Dr. Young's hobbies include traveling, photography, golf and swimming. He loves his work and intends to participate as long as his health permits.

ALEJANDRO ZAFFARONI

Without the controlled release techniques used in medication, many people taking prescribed drugs who are alive today would have died a few years ago. Moreover, in the future the rate of survival will increase for those persons taking such medication. The use of these sustained release systems was pioneered by Smith Kline and French Laboratories in 1945; by 1952, this company had introduced eighteen prescription drugs as tiny beads coated with wax of varying thicknesses. But it was not until 1961, when SK & F's Menley and James Laboratories marketed Contact capsules, that many consumers became aware of sustained release drugs.

Another technique used for sustained release of drugs is a reservoir system, consisting of transdermal patches, which release the drug at a near constant rate via diffusion through a polymeric membrane to the skin. One of the leaders in this field is Alejandro Zaffaroni, who founded Alza Corporation in Palo Alto, California, in 1968.

In 1981, Alza, which is derived from the first two letters of the first and last names of the inventor, developed a transdermal patch for the sustained release of scopolamine to combat motion sickness. Transdermal patches which release glyceryl nitrate for treatment of angina were also introduced that year. The annual sales volume for these "nitro patches" is about $175 million. Alza has also developed transdermal patches for the therapeutically controlled release of estradiol for relief of menopausal symptoms and a patch for delivering phenyl propanolamine to supress the appetite.

Alejandro Zaffaroni, who was born in Montevideo, Uruguay, on February 27, 1923, received his B.S. in chemistry from the University of Montevideo in 1941 and doctorate from the University of Rochester in 1949. After spending two years as a National Institute of Health Research Fellow at Rochester, Dr. Zaffaroni joined Syntex Corporation, where he rose to the position of President of Syntex Research Center. In 1968 he left Syntex to establish the Alza Corporation. He founded DNAX Ltd. in 1980, which firm has since been acquired by Schering-Plough Corporation; Dr. Zaffaroni continues to serve as Chairman of its Board.

Dr. Zaffaroni is recipient of the Pioneer Award (1979), President's Award from the Weizmann Institute of Science (1978), Barren Medal Award (1974), and honorary doctoral degrees from the University of Rochester (1972) and the University of the Republic, Montevideo (1983).

Zaffaroni is a member of the American Academy of

Arts and Sciences, American Association for the Advancement of Science, American Chemical Society, American Foundation for Pharmaceutical Educational, American Pharmaceutical Association, Academy of Pharmaceutical Sciences, American Society of Biological Chemists, Inc., American Society for Microbiology, American Society of Pharmacology and Experimental Therapeutics, Biomedical Engineering Society, California Pharmacists Association, International Pharmaceutical Federation, International Society for Chronobiology, International Society for the Study of Biological Rhythms, Society for Experimental Biology and Medicine, Sociedád Méxicana de Nutricíon y Endrocrinología, The Biochemical Society (England), The Endocrine Society, The International Society for Research in the Biology of Reproduction, and the New York Academy of Sciences. A fellow of the American Institute of Chemists, Institute of International Education of the University of Rochester, American Academy of Arts and Sciences, American Pharmaceutical Association, and Academy of Pharmaceutical Sciences, he is a member of the Institute of Medicine of the National Academy of Science. He is consulting professor of pharmacology at Stanford University Medical School and an honorary professor of the National University of Mexico and the faculty of Madison University in Montevideo.

He is also Chairman of the Board of the International Psoriasis Research Foundation, a Founding Life Member of MIT Sustaining Fellows, an Honorary Trustee of the Board of Trustees of the University of Rochester, Incorporator of the Neurosciences Research Foundation at MIT; and member of the Board of Governors of the Weizmann Institute of Science, of the Board of Trustees of Linus Pauling Institute of Science and Medicine, of the Council of the Institute of Medicine of the National Academy of Sciences, and of the Pharmaceutical

Panel of the Committee on Technology and International Economic and Trade Issues of the National Academy of Engineering's Office of the Foreign Secretary and the Assembly of Engineering.

The author of fifty-four scientific reports, he has been awarded fifty-five patents by the U. S. Patent Office.

Alejandro married Lyda Russomanno in 1946. He and his wife have two children: Alejandro and Elisa.

(Photograph courtesy of University of Wisconsin.)

HOWARD ELLIOT ZIMMERMAN

Howard was born in New York City on July 5, 1926, to Charles and May Cohen Zimmerman. After graduating from Stamford, Connecticut, high school in 1944, he entered the U. S. Army to serve as a tank gunner in the Armored Corps in Europe. At war's end, he enrolled at Yale where he conducted undergraduate research under the direction of Professor Harry W. Wasserman; he received both the B.S. and Chittenden Award from Yale in 1950. Professor James English guided his graduate investigations (Ph.D., 1953) on the acid-catalyzed 1, 3-diol cleavage reaction. The results of Howard's undergraduate and graduate research were published in six reports in the *Journal of the American Chemical Society.*

Thereafter, Zimmerman spent a year as a Lilly National Research Council Fellow at Harvard under the direction of Professor R. B. Woodward. Four of the next six years (1956-60) he was an Alfred P. Sloan Fellow while serving as Assistant Professor at Northwestern University. He then joined the faculty of the University of Wisconsin, where he now holds the Arthur C. Cope Chair in Organic Chemistry.

His research accomplishments include the stereochemistry of ketonization of enols, overlap control of organic reactions, control of aldolization stereochemistry six-membered ring transition states, 1, 2-carbanion rearrangements, the first synthesis of barrelene and semibullvalene, the Mobius-Huckel concept in organic chemistry, the generation of sterically hindered carbenes, the applicaiton of MO theory to organic reaction mechanisms, the di-methane rearrangement, the application of quantum mechanics and MO reasoning to prediction and rationale of organic photochemistry, metatransmission in excited aryl groups, photochemistry without light, investigation and development of unimolecular photochemical rearrangements, development of excited state reaction theory, and single photon counting methods for determining excited state reaction rates.

Recipient of the AIC Chemical Pioneer Award in 1986, he has also been honored with the Northeast American Chemical Society Section Award for Photochemistry, ACS James Flack Norris Award, and Halpern Award for Photochemistry by the New York Academy of Science. Formerly a fellow of the Japanese Society for the Promotion of Science, Professor Zimmerman is a fellow of the American Institute of Chemists, and a member of the National Academy of

Sciences, American Chemical Society, Chemical Society of London, German Chemical Society, Sigma Xi and Phi Beta Kappa. He has served on the editorial boards of the *Journal of the American Chemical Society, Journal of Organic Chemistry, Molecular Photochemistry,* and *Reviews of Chemical Intermediates.* He was named by the 1979 and 1981 Garfield surveys listing the 250 and 100 most cited authors in all fields of science.

A unique aspect of Zimmerman's career has been the fantastic number of truly outstanding students who have worked with him. He keeps a map in his office with a label "Members of the Group." Of his more than one hundred fifty graduate and postdoctoral students, seventy-one now hold professorships in colleges and universities around the world; many are internationally known. Professor Albert Padwa of Emory University is Chairman of the Organic Division of the American Chemical Society. Harry Morrison is Chairman of Purdue's Organic Division. John Swenton, Professor at Ohio State, is well known for his photochemical and synthetic research. Reuben Rieke, Professor at Nebraska, is best known for his ultrareactive metals in organic reactions. Stuart Staley, who is Professor at Carnegie Mellon, is known for his physical-organic research. New York University's David Schuster is best known for his organic photochemical research. Outstanding in photochemistry are Richard Givens of the University of Kansas, Stephen Hixson of the University of Massachusetts, and Laren Tolbert of Georgia Tech. Boston University's Guilford Jones is a well known figure in solar energy research. Gary Keck, Professor at Utah, is very active in synthetic organic research. Professor R. Dan Little, University of California at Santa Barbara, is recognized for his ability to apply physical-organic ideas to synthetic organic chemistry. A well known figure in organic photochemistry and heterocyclic chemistry is Professor Patrick Mariano of Maryland. A number of

Zimmerman's former students came from Germany, such as outstanding photochemists Dietrich Dopp, Professor at Duisburg, and Heinz Durr, Professor at Saarbrücken; and synthetic organic chemist Wolfgang Eberbach, Professor at Freiburg. One of the most active of the younger Japanese organic photochemists is Hiizu Iwamura, Professor at the Institute of Molecular Science in Okazaki. Jacques Nasielski is Professor and Head of the Department at Brussels. Reinhart Keese, who is well known for his research on Bredt's rule violations and fenestrane synthesis, is Professor at Bern, Switzerland. Professor John Scheffer of the University of British Columbia is best known for his solid state photochemical research. Known for studies on photochemical molecular rearrangements are Canadians Christopher Bender, Professor at Lethbridge, and McMaster University's John McCullough; as well as Scotland's Professor at Dundee William Horspool, who also writes for "Specialist Periodical Reports" in England. Former undergraduates in Zimmerman's group are Martin Semmelhack, Professor at Princeton, and Larry Singer, Professor at the University of Southern California.

Howard's 1950 marriage to Jane Kirshenheiter produced children Robert, Stephen and James. Following Jane's death in 1975, Professor Zimmerman married Martha L. Bailey Kaufman to become stepfather to Peter and Tanya Kaufman.

CHEMICAL PIONEERS: PAST AND FUTURE

The American Institute of Chemists Chemical Pioneers program, active since 1966, has enjoyed a magnificent history. The question now is "Will the program be equally successful in the future?"

Future Pioneers will face a formidable challenge in competing with past awardees. For, how can future programs surpass the earlier ones that named Nobel Laureates Herbert C. Brown, Paul J. Flory, Linus C. Pauling, Glenn T. Seaborg, and Harold Urey? Or Carl Djerassi for oral contraception, Roy Plunket for Teflon, Lewis Sarett for cortisone, and Max Tishler for riboflavin and sulfaquinoxaline - four members of the National Inventors Hall of Fame? Programs that recognized polymer giants Speed Marvel and Herman Mark? That named many other great inventors whose creative work contributed importantly to the manufacture of new products and the creation of new industries? That recognized talented pioneers in fundamental chemistry?

Despite the challenge, future Pioneer programs will probably equal - maybe even surpass - the successes of the past. The Awards Committee will have two excellent sources of nominees: Those creative chemists who have already distinguished themselves by important research achievements, and those successful chemists whose research in the future will be deserving of special recognition.

It is an easy task to call to mind potential award nominees who have already performed research of outstanding value: Waldo Semon for plasticized polyvinyl chloride; Thomas Gresham, originator of the dioctyl phthalate plasticizer; Percy A. Wells, who discovered corn steep liquor used in the manufacture of penicillin and as a valuable nutrient in fermentations and who developed a successful method for making sorbose, which is intermediate in the manufacture of vitamin C; Warren Niederhauser for his epoxidized glyceride oils as polymer stabilizers and plasticizers; J. David Reid for his major contributions to the development of easy-care and other improved cellulosic textiles; Jett C. Arthur, Jr., for his advances in cellulose graft copolymers and plant protein products. Bryan Bunch has listed more than forty distinguished scientists as "People Who Deserved the Nobel Prize (But Did Not Get It)" in his Science Almanac (Anchor Press/Doubleday, Garden City, New York).

Predicting the future is risky. It seems reasonable, nevertheless, to anticipate much exemplary work in the field of chemistry will be undertaken. The availability of improved instruments and techniques will greatly facilitate this work. But because research goals are influenced by economic and social needs, the nature of future research may change. There may be more achievements in energy-related research, in biotechnology, in carbon-one chemistry, and in biomass chemistry and processing. And there are other favorable circumstances to insure these goals. Budgets for research and development in this country have been increasing - over one hundred twenty billion dollars were invested in R&D in 1986 - and economists predict great prosperity for the rest of this century. This should guarantee the employment of more chemists which, in turn, will provide more potential candidates for future Chemical Pioneer Awards.